Designing
Sustainable
Packaging

Designing Sustainable Packaging

Scott Boylston

Laurence King Publishing

LAURENCE KING

Published in 2009 by
Laurence King Publishing Ltd
4th Floor
361–373 City Road
London
EC1V 1LR
United Kingdom
e-mail: enquiries@laurenceking.com
www.laurenceking.com

A catalogue record for this book is
available from the British Library.

ISBN: 978 1 85669 597 8

Project editor: Gaynor Sermon
Copy editor: Liz Dalby

Designed by Roger Fawcett-Tang,
Struktur Design

Printed in China

Mixed Sources
Product group from well-managed
forests and other controlled sources
www.fsc.org Cert no. SGS-COC-003548
© 1996 Forest Stewardship Council

Dedication:
for Makenzie Tyler and Francesca Elle

Author's acknowledgments:
The professionals who have contributed to this book
demonstrate how dedication to innovative problem
solving coupled with a sincere desire to reduce the
negative impacts of packaging can help bring about
lasting positive change. And, representing the next
generation of practitioners, the graduate students from the
Savannah College of Art and Design whose work is featured
throughout the book are more than ready to challenge
the shortcomings of an industry they are just entering;
their eager embrace of a role for graphic designers that
encompasses a broader and more influential role in design
thinking has been inspiring.

As Commissioning Editor, Lee Ripley has been dedicated
to this project since our very first meeting, and has made
the development experience a pleasure. Project Editor
Gaynor Sermon has provided insightful advice, juggling
the complicated array of evolving content with aplomb.
The text has been massaged expertly by Liz Dalby, the
Copy Editor, and Roger Fawcett-Tang has been invaluable
in helping to create a dynamic design presentation for the
book as a whole.

The Savannah crew has been equally invaluable. Clark
'fingers' Delashmet, in building what was needed to be
built and then performing as hand model for his own
creations, quite literally has his hands all over a number
of spreads in this book. Thanks to Larissa Thut and Bailey
Davidson for their enthusiastic and expert contributions
to much of the photography in the book that not only
sets the tone, but does such a masterful job of illustrating
key concepts. Photography professor Tim Keating and
his students, meanwhile, contributed greatly to the
presentation of some of the final package prototypes.
Finally, thanks to my wife, Kristin, for bearing my
persistent disappearance into the attic during the course of
this project's development with smiles, support and love.

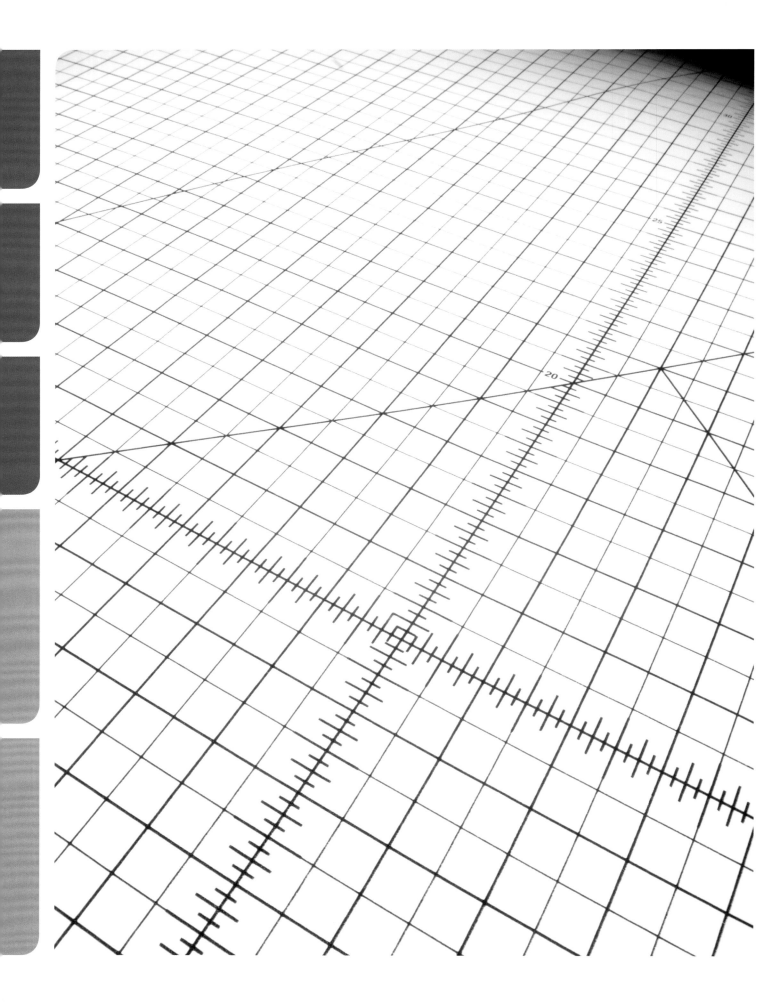

Foreword
Scott Boylston

Package design, like many industries, is in the throes of change that is occurring not just rapidly; not just comprehensively; not just irrevocably; but with no small level of ferocity. This is not to say the change was wholly unexpected, or that earlier shifts in the landscape emerged at an equally frenetic pace. It's just that subtle change can be endured through denial for only so long. Subtle change, consistently ignored, builds to sudden change that cannot be denied, and this particular kind of change has a way of thinning the field, with ignorance being an early casualty.

Even as this foreword is being written, the naysayers in the industry – who insisted sustainable package design was either a specialty niche or a contradiction in terms – are struggling in vain to keep up with the spry innovators who have dared to buck the old, inefficient system and are in the process of reinventing the very concept of package design.

While packaging technologies are in a constant state of flux, the range and rate of flux is often modest, and this has been the case over the last decade or so of clamshells and multi-layer cartons. But occasionally there are jolts to the system, and the pace of change accelerates beyond what many thought possible. And this is surely the present case.

There is, of course, a very long way to go. There is still far too much packaging. There are still far too many wasteful secondary packaging schemes, and far too many shortsighted delivery systems. There are still far too many toxins in packaging material, and far too few efficient recovery systems. There is still insidious foot dragging in the industry. New methods and new methodologies are necessary, but not nearly as necessary as new ways of thinking, and young, energetic designers.

Yesterday's package design systems will not remain the same; they have the capacity within their natural cycles of evolution to become significantly more sustainable. The choice, therefore, is not change or no change, but instead, what kind of change. This book aims to demonstrate that the industry is in a state of flux and can be influenced by pressure exerted upon it by those entering its sphere, and provide young designers and old hands alike with the impetus to make a positive impact.

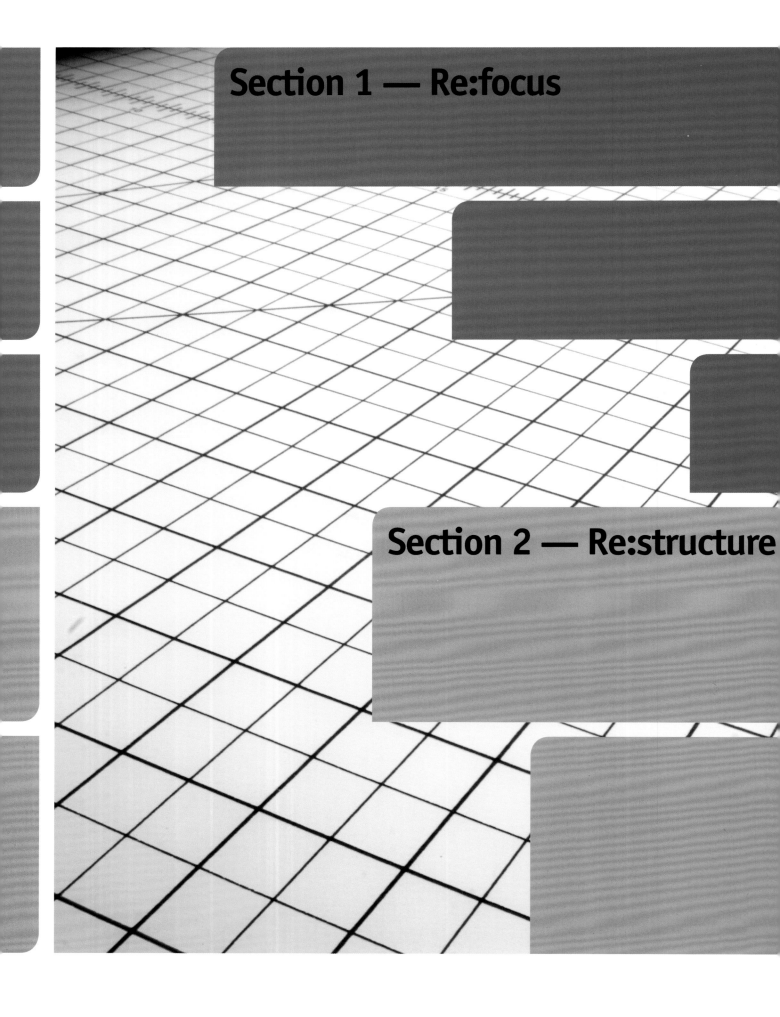

Section 1 — Re:focus

Section 2 — Re:structure

Introduction:
About this book

There are two primary objectives to this book. The first is to challenge the next generation of graphic designers to re-envision package design as a less environmentally destructive practice than it presently is. The second is to provide methodologies and techniques for creating prototypes for innovative and sustainable package designs.

The two objectives for any reader of this book should be: first to see, then to act; and to conceive of a new vision, then bring structure to that vision. A keen focus is necessary at the outset of any endeavour in order to discern what *may* be, but only in the defining of the structure can we determine what *will* be.

Section 1 – Re:focus

The acclaimed management writer Peter Drucker was fond of stating that doing the job right is vastly different from doing the right job. For instance, in working to the constraints of large container stores over the last several decades, the package design industry might have been doing the job right, but from a more holistic point of view (one that takes into account factors other than corporate profit) the job they were doing so well was not necessarily the right job. Unfortunately, doing the wrong job right in this case has led to an environmentally unsustainable packaging paradigm. Focus, then, is only helpful when the proper outcomes are the object of attention, and, before considering how to refocus, the problems of the present focus must be understood.

Emphasis on selling more and cheaper goods has long been the objective of the package design industry, and, to their credit, they have found impressive ways to create inexpensive, strong and theft-proof packages. If the focus on this framework is widened, however, it becomes clear that this myopic view has led to a range of negative impacts, including natural resource depletion, inefficient energy consumption and long-term toxic by-products. A refocusing of the industry's priorities is overdue.

Such a refocusing does not aim to exclude profitability as a motivating factor. Neglecting to consider financial incentives is no different from neglecting to consider environmental impacts – both fail to address the larger picture. Instead, there is a need to embrace the complexities of the larger system, and incorporate the industry's 'triple bottom line', which accounts for the *social,* the *environmental* and the *economic* considerations of operating a business. Thankfully, this is already underway. Package designers must wholeheartedly join this movement, and commit their substantial talents as creative thinkers to this change.

The first section of the book provides information and tools to enable designers to become proactive in refocusing the objectives of their package design endeavours. A plethora of sustainable knowledge has entered the field over the last decade, and the potential range of sustainable practices has recently come into sharp focus. This knowledge was not obtained in a vacuum – it has required the effort of innovative and dedicated individuals. As a model for successful integration of these sustainable ideas, numerous examples of the work done by these visionaries comprise the later part of this section.

Section 2 – Re:structure

While the first section of the book aims to convey the diverse sustainable information available to graphic designers and the practical outcomes of companies already committed to sustainable change, the second section features examples of bringing sustainable packaging ideas to fruition in the most concrete sense. After all, someone has to build the prototypes that impress the client, and not every designer works in a firm large enough for that duty to be delegated to a committed department or an outside service.

Section two aims to help graphic designers to conceive, develop, design and construct fully functional packaging prototypes that provide secondary uses as a part of their primary objective. The subject of the case studies provides examples of how a package can be re-envisioned as an after-market product in its own right, while the presentation of the design process provides insight into troubleshooting the creative process, and the development of successful prototypes.

While there are special modelling foams and high-end technologies that allow for astonishing prototype results, this book focuses on what can be achieved with a traditional set of tools to create working prototypes. These can then be used for client presentations, as well as physical stand-ins during photoshoots for packages that have not yet been manufactured. The methods and techniques demonstrated here provide guidance to anyone interested in elevating their vision of a packaging idea to a highly accomplished physical form. In short, whether you consider yourself a career package designer or an occasional designer of packages, this book will provide information and inspiration.

Is package design suffering from a dead-end mentality?

Individuals who design packages have much to learn from those who design other ordinary objects. Take the example of a pop-up tent: imagine going on a camping trip, and carrying a handsomely designed and lightweight tent. Imagine marvelling at its compact nature as you hike; the ease with which it opens and pops up at the campsite. Imagine the comfort and shelter it provides through a rainy evening. Then imagine realizing in the morning, as you prepare for another day's hike, that the designer of the tent neglected to consider its ability to collapse back into a portable form (it's a pop-up tent; no-one ever said anything about pop-down). This clearly shows that what's considered to be a dysfunctional model for one group of designers is actually regarded as the ideal model for another group of designers: package designers (unlike tent designers) make satisfactory one-way packages, but very few have focused on what could be done to facilitate a round trip.

Of course, package designers would protest that it's not as easy as that. The typical design brief for a package simply doesn't address anything beyond the package's success in delivering its contents to the consumer. Once a package performs its last intended use within the present system (getting the product safely into the consumer's home), it becomes a genuine nuisance to those who had never asked for it to begin with. Once the product is wrestled from its excessive layered wrapping, what remains is a heap of refuse that no-one wants. It's not necessary to ask how we've come to a point where the original objective of product protection has led to a massive environmental burden. Instead, we must question how this model can be reimagined in a way that retains its positive attributes even as its negative attributes are... discarded.

So, package designers have failed to consider a 'second life' for their creations for good reason; packages were simply never intended to be reused. Yet, this rationale fails to stand up to scrutiny not only from a forward-looking mindset, but also from an historical point of view. The present era of disposable convenience, which has lasted less than half a century, is quickly approaching its end – by necessity. Before this era, people imaginatively used and reused any object they could obtain, including packages for consumer goods. Our recent shortsighted splurge on disposability for disposability's sake is a luxury that the world can no longer afford. Package designers, who have long enabled their clients to create magnificent containers intended only to protect and dazzle, are facing a moment in their careers where they either doggedly hang onto that outmoded model – and risk becoming obsolete – or enthusiastically embrace the new prerequisites of their profession.

It's no longer risky for graphic designers to suggest pursuing 'green' printing options to clients. Only a few years ago, such suggestions elicited derision and cynicism.

Understanding the material needs of the product performance arena, the designer can imagine a secondary use for the retail package that adds to that experience. Here, the retail package transforms into a functional smock. Elastic bands serve to hold the product as they're being shipped and as they're being used, and the waist band for the smock performs as a strap for the package-as-product as it's being delivered to the consumer. The set is also fully functional as a mobile silk-screening kit.

Now however, companies around the world are searching for sustainable alternatives to their printed matter and packaging, and graphic designers have an opportunity to reimagine the end of a package's life as nothing less than the beginning of another one. The dead-end, one-way street that our contemporary packages end up on happens to be the only street that we, as a species, have. The present cradle-to-grave packaging paradigm is not just environmentally damaging; it is economically inefficient. So, devising innovative methods of reuse can be beneficial in more ways than most could imagine.

The catch is that now graphic designers must expand their field of expertise and accept this new responsibility. They must learn to navigate this new terrain, and incorporate a solid understanding of sustainable options into every project. This trend can empower savvy graphic designers to provide a valuable consulting service to their clients, thus helping increase the company's 'triple bottom line'. This triple-bottom-line focus acknowledges that if one of the areas is neglected, they all eventually suffer. The larger the project, the more significant the potential benefits. Packaging constitutes the single largest expenditure for many large product companies, and so represents a point of great opportunity for reinvention.

Sustainability is an idea that suggests a perpetual birth of functionality for all things designed, which, considering nature's prehistoric ability to regenerate, shouldn't come as much of a surprise to us, who comprise the 'higher species'. We must design all things so that they feed our future needs rather than compromise them. Accordingly, much information on material and systems innovation is presented in this book. At their core, the various sustainable philosophies have one concept in common – they espouse the need for creating 'closed loops' of material usage and reusage that do not contaminate other loops of usage. In this manner, materials can be reconstituted endlessly, thus greatly reducing – if not outright eliminating – the need for further material extraction and depletion. These closed loops will also ensure that chemicals do not escape their productive loops to become destructive agents, harming nature and humankind.

But a designer's horizons can be even broader than that. Rather than simply keeping the garbage out of the package, why not also keep the package out of the garbage?

Innovative secondary uses for packages have the potential to revolutionize the industry. If materials must be used to begin with, why not make the most out of them before they're eventually reintroduced into the closed loops they're intended to eventually feed? Secondary use is intended as a means not only of preventing inferior materials from entering the waste stream, but of helping the new and innovative material cycles to function much more efficiently.

Package designers, who have long enabled clients to create magnificent containers intended only to protect and dazzle, are facing a moment in their careers where they either doggedly hang onto that outmoded model – and risk becoming obsolete – or enthusiastically embrace the new prerequisites of their profession.

Why are physical prototypes necessary?

After reading the previous pages, you might be tempted to scoff at the notion of using a lot of material to build physical packaging prototypes. Instead, wouldn't it be more environmentally sound to use digital prototyping as a means of reducing waste in the early, exploratory stages of packaging development?

This is a key question, and in cases where the designer works in a dedicated package-engineering environment, and has access to the modelling programs created for such tasks, digital prototyping is common. When primary packages such as bottles, tubes and canisters are being developed, this is also often the case. Additionally, there are industrial design systems that cut three-dimensional foam prototypes generated by computer models. All of these reduce material usage (although not necessarily energy use), and reduce the need for physical building.

Yet, just as the utopian 'paperless office' has yet to be realized in any far-reaching way, paperless package development is still far from being implemented. The objective here is not to urge resistance to computer modelling as much as to offer alternative prototyping skills to the many designers in the world who, for numerous reasons, are required to create their packages without the aid of expensive computer software, let alone the hardware that may be required.

A comprehensive, or 'comp', is an individually crafted simulation of the proposed production piece – the term is used somewhat interchangeably with the word 'prototype'. Comping skills comprise a craft of great acumen, and, once learned, they will come to the aid of the designer more often than you might expect. Not all package designs are conceived by large package design firms; many are created in smaller studios that provide package-design

services as one of many other design services. Because of this versatility, many of the mid-sized and smaller design firms simply don't own modelling software. Also, short-run promotional boxes and packages of all kinds can be created in-house in an economical and professional manner by anyone well-versed in three-dimensional comping. Perhaps most importantly, there is nothing that will convince a client of a package's worth more readily than a fully realized, exceptionally built, three-dimensional comp.

Shopping is a visceral act that involves feeling, turning and holding, and as such the power of touch is integral to the success of package design in the marketplace. Packages that create a compelling physical experience have a distinct advantage over packages that are awkward in the hand or uninspiring to hold. So, while considerable effort, skill and materials are required to create such a lifelike model, the real-world tactile experience of form, weight and surface simply cannot be matched.

Furthermore, when presenting final ideas to a client, a single comp will rarely suffice. In larger organizations, the decision-makers might work in several offices around the world, so comps are built to allow each the opportunity to physically handle the prototype.

Finally, photographs that are seen in advertisements and catalogues are not always actual production pieces; more often than not they are flawless, hand-crafted comps. Business-to-business catalogues are especially familiar with this practice; it is only after the large stores commit to an order that the client will venture into an actual production run. For both the initial client presentation and the photographic representation of the package itself, it is therefore necessary for someone to build the perfect three-dimensional facsimile.

The process of prototype development provides the designer with an unmatched opportunity to become intimate with the physicality of the products and the proposed package form, volume and texture.

So, who builds these comps? In larger package-design firms this task is delegated to either an in-house or stand-alone comping studio. These service studios are comprised of seasoned experts and young designers with ambitions to move up the ladder to the more creative arena of conceptual development, and these artisans churn out perfect comps on a day-to-day basis. In turn, these studios employ or contract a range of primary services such as foil-stamping, embossing, silk-screening and other high-end outputs.

Smaller design firms that develop a range of graphic design projects beyond their packaging assignments usually rely on their own designers to build their comps, and it is in these studios that you see individuals taking the project from its earliest conceptual stages to the final, full-scale comps. Freelance designers and graduating students who hope to develop convincing portfolio pieces are also charged with this full-spectrum task.

The building of comps requires finesse and a lot of hands-on experience. And, unlike the present technologies for computer modelling and foam prototyping, there are certain hand skills and techniques that will never become outdated. These are discussed in the second section of this book, and embody long-term knowledge that will not become irrelevant due to a software upgrade.

Computer modelling (left) is an essential part of package design. Once basic structures are determined, surface graphics can be added and edited as often as necessary. Computer modelling also allows for the study of surface qualities for bottles and packages, and in this way can provide valuable aesthetic information when considering materials. However, in an industry built on tactility and human-scale interaction, computer models still have their shortcomings, and hand-made comps (right) can often be invaluable.

15

Section 1

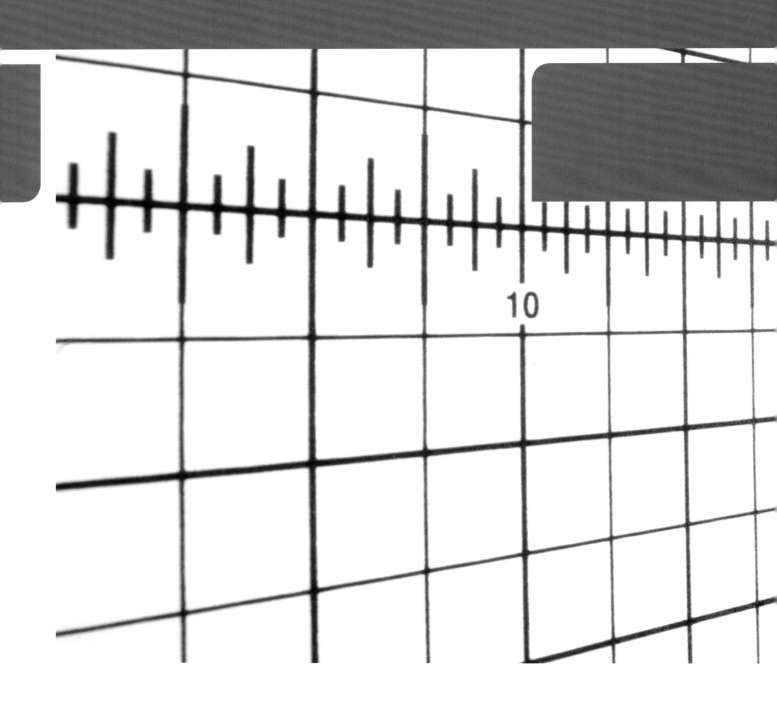

Re:focus

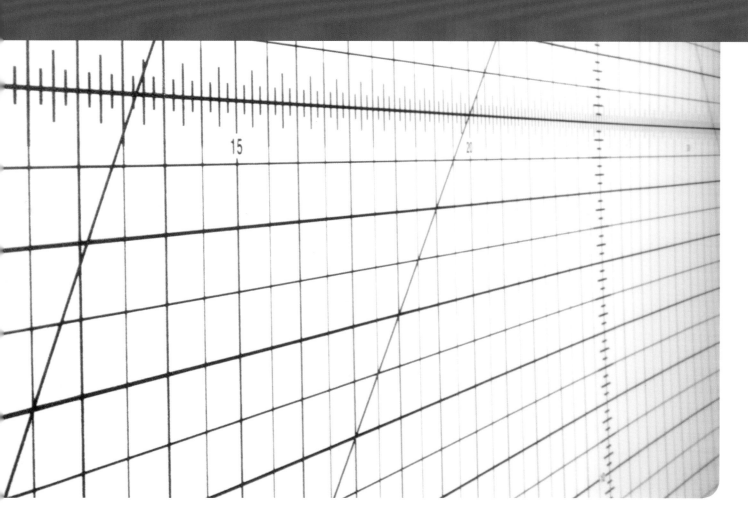

'Creativity is any act, idea or product that changes an existing domain, or that transforms an existing domain into a new one. And the definition of a creative person is: someone whose thoughts or actions change a domain, or establish a new domain. It is important to remember, however, that a domain cannot be changed without the explicit or implicit consent of a field responsible for it.'

Mihály Csíkszentmihályi

1: Package design and commerce: a foundation on which to build
2: Package design and sustainability: constructing a future
3: Sustainability in the professional realm

Re:focus

In the quote on the left, the acclaimed author and psychologist Mihály Csíkszentmihályi provides both inspiration and caution. The caution lies in the description of a field's potential resistance to change in the face of creative innovation. Design, in its most ambitious sense, represents a domain, while packaging constitutes a single field within that domain. And while the domain of design has always been responsive to transformation, the industries that have historically patronized it have been open to transformation only inasmuch as it assured financial success.

Csíkszentmihályi explains that, because the gatekeepers of any field are deeply invested in the status quo, great ingenuity and persistence are required to alter the traditions that define it. Package design, long enamoured with inexpensive materials and extravagant appearances, has historically resisted sustainable innovation, despite the efforts of incredibly creative individuals intent on reforming it. Visionaries such as Buckminster Fuller and Victor Papanek for instance, in attempting to redefine the larger domain of design as a less ecologically and socially harmful endeavour, personify Csíkszentmihályi's 'creative person'. Yet, during their lifetimes, the stiff resistance within the fields that inform design (packaging being one of them) prevented major shifts from occurring. However, without the groundbreaking successes these individuals did have, today's quickened pace of sustainable change in packaging may have taken much longer to establish.

Another keen observation Csíkszentmihályi has made is that creativity generally involves 'crossing the boundaries of domains'. And here, graphic designers of all ilks – even those with limited experience in the package design field – might find a way to contribute to the ongoing shift towards sustainable package design. It's not just experienced package designers who have the capacity to reimagine packaging as a more sustainable venture; the capacity to change the industry lies within all designers, and in fact, it may be individuals outside the field that have most new insights to offer.

In his seminal essay, 'Wicked Problems in Design Thinking', Richard Buchanan defines a broad strategy for designers as they attempt to translate their creative energies into actionable results. His Doctrine of Placements describes a designer's inherent ability to understand larger problems – even problems in fields that they do not have expertise in – by creatively relating the general structure of the problem at hand to problematic structures that they've had experience with in their own fields. *The inventiveness of the designer',* Buchanan explains, *'lies in a natural or cultivated and artful ability to return to those placements and apply them to a new situation, discovering aspects of the situation that affect the final design.'*

Graphic designers have been known to shy away from the structural challenges of package design, leaving such work to the engineers. Perhaps designers should instead apply their abilities to broadly interpret their own knowledge in order to help solve the sustainable packaging dilemma. As they learn, they may also teach. The early chapters in this section provide a very general overview of the package design industry, while the later chapters provide a roadmap for sustainable change. The section ends with inspiring real-world case studies.

Is a package still a package if it's designed as a value-added product? This package by Zatzu includes everything you'd need for a picnic, including a rain poncho, sunscreen, wipes, a blanket and removable hydration pack. All of these, including the blanket, are presented in a useful saddle-bag type package. By imagining how a package can be used in a post-purchase scenario, designers can jump boundaries into product design and fabric design.

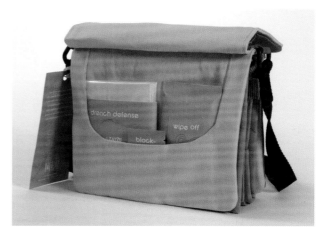

EQUIVALENT VALUES
CONVERSION TABLE
X-ACTO GRIPSTER
FAIRGATE
MADE IN U.S.A.

1 Package design and commerce: a foundation on which to build

Package design as an integral part of a system

We are packaged in our skin. We do have some small degree of control over this utilitarian packaging, which is primarily there to protect us. People around the world have found ways to decorate and use it as a form of communication.

We are packaged in clothes. While clothes also serve a protective function, they provide us with a greater opportunity to tell stories and express values. Unlike our skin, we can shed our clothes.

We are packaged in structures, or buildings. Protective structures serve our biological needs, but they too can be used as a tool to convey information. Buildings are also intended to express values, status and authority.

We are packaged by our thoughts. Or more concisely, by the ways in which we convey or receive these thoughts. We sell ideas by packaging them with words.

Then there are the types of 'packaging' we most associate with the word. There is retail packaging and wholesale packaging, paper packaging and plastic packaging, primary packaging and secondary packaging. There is sterile packaging and ventilated packaging, minimal packaging and excessive packaging, functional packaging and ceremonial packaging. There is even 'carefree' packaging and, much to our chagrin, frustrating packaging. This diversity reflects the range of products that require packaging, and each product requires a different mix of the variable attributes that packaging can provide.

When presented with a legal case to defend, a good lawyer begins with the purest of all questions – one not tainted by assumptions. The question is this: is there a case at all? Likewise, when a package designer is presented with an assignment, the first question should be equally untainted by assumption: is a package even necessary?

Placed as it is at the beginning of a book on package design, this kind of question might seem counterintuitive, but a core understanding of need is necessary from the start. Asking this first question enables an understanding of the 'needs' of the product to be packaged.

This chapter considers the foundations of package design, and explores how the tasks of package designers stem from the larger demands of commodity placement and brand identity.

The integral relationship between analysis and synthesis is at the core of any solid research methodology. The designer begins with an investigation into the targeted consumer's behaviours and preferences; then moves onto research that helps define the product's brand essence and the relevance of its price point to its perceived quality; then into the product's competitive market stance and its intended retail environments. This research defines the design brief which, of course, defines the design direction.

There are many methods of discerning the relationship between brand essence (as defined by package design) and a target audience's search for meaningful connections. Consider the designer as part of a 'dating service' hired if a brand were to go looking for a date (multiple dates, in fact). Compatibility with a target audience can only be determined if both the audience and the brand are methodically analyzed and understood.

The process just described could be considered the first 'segment' of a much larger loop – and the second segment should begin with instituting a feedback mechanism that allows the designer to determine whether or not the design is eliciting the expected responses from individuals within the target audience. Once it has been determined how well the package is being received, the designer engages in another round of design to address any shortcomings.

While packaging is one part of a much larger marketing mix which includes advertising, e-commerce and direct marketing, once the consumer has arrived at a retail site, a more immediate relationship between package, product and consumer predominates. A package on the shelf is much like an actor on the stage – the potential connection between this 'stage player' and the audience will only occur if the stage player lives up to all the promised hype. This analogy is however, somewhat simplistic, because it neglects to consider that while real actors work in concert with each other, packages must compete with other 'actors' right next to them, and each of these actors possess as much motivation to connect with the audience as they do. Imagine numerous actors reciting their own distinct lines on the very same stage, and you have some idea of how 'talented' commercial package designs must be in order to break through all of the retail clutter. Achieving 'shelf pop' or 'shout' is of primary concern for any package designer. A clear point of departure – or point of difference, unique selling proposition, or whatever else you want to call it – must be evident in order for customers to make that

The schematic on the right defines both packaging characteristics and consumer characteristics. In packaging design, a clear understanding of both is necessary. The centre circle defines the internal drives of the individual; the middle circle describes the characteristics of packaging; and the outer ring details consumer behaviours.

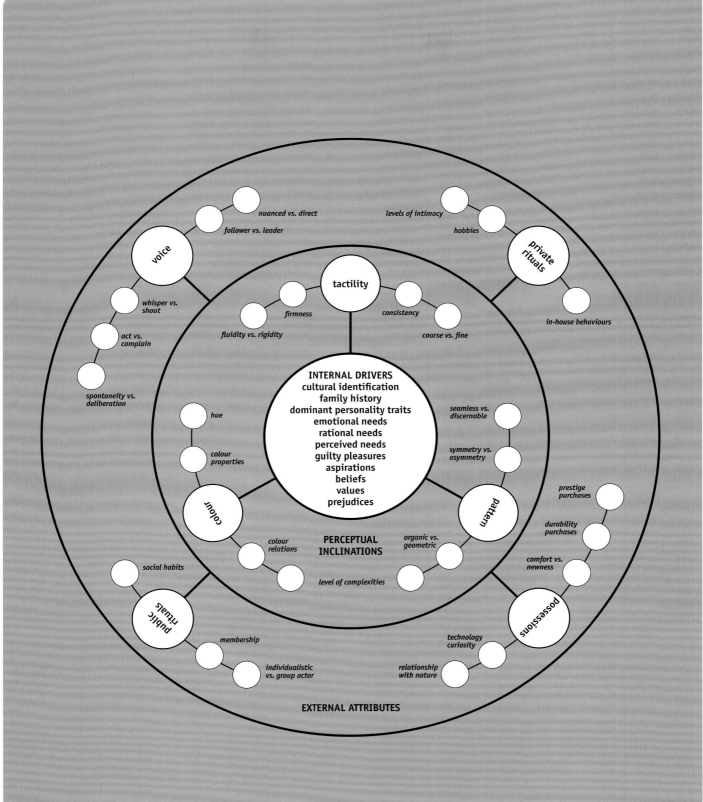

nuanced vs. direct
follower vs. leader
voice
whisper vs. shout
act vs. complain
spontaneity vs. deliberation

levels of intimacy
hobbies
private rituals
in-house behaviours

tactility
firmness
fluidity vs. rigidity
consistency
coarse vs. fine

INTERNAL DRIVERS
cultural identification
family history
dominant personality traits
emotional needs
rational needs
perceived needs
guilty pleasures
aspirations
beliefs
values
prejudices

hue
colour properties
colour
colour relations

seamless vs. discernable
symmetry vs. asymmetry
pattern
organic vs. geometric
level of complexities

PERCEPTUAL INCLINATIONS

prestige purchases
durability purchases
comfort vs. newness

social habits
public rituals
membership
individualistic vs. group actor

technology curiosity
relationship with nature
possessions

EXTERNAL ATTRIBUTES

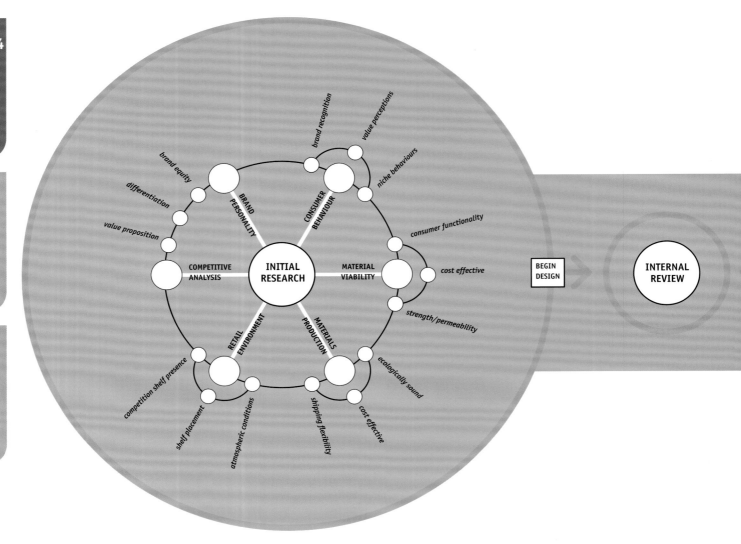

split-second decision to walk away from the shelf with your product in their hand. That point of difference must resonate in some way with the consumer.

The process of on-site persuasion that begins with the visual allure of a package – its size, shape, colour scheme and graphic and typographic charm – must then live up to the physical experience consumers have once the package is in their hands. The proof is in the touching. It is that moment of physical interaction that can instantaneously trigger a consumer's decision-making process. There's one thing that even the best advertising and marketing campaigns cannot do (even guerilla or viral advertising), and that is to physically touch a potential consumer. This visceral connection – the texture and polish of the surface, the distribution of weight, the comfort or novelty of the proportions in relation to the human hand – all are compelling factors that influence the consumer's critical considerations. Packages that 'feel right' in the hand usually live up to the best advertising and marketing and, furthermore, can often transcend all but the worst advertising and marketing.

Once the design process has begun in earnest, it is important to get prototypes in front of test audiences and observe how well the intended objectives have been met.

Certain action standards can be defined beforehand to provide criteria that would guide any changes that may result in focus-group feedback loops.

'Focus groups' – small groups of individuals who are invited to interact with and respond to packaging prototypes – are only so effective. They tend not to be consistently reliable in their feedback, mostly because individuals who know they're being observed respond to the packages in question with more cynicism than they otherwise might. Focus-group behaviour is habitually influenced by an understanding by the group that they themselves are being scrutinized.

'Behavioural studies' – observing consumer behaviour in settings that obscure the fact that the subjects are being watched – usually provide a more accurate reflection of normalized behaviour. It's been shown however, that even in actual retail environments, small case studies can only moderately predict mass-market behaviour. Individual recall and product recognition have been found to be deeply biased, derived from personal histories and brand favouritism, so much so that an accurate baseline of package-to-consumer relationship is difficult to determine.

Because it has been shown that almost 30 per cent of shelf brands are not even viewed by consumers (optical

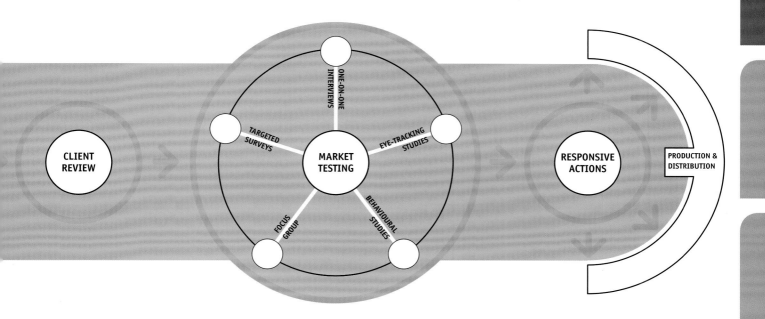

CLIENT REVIEW

ONE-ON-ONE INTERVIEWS

TARGETED SURVEYS

EYE-TRACKING STUDIES

MARKET TESTING

FOCUS GROUP

BEHAVIOURAL STUDIES

RESPONSIVE ACTIONS

PRODUCTION & DISTRIBUTION

scans have shown that only familiar or truly unorthodox packages are acknowledged by shoppers), researchers have attempted to combine eye-tracking data with behavioural responses. In this way, it can be determined whether packages are not handled because they are unattractive or because they are completely invisible to a consumer's quick shelf-scan.

While no single particular feedback methodology can assure an accurate reflection of real-world consumer behaviour, they are nonetheless important to consider, and most companies do make use of one or more of them before putting a package into full production.

Shelf visibility is different from shelf appeal, and both of these are different from shelf communication. 'Shelf visibility' is the amount of shout, or visual punch, that a package provides. Not everyone likes screamers however; and 'shelf appeal' addresses the connection a package makes with a target audience. Finally, 'shelf communication' refers to the accuracy between product expectations (as defined by the package design) and actual product performance.

The above schematic represents a research methodology that considers the many factors involved in developing successful packaging strategies. Note that the design stage begins after a period of intensive and comprehensive research. Refinement in the design process continues throughout the feedback process – each step of the way, as more and more response data is collected, the details of design work may change accordingly. This does not mean that major changes should be expected – that would reflect shortcomings in the initial research process. Rather, the feedback mechanisms should allow for very specific and targeted shifts in the package design.

Fundamental concepts of package design

Distinctive package form can help define product personality and brand essence. Several important considerations regarding various aspects of package design, from technical prerequisites to human perception are discussed here. A package is a functional tool that fulfils the various requirements of commerce. Package designers must take into account the entire lifecycle of the package they are proposing, from its place within the brand hierarchy to the practicalities of transportation, containment, storage, display, end-use and disposal. Packages must also attract, dispense, identify, inform and persuade.

A well-designed package must provide the consumer with convenience even as it strives to define style and essential brand qualities. The following bulleted list highlights the key considerations that should be taken into account when designing packaging.

• The challenge for a package designer is not only to make a truly unique package, but to make one that works within the parameters of the project specifications. Unique constructions are commendable only if they can be mass-produced efficiently, and they accommodate the distribution schemes available to the company.

• The design must comprehend the technical feasibility of what is being proposed, and be able to predict any potential pitfalls along the way. Nothing will upset a client more than proceeding smoothly through the early stages of design development, only to have a production manager state that such a design simply cannot be manufactured with the materials specified, or within budget.

• The design of the package is the last thing the consumer sees before making a decision. The next time you're in a store buying a product that you haven't already developed brand loyalty towards (the next time you're browsing) try to follow your natural thought sequence as you go through the process of deciding which brand to buy. When most other things, including quality (or perceived quality), are equal, packaging has a power bordering on the absurd.

• Ingenious package design frequently becomes the cornerstone for entire marketing strategies. Developing an alluring form or a uniquely functioning package can easily influence a future advertising campaign. Once the target audience has been determined, it is not uncommon for designers to begin with the form of the package before deciding anything else. Once a three-dimensional form has been agreed upon (and focus groups have shown which perceived qualities are attributed to it) all facets of design branch from that form. From the obvious (surface graphics) to the less obvious (advertising campaigns, point of purchase displays, etc.), the package can make the product.

• Three-dimensional form – something the consumer can actually wrap their hands around – has an undeniably sensory impact. Packaging alone can make the consumer feel that they are buying not just a product, but an experience; not just goods, but value.

Opposite and left – This fondue set is held together with a wrap that is scored strategically so it can be folded into a booklet; the inner surface contains directions and recipes. The accordion hinge allows the boxes to open flat on the table, and the green striped tongue flap (seen flat on the table in the image) is designed so that the individual box containing the sterno unit can be removed from the other two boxes. Slot-and-groove closures prevent the contents from slipping out when the boxes are opened and closed. One box contains chocolates, one box contains the dish and the other contains the sterno can and metal grating.

Who says a package designed to hold medical supplies couldn't be adapted to hold stockings?

• The average advertising campaign runs for approximately eight to ten weeks, while the shelf-life of a particular product has no set time limitations. Think of the Coke bottle; although this is an exceptional example, the form of a package can easily remain the same for five years or more, depending on its effectiveness. While most companies redesign their packaging on average every two years, an innovative approach to the design could extend that timespan much further.

• Waste is a by-product of affluence, and packaging contributes greatly to the overuse of natural resources on the front end, and excessive waste on the back end. Kaj Franck, a Finnish designer, once asked '... *of what use for man to stand on Earth and reach for the stars if he is standing up to his navel in garbage?'* Package designers should always be searching for solutions that address the issue of harmful by-products and excessive waste. Chapter three looks more closely at this issue.

• Studying successful forms from the past – not just of direct competitors but of products that are removed from the market segment in question – is paramount to success in package design. Who says a package designed to hold medical supplies couldn't be adapted to hold stockings?

• 'Primary packaging' is the material that is closest to the product. In most cases, it represents that outer surface of what would be found in the retail environment. This is the packaging that is designed to visually enhance the product, and to convince a consumer to pick it up off the shelf – despite all the competition directly surrounding it – and commit to the purchase. 'Secondary packaging' is the packaging used to bundle multipack items or to transport the merchandise from the factory to the retail outlet. In the case of the former, shrinkwrap plastics or paperboard and boxboard sleeves allow for a design-friendly surface for high-end graphics intended to reach the consumer. The latter – sometimes referred to as 'tertiary packaging' – is often bulk packaging intended to safely transport the cargo, and therefore a premium is placed on function, with surface graphics employed as information graphics for transportation handlers. Cardboard is the most frequently used external structure for this type of packaging.

What's the problem?
Part 1: Organizational procedures without vision

Considering John Thackara's statement that *'eighty per cent of environmental impact of the products, services and infrastructure around us is determined at the design stage'*, designers are not as helpless in the area of sustainable change and client influence as they often think. While not altogether helpless, package designers are traditionally somewhat isolated from the entire range of expertise within the package-development process.

This leads us to the first problem to overcome when considering the move towards more sustainable practices in package design; that of connectivity and communication. As businesses grow in size, layers of specialization and bureaucracy pile up, and as this occurs, organizational and budgetary 'silos' develop. The term 'silo' here refers to the tendency towards isolation between departments in organizations. Overspecialization can create a disjointed whole that lacks the necessary level of communication between all of the individual parts.

What results from this isolation is an uncoordinated – and often divisive – stumbling towards a successful business practice, rather than a more agile and holistic approach where each department moves forward with a clear understanding of the other departments' agendas and operational methods.

A properly executed lifecycle analysis (LCA) of a package's hidden costs is essential when assessing the degree of ecological damage attributed to its entire lifespan. An LCA looks closely at the entire range of factors, from 'upstream' costs such as energy consumption, raw materials extraction, transportation, infrastructure, toxic by-products and habitat and climate impacts,

to 'downstream' costs such as distribution, consumer convenience, product protection (from criminal encroachment as well as breakage and spoilage), shelf storage, marketing needs, disposal and recyclability. While the project development process of package design is linear, the coordination of the process should never be.

What role does the graphic designer have in this cycle? How can someone who is often squeezed into the cracks of this larger business model provide constructive advice? These questions speak to the larger dialogue regarding the designer's place in the workflow. While the traditional role of a graphic designer places them somewhere between the marketing and advertising departments and the production department, graphic designers who are engaged with the larger playing field of visual communications, and who take their role as a systemic thinker and problem-solver seriously, understand that their expertise transcends mere surface decoration, and can inform all facets of project development. Designers who hope to contribute to the paradigm shift towards sustainability must make design decisions based on what they understand of the entire process to which their work is applied. There are many books, forums and online locations that can provide the interested graphic designer with a world of relevant information, and if they are willing to become familiar with such a wide scope of information, they can offer expertise that is otherwise difficult to come by.

A properly executed lifecycle analysis (LCA) of a package's hidden costs can be tremendously helpful when assessing the degree of ecological damage attributed to its entire lifespan.

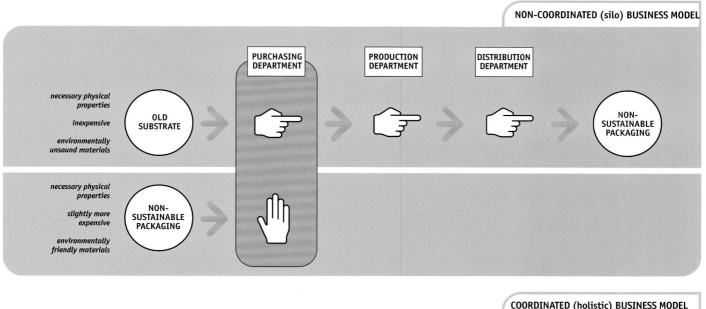

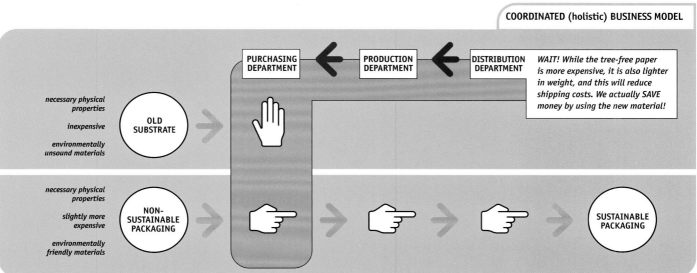

The above graphic is a simplified yet informative example of how business practices that lead to isolation between departments can work against innovators who hope to introduce sustainability into a company's packaging practices. Let's say an individual has found a tree-free substrate as an alternative to the present paperboard they use for a package. The tree-free alternative possesses all the physical properties of the old substrate, but it's more expensive. In many traditional business models this would be enough to prevent the new materials from being used. However, consider that the material, while more expensive, is slightly lighter in weight than the old material. While the purchasing department may not be accounting for that small difference, the distribution department may be hyper aware of such details. In a more holistic business environment, the weight factor would be considered early in the process. When the difference in weight saves in shipping costs that outweigh the extra cost of the new material, there is a net gain.

What's the problem?
Part 2: Packaging procedures without vision

Why sustainability? Why is change necessary? Does the package-design industry really present an environmental problem? And why would designers need to be involved in any changes? It's always helpful to break down an issue into digestible parts in order to understand the larger picture. In this section, the problems are divided into eight different categories.

SOLID WASTE

Over 68 million tonnes (75 million tons) of packaging material enter the US waste stream every year (the total amount of municipal solid waste in the US for 2005 was 222 million tonnes (245 million tons) – EPA). Imagine 330,000 new Statues of Liberty built in the US – or 6,600 for each state in the Union – every year! At such a rate, we could build a full-sized Lady Liberty for every house in the state of Rhode Island in less than two years. This unfathomable amount of rubbish does not just sit there. As it slowly breaks down, toxins from inks, adhesives, bleached pulp and plastics leach into surrounding soil and water sources.

WATER POLLUTION

At the same time, fresh water supplies are being depleted due to increased worldwide demand, and they are more prone to encroachment from sources of pollution. According to a joint World Health Organization and UNICEF report, more than one billion people use unsafe sources of drinking water. The manufacturing of paper – a primary substrate for packaging – is extremely water-intensive, and according to Daniel Imhoff, author of *Paper or Plastic*, it *'ranks third in hazardous effluent due to the pulping and bleaching processes'*, which places it behind only the chemical and steel industries. If you then consider the negative impacts on the water supply of the plastics, inks and adhesives lifecycles, you can begin to imagine the size of the problem.

AIR POLLUTION

Pollution generated by packaging is not limited to the materials that comprise the package and it manufacturing by-products. Each step of material development requires massive amounts of energy, and the energy burned creates significant amounts of air pollution. The ill-health effects that result from breathing air pollution are too numerous to list here, but the World Health Organization estimated that in 2002, three million deaths resulted from all sources of air pollution. As a point of comparison, car deaths in that same year were responsible for one-third of that number.

FOREST DEPLETION

The Rainforest Alliance estimates that 40 hectares (100 acres) of tropical rainforest are lost every minute. That's about 33 trees every second; second after second after second. Destroying old-growth forests decimates biodiversity, spews tremendous amounts of pollution into the air, and exacerbates other problems, such as the availability of clean water (forests act as water-filtration systems), and climate change (forests sequester carbon). Forests have been called the 'lungs of the world', yet we are polluting them even as we cut them down.

DEPLETION OF OTHER RAW MATERIALS

John Thackara, in his book *In The Bubble: Designing For A Complex World*, notes that a product or package represents approximately eight per cent of the actual material used to create it. How many people would be happy with getting a meal that represents less than ten per cent of the food that went into making it? Present manufacturing and production processes could hardly be less efficient. Inefficiency is crime enough, but when the monumental environmental problems that result from these methods become apparent, it is clear that this gross inefficiency is not just costly in a financial sense – it is environmentally unsustainable, and morally suspect.

ENERGY CONSUMPTION

As much physical evidence as there is in the form of material waste on the one hand, and depletion of resources on the other, the primary environmental problem with packaging is in the energy consumption within its lifecycle. Ironically, then, the most damaging aspects of package design are the ones that relate to things that we as consumers don't even ask for and never actually use: energy use throughout the manufacturing cycle and the energy required for transportation. The paper industry for instance, is the fourth-largest consumer of energy. Add to that the energy required to extract petroleum and manufacture plastics from it, not to mention the energy in shipping these materials from one processor to the next.

SOCIAL DISTRESS

This particular area of concern is too-often overlooked, but the process of extracting raw materials and the operation of low-wage manufacturing plants have always had serious negative repercussions on the citizens of third-world countries where these processes are undertaken. This phenomenon of corruption is so common, it has a name – the 'resource curse'. Large corporations deal with dictators in order to keep the supply-lines open, and dictators oppress their populace in order to keep the revenues for themselves. The social injustice that results is as brutal as it is predictable.

CLIMATE CHANGE

Before anyone feels inclined to label the concern over climate change 'overexposed', understand that it took two decades for it to become part of the cultural dialogue. Considering the first comprehensive global warming warnings were issued in the late 1980s, it's not that the topic is on everyone's lips now that is the curiosity, as much as why it took so long for it to get there in the first place.

'We have lived by the assumption that what was good for us would be good for the world. We have been wrong. We must change our lives, so that it will be possible to live by the contrary assumption that what is good for the world will be good for us.'

Wendell Berry

2 Package design and sustainability: constructing a future

Striving for innovation: the credo of any good graphic designer

The earlier question of whether a package is even necessary is important for a reason beyond the one originally discussed. It offers us a window into our changing commercial and ecological environments. Package designers are confronted with an undeniable dilemma: very few other disciplines are engaged in the process of material consumption as a means of encouraging further material consumption. We use natural resources in our packages as a means of persuading consumers to purchase products which are themselves the culmination of material extraction, consumption and production. Plainly put, package designers have been in the habit of compounding material consumption in ways that are simply not sustainable.

This chapter will delve into the complex world of sustainability as it pertains to package design. Package design, before anything, is about materials. Any discipline engaged in the application of materials must understand the full range of repercussions behind material choices, and material application, rather than, literally, the surface – or graphic – effects of the practice.

Why not a package that benefits nature when discarded, rather than one that pollutes it? Pangea Organics has developed packaging seeded with organic herbs, like the basil shown here, for their product line. Information on Pangea Organics can be found in the next chapter, on pages 76 and 77.

Books that encourage the next generation of graphic designers to break from the stylistic tendencies of the generation before them are commonplace. Young designers everywhere strive to redefine visual communication; to put their own stamp on the field of graphic design. What is often overlooked is the notion that breaking from tradition in graphic design can be embodied in something other than stylistic innovation. The creation of a unique style provides proof that its originators are adept at imagining new ways to communicate, but it's only embodied in things such as new colour schemes, new compositional approaches or new typographic manipulations. These are revolutions of the surface. What is needed is a revolution of the form itself; not the package form as much as the form of the package. Rethinking the very methods of imagining form and function will help address the changing ecological and social needs of our world cultures.

The old ways of thinking about package form address old problems. It can be argued that the old ways of thinking have, in fact, created the need for new ways of thinking. Our present methods of production, consumption and disposal are destroying our global life-support system. In their book *Natural Capitalism*, authors Hawkins, Lovins and Lovins put it this way: *'In the past three decades alone, for instance, one-third of the planet's resources, its "natural wealth," has been consumed.'*

When it comes to a trend that young designers might want to rebel against, this seems a more relevant place to begin than, say, layered typography. Here is something else these authors tell us: *'A major German retailer found that 98 per cent of all secondary packaging – boxes around toothpaste tubes, plastic wrap around ice-cream cartons – is simply unnecessary'*. That is a remarkably high percentage; even at 50 per cent, such a trend embodies gross inefficiency.

In 2001, Edward Denison and Guang Yu Ren wrote the book *Packaging Prototypes 3: Thinking Green*, a genuinely helpful text for anyone interested in the effects of

Rethinking the very methods of imagining form and function will help address the changing ecological and social needs of our world cultures.

As a way to promote their dedication to LEED certified building, Greenline Architects developed a promotional package that educates new clients and would-be clients about the certification process. The package, a wooden birdhouse specified with FSC woods, contains four home products, each providing an educational lesson about categories in the LEED certification process. In this way, the home investor not only learns about sustainable building, they are provided with the ability to actually see it: a water gauge illustrates water-efficient landscaping; LED candles demonstrate how to optimize energy performance; starter pots with indigenous seeds and a box of bird seed illustrates how to reduce site disturbance. Each product is used as an educational tool as well as an invitation to participate.

ecologically unsustainable packaging, and the positive steps that were being taken at the time to alter ways in which we thought about material consumption. Early in the book, they discuss the trends of the previous 20 years, observing that consumers in the late 1980s could no longer ignore the negative repercussions of their consumptive habits. Discussing the visible negative impacts of overconsumption, they state that *'such signals could no longer be ignored and the ecological agenda became firmly etched in economic, political and social ideology'*. They conclude: *'We are now in a period of response whereby we should be implementing that which we have learnt in order to achieve a quality of life that is not in any way detrimental to the environment around us.'*

One might be inclined to conclude, given the still-accelerating state of environmental degradation, that Denison and Yu Ren were overly optimistic in their assessment of the global mindset, and in their hopes for significant change. Despite their warning *'that the momentum established by these early environmental success are not lost to subsequent waves of economic and consumer rationalism'*, very little substantive improvement can be observed in this area. Yet, despite the increased environmental damage our consumptive habits have since wrought, much has changed; if not in the concrete actions of individuals around the world, then at least in the collective conscience. As with any cultural paradigm shift, this one has been occurring slowly – at times imperceptibly – yet it is now occurring at a steadily increasing pace. As we near the end of the slow period of change, graphic designers must help facilitate this trend towards sustainability.

As designers search for inspiration in the great modernist movements of the past, they must remember that the innovators in these movements were not merely exploring new styles; they were suggesting new ways of thinking about design's relationship with its culture. The visual styles that stemmed from these movements were the result of their ideas, not the ideas themselves. And so, designers with the ambition to 'make their mark' should consider what design should and could be in the larger context of a culture, rather than what new typographic distortion they can make up for the sake of its own visual novelty.

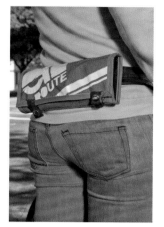

This tyre repair kit is constructed with 100% post-consumer materials that have been built to last. The pockets, straps and hip belt are die-cut from old tyre tubes, while the inner and outer panels are cut from discarded sediment and runoff barriers which are temporarily erected at construction sites. These materials are not only abundantly available, but their strength, durability and lightweight nature make them perfect for the needs of such a product-as-package.

Sustainability: an introduction

Sustainability is not a new concept. It fits in with the writings of every historical philosopher, and the principles of every world religion. Humankind has engaged in high levels of sustainability for a majority of its history, and it is only recently that our behaviour has changed so dramatically and in contradiction to the symbiotic flows of nature that we've even needed a word like sustainability to define what we have, in large part, forgotten.

How's this for simple: 'A sustainable society is one which satisfies its needs without diminishing the prospects of future generations.' That comes from Lester R Brown, the Founder and President of Worldwatch Institute. To add to that, we can say that a sustainable culture is one which satisfies its needs without diminishing the needs of other cultures, and a sustainable economy is one which satisfies its needs without diminishing the needs of other economies. What could be more plain-spoken than that?

It is not the definition of sustainability that is so important, as much as that wide expanse of possibility that the definition alludes to. The moment we attempt to reduce its meaning to simple terms is the moment of most peril – the moment when we lose sight of the fact that true sustainability can only occur when individuals resist the call to limit their field of vision when considering a course of action. This is because sustainability is not about one limited range of thought or interaction. Instead, it is a holistic attempt to mimic the best behaviours of the natural environment. And within the greater weave of complex relationships in the natural world, we can witness a nuanced web of symbiotic relationships. The notion of sustainability simply asks that we engage in such relationships.

While the definition of sustainability is simple, the process required to devise sustainable design thinking is a little more complex. The opposite page graphically represents the factors that impact on sustainability in package design. Because packaging requires the coordination of numerous industries, the application of sustainable ideas requires coordination and communication.

Rather than being a cause for alarm, this degree of complexity should be a signal to designers that there are many ways to reduce the negative impacts of their practice.
What is desired is not a positive change in every area, as much as a positive change in as many areas as possible and an end result that is less detrimental than the original process.

Stewardship

Clear-cutting century-old forests to make toilet paper doesn't sound reasonable to anyone. Neither do flattening mountain-tops, polluting rivers, poisoning fish or devastating third-world economies. Yet these are the well-documented results of unsustainable extraction methods that have served our desire for material goods. There are now third-party organizations who can certify that extraction procedures do not destroy local habitats, cultures or economies.

Locality

If materials are mined in Indonesia and converted in factories in China, so products can be produced in factories in India and distributed to stores in the United States, imagine how much fuel is used throughout the entire process. Buying local can greatly reduce greenhouse gas emissions as well as nurturing local communities. Other than renewable energies, support for local materials is the only action that can influence all of the above stages.

Low Toxicity

While cradle-to cradle-practices make some allowance for the potential reuse of toxic chemicals, less caustic materials can often be substituted. In a theme common to sustainable thinking, an improvement in one area is often related to improvements in others. For instance, the use of less-toxic inks allows for higher rates of recycling and compostability. Advancements in production have made less-toxic substitutes cheaper and more accessible.

Rightsizing

'Rightsizing' is the term for reducing the size of a package within reason. Reduction to the point of elimination is the best practice, but it is not always reasonable, nor is reducing the amount of packaging to the point where the product is vulnerable to spoilage or breakage. This is why this particular term is used; 'size minimization' ignores the fact that there are factors that must be taken into account when reducing package sizes.

EXTRACTION

CONVERSION & PRODUCTION

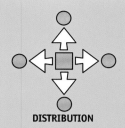

DISTRIBUTION

DISPOSAL

SUSTAINABLE OPTIONS

QUESTION:
Where does design enter
into this process?

ANSWER:
Design decisions
influence EVERY stage.

Lightweighting
While the concept of 'lightweighting' is simple – making the package lighter – achieving it can be complex. If lightweighting is achieved through reducing the amount of material used, it is a net gain. But if it is achieved by using materials that are more toxic than the original material, or if the extraction of the new material is more energy-intensive or environmentally damaging than those of the old material, a net gain may not be realized.

Renewable Energy
The market for renewable energy continues to grow, so much so that there are many paper companies and printing facilities that provide services that make use of renewable energy sources. Third-party certification, such as that awarded by Green-e, is available.

Reuse/Recycle
Reuse is a common practice on factory floors and residential neighbourhoods, and everywhere in between. The rate at which certain materials are recycled can be improved with the initiation of comprehensive collection systems. Without the proper systems, individual recycling practices can be less than productive.

Compostability
It is common knowledge that organic materials trapped in traditional dumps do not break down efficiently. Creating packaging that can go directly into the compost heap – or at least to an industrial composting company – can significantly lower the solid waste stream. Composting is also a way to give back to the natural systems that provide so much for human survival.

Chapter 2: Package Design and Sustainability

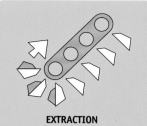
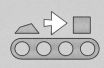

The US Environmental Protection Agency suggests honouring the following principles in order to create more sustainable packaging systems. Graphic designers have the potential to influence client decisions in each area.

— **Eliminating toxic constituents**
— **Using less material**
— **Making packaging more reusable**
— **Using more recycled content**
— **Making packaging more readily recyclable**

So, no more hesitation when confronted with the 'sustainability' word. The idea is as simple as can be. It is only the deliberation of action required to live up to it that is potentially complex – it involves taking responsibility for repercussions that occur throughout the lifecycles that feed and ultimately result from our actions. And that, while being a simple demand, requires something much more than one-dimensional concepts. Sustainability asks that we understand the world as the complex system it is, and that we interact with it accordingly.

Luckily for us, artists are rarely comfortable with restrictive definitions and one-dimensional concepts. Artists understand that intuition, and a firm grasp of the many and nuanced influences of any one idea, are the only means of fully comprehending that concept. They are uniquely suited to leading our societies towards a more sustainable existence.

The myth that there is not enough information available on sustainable printing practices must be challenged. In fact, there is so much recent literature on sustainable materials that an individual could get overwhelmed by information and succumb to a functional paralysis. If one does not know exactly how to begin, after all, how can one know where to begin? So designers must not shirk their obligations by decrying a lack of resources, but instead pursue the accumulation of knowledge just as they would when learning about other essential design issues.

While we have explored how attempts to break down complex processes into specialized units can lead to an inability to run the larger system efficiently, the bigger picture can only be perceived through intimacy with the individual ingredients, and so these must be understood on their own terms before their impacts on the larger system can be fully understood. The following pages look at some of the pieces of the puzzle.

To begin with, five of the initial eight categories are discussed in greater depth on the opposite page. The other three (rightsizing, lightweighting and locality) are not covered here. Issues of rightsizing and lightweighting, while key factors addressed throughout the book, are very specific to the needs of the project in question, and the matter of locality (or the distances that materials must travel throughout the packaging lifecycle) is simply too big to address in a paragraph. Suffice to say that the shorter the distance any materials have to travel, the better.

While the preceding pages categorize sustainability issues by areas of potential impact, the following pages focus on specific areas of material usage, from paper and plastic to inks and adhesives. The hope is that readers will be able to consider how each of the aforementioned areas of impact can be considered when choosing the subsequent categories of packaging materials.

Graphic designers have long understood the importance of visiting the printers they use for their projects. So, discussions regarding sustainable practices should be easy to prompt for those graphic designers who have already sufficiently nurtured these professional relationships.

'Perhaps there should be no special category called "sustainable design". It might be simpler to assume that all designers will try to reshape their values and their work, so that all design is based in humility, combines objective aspects of climate and the ecological use of materials with subjective intuitive processes...'

Victor Papanek

Stewardship

Whether it be petroleum extracts for plastics, mineral extracts for ink pigments, wood-pulp products for papers and cardboards or materials for newer bio- and agro-based polymers, the raw materials for packaging have to come from somewhere, don't they? Safeguarding the environments and protecting the workforces that are local to the extraction of materials is necessary for sustainability in package design. Furthermore, precious natural resources such as old-growth forests should not be consumed, but preserved.

Low Toxicity

This covers a wide range of packaging processes. For paper products, the primary concern is the use of bleaching and pulping processes. For inks, there are concerns with volatile organic compounds (VOCs) in processes that are used throughout the printing cycle. And for plastics there are myriad concerns regarding not just the toxicity of the plastics themselves, but the methods of reconstituting the materials. Massive quantities of toxin-leaching waste can no longer be ignored – the world is literally choking on discarded plastic.

Renewable Energy

The market for renewable energy is exploding, and companies across the packaging industry are embracing these technologies. Renewable energy includes solar, wind, biomass, geothermal, methane extraction from landfills and hydroelectric. Due to the energy-intensive nature of packaging production and distribution, improvements need to continue. While not a form of renewable energy, carbon offset initiatives provide a means of addressing some of the negative repercussions of using nonrenewable energy sources.

Reuse/Recycle

All materials used in the development of package designs have the potential to be reused in some fashion. Companies have long practised the art of factory-floor recycling as a means of limiting waste and increasing material productivity. Municipal systems, while increasingly efficient in countries around the globe, still require far more attention, and far more systemic coordination in order for the global solid waste stream to be exploited for its rich material wealth.

Compostability

The oldest method of disposal is quickly becoming the newest trend in package manufacturing, but what does it mean for a package to be 'compostable'? Conscientious consumers have long made use of organic waste matter to feed their home gardens, but some companies are taking a previous liability – waste packaging – and discovering ways to make it a form of brand differentiation. Even those companies not yet fully capable of making their packages compostable are expressing interest in industrial-grade composting, which is creating a vibrant market for biodegradable packaging materials.

Paper and paperboard

The What

The How and Why

USE HIGH PERCENTAGES OF POST-CONSUMER RECYCLED CONTENT

The world's paper stream is a mighty force to be reckoned with – there is simply so much of it out there that the world is choking on it. Demanding high levels of post-consumer waste (PCW) in paper stock choices should be of the highest priority. This encourages the efficiency of collection systems by creating demand, and reduces energy consumption and further devastation of the world's forests. According to the Environmental Defense Fund, every tonne of recycled paper saves over 1,500 litres (400 gallons) of oil due to the significantly lower energy loads required.

Organizations such as the 100% Recycled Paperboard Alliance (RPA-100%) have streamlined the collection systems for these materials and, in doing so, have significantly reduced the load on landfill and incinerators. The RBA claims that 14 trees are saved for each tonne of paperboard converted to 100 per cent recycled paperboard.

A number inside the Möbius loop – the universal symbol for recycling – designates the percentage of recycled content. Beware of the Möbius loop when it is not accompanied by any other information; because the symbol is in the public domain, anyone can use it. Many consumers believe that 'recyclable' has the same meaning as 'recycled', but the symbol unaccompanied by any explanation simply means that the product could theoretically be recycled.

PCW should be given highest priority, while pre-consumer, or post-industrial waste (PIW), consists of scraps, trimmings and other waste products resulting from the production stream. While not detrimental, PIW does not have the positive impacts that PCW has, and if a product does not claim to be comprised of post-consumer recycled materials, the chances are that any recycled content claim is from post-industrial collection.

EXPLORE TREE-FREE ALTERNATIVES, SUCH AS FAST-GROWING PLANTS AND AGRICULTURAL BY-PRODUCTS, AS WELL AS FUNKY STUFF LIKE OLD JEANS AND BANANA SKINS

Benefits of plants such as hemp, kenaf, switchgrass and straw include: quick growth, little or no need for chemicals and low water needs.

'Waste' from agricultural processes (what remains after the 'valuable' parts of a farmed product are harvested) would otherwise be burned, increasing greenhouse gas emissions. For example, the redirection of waste by-product from empty fruit bunch (from palm-oil processing) to tree-free paper products is a new and highly competitive market because there is so much of this waste product. There is also a natural wax in the fibre that can serve as lamination for certain paper products, and because this is a natural part of the substance, it biodegrades – unlike many existing laminates.

From a marketing standpoint, more unique tree-free products provide an innovative opportunity to create a line of 'paper' products because the differentiation is very visible – banana-skin boxes are inherently more interesting from a consumer's point of view than boxes that meet FSC specs.

The What

The How and Why

SUPPORT SUSTAINABLE FORESTRY. STOP VIRGIN WOOD HARVESTING, ESPECIALLY OLD-GROWTH FORESTS AND RAINFORESTS

What was once considered hard to find has now become hard to ignore – a graphic designer interested in finding paper from renewable sources simply has to visit the website of any major paper manufacturer in the world to find a wide array of product that is not produced from virgin harvests or comprised of post-consumer waste.

This is not just an environmental issue, but an issue of global justice as well. For example, the World Bank estimates that illegal logging in developing nations robs the citizens of these countries of £5 to 7.5 billion ($7.7 to 11.6 billion) annually. Using certified pulp sources will help to ensure that everyone in the supply-chain gets a fair share of the profits.

The Forest Stewardship Council (FSC) provides certification for any materials derived from wood. FSC principles account for the sustainability of timber growth and harvest, but also monitor indigenous people's rights, and workers' rights. The organization certifies paper merchants, manufacturers, printers and pulp suppliers and an annual basis. 'FSC 100%' are products that meet the Chain-of-Custody (COC) principles of FSC. COC defines *'the path taken by raw materials harvested from an FSC-certified source through processing, manufacturing, distribution and printing until it is a final product ready for sale to the end consumer'*. Other FSC certificates include 'Recycled Content' and 'Mixed Sources'.

The PFEC (Programme for the Endorsement of Forest Certification), is another nonprofit organization that offers third party certification around the globe.

INSIST ON CHLORINE-FREE PAPERSTOCK

Processed Chlorine Free (PCF) is reserved for recycled-content paper and requires that the product contain at least 30 per cent post-consumer content. The method by which the percentage of the recycled content is determined must also be certified.

Totally Chlorine Free (TCF) is reserved for virgin-fibre paper, and requires that the mill does not use old-growth forest or any other virgin pulp. TFC can only be used to designate virgin paper simply because its impossible to verify the amount of bleach that may have gone into the production of recycled waste paper.

The Chlorine-Free Products Association (CFPA) provides ongoing testing, inspection and enforcement for products that carry their certification for both PCF and TCF papers. There must be no chlorine or chlorine compounds used in the papermaking process, and no current or pending violations at the mill. Comprehensive mill audits by industry experts are required, and the CFPA provides recommendations on product quality and increased productivity.

Elemental Chlorine-free (ECF) uses chlorine dioxide rather than elemental chlorine, and thereby reduces harmful by-products by approximately 90 per cent.

41

Inks etc.

The What ## *The How and Why*

USE LESS INK COVERAGE OVERALL

This is maths that all graphic designers can manage, even though they may not always like the answer. The more flood-colour usage, and the more full-bleed ink coverage, the less ecologically sound the job will be. Not only is more ink consumed in the process (more intensive extraction and manufacturing), but more post-industrial and post-consumer waste is produced that must be de-inked before being recycled.

ASK FOR THE 'GOOD' BLACK, AND OTHER COLOUR-AWARE IDEAS

What has long been embraced by printers as a way to save money has quickly become another method of reusing more ink – any artist knows that when you mix enough colours from the spectrum, the ultimate result will be black. By mindfully reusing inks from every job, and mixing them all into a large vat, many printers can reduce the amount of black ink they need to purchase. This results in a bonus in two areas – it reduces demand for black ink, and it reduces the amount of waste flowing from printing facilities.

As can be seen in the sidebar for the Celery Design Collaborative on page 89, approximately 20 per cent of the Pantone Matching System® colours contain especially harmful chemicals. Avoiding designing with these spot colours can reduce the toxic load of a print job. Metallic colours, for instance, contain high levels of copper and zinc compounds, while many warm reds contain barium. Fluorescents should also be avoided.

SPECIFY SOY-BASED INKS

Petroleum-based inks require destructive extraction techniques, and are made from a nonrenewable and increasingly precious resource – oil. They do not biodegrade, but remain toxic in both the resulting post-industrial toxic waste (solid and effluent), and post-consumer waste. They also require toxic solvents and cleaners, which can be comprised of 90 per cent VOCs (see opposite top for more information).

Soy beans, on the other hand, are an abundant and relatively low-maintenance crop. For example, approximately 50 per cent of all soybeans produced in the US require no irrigation. Soy printing allows for biodegradable cleaners for clean-up and disposal. In terms of performance, soy inks have a high level of rub-resistance, and result in less dot-gain than petroleum-based inks.

Soy inks generally spread 15 to 20 per cent further than petroleum-based inks, and soy pigments are usually more intense, thus requiring less ink to begin with.

Soy ink can be cleaned with water-based solvents, thus further reducing the VOC load.

Soy ink can be more readily removed from paper in the recycling process (de-inking), and does less damage to the pulp – so more fibre is saved for reuse. Soy waste is considered much less hazardous by government standards.

INVESTIGATE OTHER VEGETABLES INKS

Sustainable inks can be produced from a wide variety of vegetable oils, including corn, walnut, coconut, linseed and canola. These possess the same positive attributes as soy.

The What	The How and Why

SPECIFY LOW-VOC INKS

Not all soy-based inks are created equal. For example, an ink can contain 90 per cent petroleum and still qualify for certain soy-ink labels, so low-VOC inks must specifically be requested. VOCs (Volatile Organic Compounds) are chemicals that vaporize and enter the air under normal atmospheric conditions. Their vapours contribute to a range of air pollution, including smog, ozone and greenhouse gases. Those particles that remain in solid form pollute ground water and soil, and many are carcinogenic. Soy-based inks generally contain 1 to 10 per cent VOCs, while petroleum-based inks contain approximately 25 to 40 per cent VOCs.

ASK FOR AQUEOUS VARNISHES

Standard varnishes and adhesives contain high levels of VOCs, and result in toxic by-products and 'end-of-life' residues.

Aqueous varnishes are water-based and low-VOC. Clean-up does not require solvent-based toxic cleaning detergents or high temperatures. Paper with aqueous varnish can be recycled and re-pulped without harmful by-products.

Catalysts that allow the aqueous varnish to dry quickly without curing emit formaldehyde, and should be avoided.

UV-cured aqueous varnish is high in energy use, and the resulting paper is difficult to de-ink, and thus not easily recyclable.

USE WATER-BASED ADHESIVES

Adhesives used in binding are often petroleum-based, emit high levels of VOCs and are difficult to remove in the de-inking process. Water-based glues that do not use VOCs and dissolve in the de-inking process during recycling are quickly becoming available and much more dependable, and should be requested when possible.

MISCELLANEOUS

Waterless printing (dryography) does not require dampening solutions to prepare plates for printing. It is fast and clean, and reduces paper waste and energy use.

Computer-to-plate (CTP) or direct-to-plate (DTP) technology has reduced VOC-release and energy-use significantly because it completely eliminates film production. This technique has become commonplace due to the reduced costs associated with it.

UV inks do not require high temperatures to dry the inks, which is good because high temperatures evaporate VOCs, releasing them into the air. There is a down side to UV printing, however; it can be difficult to remove the pigment from the substrate in recycling situations because it is more firmly bonded to the pulp.

Certain large-printing facilities provide methods of recapturing VOCs, and some readapt this energy loss to create new energy. It's important to inquire about VOC-capture when researching printers for an upcoming job.

Rating plastics for their 'less bad' qualities

RESIN CODES

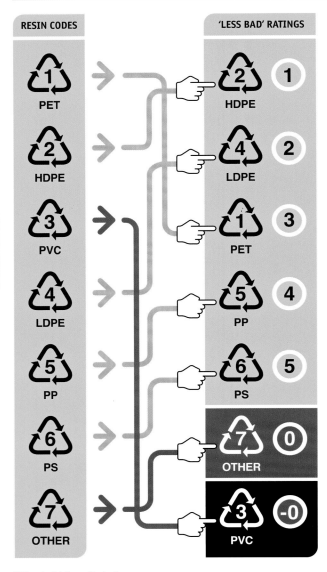

'LESS BAD' RATINGS

This prioritizing reflects the ease in which certain resins can be recycled, and relative toxicity. It's important to note that this is a loose guide and certain plastics cannot be used for certain purposes, and that regional collection systems can make certain resins more desirable than others.

Plastics are a necessary evil at this point, but must eventually be phased out.

Everyone recognizes plastic as a source of great environmental stress – in its petroleum-based extraction, in its toxicity and in its ecological persistence. Plastics are also not amenable to repeated recycling (and can be rendered useless if cross-contaminated). Instead, they 'downcycle' to less functional forms of plastic. Plastics have historically been difficult to recycle into a form that matches their original chemical integrity, either being 'downcycled' into park benches and other crude materials, or being judiciously added in small percentages to virgin plastics. Even though recent developments have improved the reuse of higher percentages of recycled plastics, they still cannot match the performance of other materials such as metals and glass, which can be effectively reconstituted indefinitely, and paper and paperboard, which can be reconstituted about seven times before losing adequate fibre strength.

Despite their negative attributes, plastics can still contribute to sustainable packaging schemes for the near future. They are significantly lighter than glass, for instance, and can thus contribute to a dramatic saving in fuel consumption (this was a major reason for its popularity as a packaging material to begin with). Also, packaging that uses recycled plastic helps in two significant ways: it reduces the need for extracting new raw materials; and it encourages the reclamation of existing waste plastic. Despite these 'benefits', plastics should not be viewed as a long-term solution for sustainable packaging; the information on page 45 represents a listing of lesser evils rather than ideal aims. Biopolymers should slowly replace the use of plastics, but this cannot happen overnight.

KNOW YOUR NUMBERS

The resin code system (left) was developed in 1988 by the Society of the Plastics Industry in order to help manufacturers and recyclers categorize the different kinds of plastics.

1	**Polyethylene Terephthalate (polyester)**
2	**High Density Polyethylene**
3	**Polyvinyl Chloride (vinyl)**
4	**Low Density Polyethylene**
5	**Polypropylene**
6	**Polystyrene**
7	**Other**

Plastics

The What

The How and Why

USE POST-CONSUMER RECYCLED (PCR) PLASTICS

Arguments that still decry the costs of instituting effective recycling systems stubbornly disregard the costs, energy consumption and pollution that result from extracting and processing virgin materials. As Daniel Imhoff in his book *Paper or Plastic* points out, virgin HDPE requires over seven times more energy to make than recycled HDPE. While few recycled plastics can maintain their original integrity through the recycling process, technology has made it easier to mix percentages of recycled content with virgin content. Progress has recently been made in depolymerizing plastics, so they can be reconstituted at their original quality. Imhoff also points out that producing virgin unbleached paperboard requires three times more energy than producing the recycled equivalent, and producing virgin aluminium requires 18 times more energy to produce its recycled equivalent.

DESIGN PACKAGES WITH RECYCLING IN MIND

Design-for-Recycling (DfR) is a subset of the Design-for-Disassembly (DfD) or the Design-for-Enviroment (DfE) movement. Plastic waste streams can be contaminated by the presence of other materials attached to the resins, including other plastics, paperboard, wire and adhesives. Because package designers rarely consider this, a lot of plastic will never be recycled – the disassembly and ensuing isolation of the individual plastics is simply too costly.

Organizations such as the Association of Post-consumer Plastic Recyclers provide information on the development of protocols that account for recycling demands at the outset of the package design process, which allows recycling organizations to effectively collect and reconstitute resins more efficiently. Generally speaking, plastics used in packages should be easily detached from the package, and marked with the appropriate resin symbol so that people who want to recycle are empowered to do so.

SUPPORT BIOPLASTIC INNOVATION

'Bioplastics', an umbrella term defining biodegradable plastics from renewable sources (botanicals), is quickly becoming a viable and environmentally friendly alternative to our petroleum-based plastics. Considering the amount of agricultural by-product (husks, stalks, leaves, shells, starch residues, etc.) created in farming enough food for six billion people, there's good cause to explore these potentials. It's another example of McDonough's 'Waste = Food' concept (see page 61).

The corn-based PLA (polylactic acid), a resin developed by and marketed under the brandname NatureWorks, has varied uses (from hard and rigid packaging to pliable and thin films). It can be reprocessed effectively and efficiently and it has been engineered to biodegrade in a matter of months. Another biopolymer, Plantic, is a cornstarch that can be modified for thermoforming, injection moulding, film extrusion and blow moulding, as well as rigid and flexible packaging. Plantic is water-soluble, and so it is not just compostable, but flushable.

Biopolymers are presently grouped into the number '7' resin designation, and very little can be done with the resulting recycled content. As biopolymers grow in popularity there will be a need to create a new resin category so that bioplastics can be treated together.

It must be stressed that 'second-generation' biopolymers, which are derived from agricultural waste, are developed so as to prevent competition with needed food sources.

Following the stream:
cleaner at the outset often means cleaner at the end

All the categories that have been discussed up to this point influence the upstream and downstream impacts of the packaging lifecycle. 'Upstream' refers to absolutely anything that transpires before the package reaches a consumer's hands. This would include the energy loads, labour stresses and ecological wastes that are connected to material extraction, processing, production and distribution. As the diagram below illustrates, upstream impacts (which can also be referred to as 'front-end' or 'pre-consumer' impacts), far outweigh 'downstream' impacts, or those effects that occur once the package leaves the consumer's hands (also referred to as 'back-end' or 'post-consumer').

Unsustainable packaging is a double-edged sword, in that it negatively influences the upstream impacts even as it intensifies the downstream problems. If harmful pollutants such as bleach, heavy metals, petroleum ink residues and plastics are designed into a package, they inevitably become a part of the toxic burden that stays with it. This equation, however, also provides the best hope for reducing the ecological burden of package design; for every reduction in toxic materials within the upstream cycle, a proportionally equal reduction results in downstream residue. In fact, this inter-relationship is cause for even greater hope. If more material is designed to be reclaimed and reused from the outset, far less material will have to be extracted to begin with, which substantially reduces the upstream impacts. So, upstream impacts – far more substantial than downstream – can be reduced not only by designing with less material and less toxic material, but by designing reuse into the materials from the outset.

Abundance, in and of itself, is not bad; it's possible to have a lot of packages without having a lot of waste. The categories on the opposite page can ensure that packaging materials are designed with the principle that they remain in isolated loops of production, remaining both unadulterated and unadulterating.

The phrase 'end-of-life' has too often implied landfills as a final resting place. But designers must learn to define the 'end' of a package's life, not as something that creates waste, but as something that facilitates a new beginning.

The Natural Step, a sustainable consulting company discussed at greater length in the next chapter (see page 60) has a name for any effort to keep manufactured materials out of the waste stream: 'value recovery'. Within that phrase we can discern a better understanding of how we might continue to live comfortably in the world without destroying its life-giving qualities. When we realize that our waste stream has value, we will find innovative methods of redirecting that stream towards persistent reuse, thus eliminating waste.

This discussion of the concept of a 'next life' for materials has primarily focused on methods of sending those materials back to a manufacturer so that they can reuse them. In the coming chapters, we will consider another kind of next life – a more immediate next life that consumers themselves benefit from – that of secondary usage.

'The most serious external costs of packaging lie in the extraction of natural resources, energy consumption and the emission of air and water pollution throughout the manufacturing processes.'

Daniel Imhoff

Next life

The What

The How and Why

CRADLE-TO-CRADLE

The question as to whether cherry blossoms that fall from the tree and never take seed should be considered waste reveals the essential core of cradle-to-cradle thinking. A blossom that does not take hold as a new seedling is not waste because it becomes nutrition for the ecosystem that feeds the tree to begin with.

Waste = Food, a philosophy espoused by McDonough and Braungart (see page 61), encourages the isolation of two closed-loop systems of materials use so that each loop can run in a perpetual cycle of reuse. The biological loop includes all biodegradable materials. The technological loop includes nonbiodegradable synthetics and hazardous materials that are either toxic to the biosphere or simply do not biodegrade. This is not recycling, because recycling downcycles materials, in that the quality of the material is less than its original quality. In cradle-to-cradle systems, quality is not compromised within the regenerating cycles.

DESIGN FOR DISASSEMBLY (DFD)

Companies are learning to view the materials in their products and packages as valuable commodities in their own right, and are finding ways to design them so that, when the consumer is done with them, the company can reuse the materials for continuous rounds of production. DfE (Design for Environment) is a global movement to design products and packages that can be disassembled once their lives as consumer products are over, and their individual components can be used again, melted down or reconstituted for a new generation of use (consider the technical nutrients above).

COMPOSTABILITY

The most common elements that prevent paper products from being certifiably compostable are inks and adhesives. While most home composting is of disposable organic matter such as fruit and vegetable leftovers, commercial-grade composting is quickly becoming a standard business operation. Within these commercial composting facilities, packages that make use of new bioplastics, like the bottles that Biota water comes in, can biodegrade in a matter of months without leaving any toxic residue.

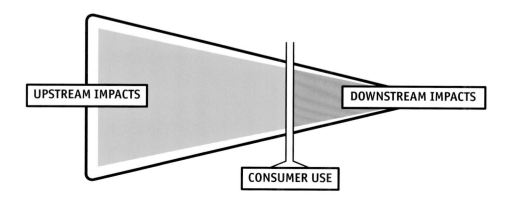

There are laws that require reduced packaging and greater recycling of packaging waste in at least 28 countries around the world (the United States is not one of them). While the European Union has set strict 'take-back' regulations for product manufacturers, other countries such as South Korea place the liability on the consumers, charging for waste disposal and thus encouraging consumer behaviour that favours products with less packaging.

The European Union's 1994 directive on harmonizing the collection of package waste, which required union members to create country-wide packaging waste collection systems that would *'gather no less than 60 per cent by weight for glass, paper and board; 50 per cent by weight for metals; 22.5 per cent by weight for plastics and 15 per cent by weight for wood'* by the end of 2008, is an example of an ambitious and comprehensive plan. By 2002, all member states had recovered 58 per cent of glass, 68 per cent of paper and board, 57 per cent of metals and 24 per cent of plastics.

Along with providing impressive concrete results, government commitment in the form of regulations and incentives signals to the business world that the issue is of substantial import, and this drives private sector innovation.

Regulation, as William McDonough often states, is a sign of design failure. *'You don't filter smokestacks … Instead, you put the filter in your head and design the problem out of existence.'* So, the need for regulations should signal to the business world that there are better, more creative methods at their disposal. However, until the time when business makes that shift, regulations are necessary. Complying with governmental regulations costs corporations billions of pounds a year, as does the cost of non-compliance. It stands to reason then, that if these corporations were provided with design solutions that did not run counter to governmental regulations, they would be eternally grateful to those who created the designs.

The diagram on the opposite page depicts part of the broader outline for companies interested in attaining

An awareness of the existence of these available tools and their basic principles can empower designers to promote sustainable thinking with confidence.

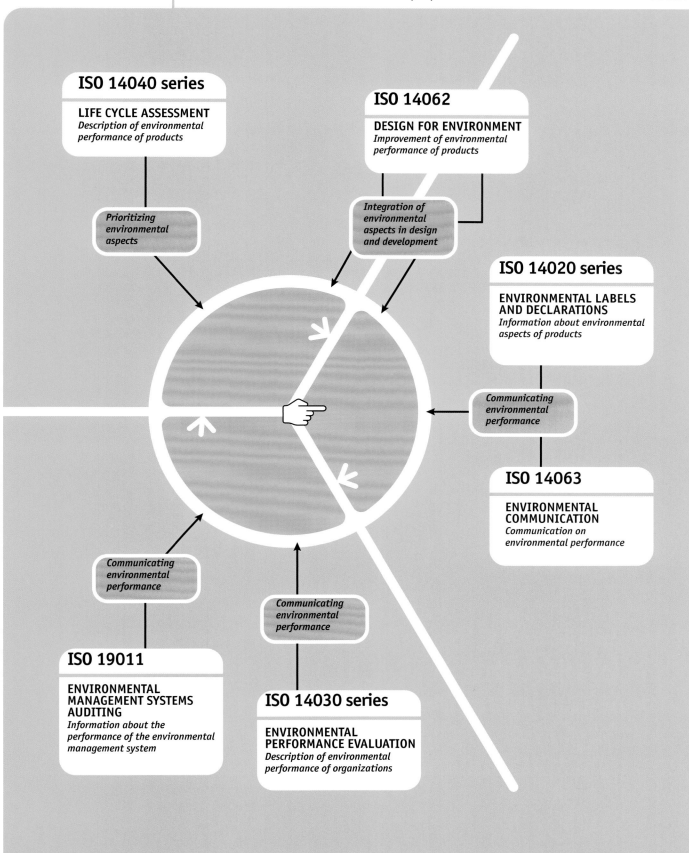

ISO 14040 series

LIFE CYCLE ASSESSMENT
Description of environmental performance of products

Prioritizing environmental aspects

ISO 14062

DESIGN FOR ENVIRONMENT
Improvement of environmental performance of products

Integration of environmental aspects in design and development

ISO 14020 series

ENVIRONMENTAL LABELS AND DECLARATIONS
Information about environmental aspects of products

Communicating environmental performance

ISO 14063

ENVIRONMENTAL COMMUNICATION
Communication on environmental performance

Communicating environmental performance

Communicating environmental performance

ISO 19011

ENVIRONMENTAL MANAGEMENT SYSTEMS AUDITING
Information about the performance of the environmental management system

ISO 14030 series

ENVIRONMENTAL PERFORMANCE EVALUATION
Description of environmental performance of organizations

This chart is based on the 14001 and 14004 standards, which are general guidelines for environmental management systems ©ISO

Certification organizations

ISO 14000 certification. The International Standards Organizations (ISO) has devised a comprehensive set of standards for creating, managing and improving environmental management systems. The ISO 14000 family of standards resulted from the United Nations Conference on Environment and Development in Rio de Janeiro in 1992, and has since been accepted globally. The goal of the standards is to provide tools for organizations to manage their environmental profiles and improve their performance in this arena. An awareness of the existence of these available tools and their basic principles can empower designers to promote sustainable thinking with confidence.

Governmental standards for package design, which vary considerably from country to country, provide a helpful starting point. The programmes range from the European Union's 'Eco-Label' to the Japan Environment Association's 'Eco Mark'. But there are also many 'independent' certification programmes that can verify the sustainable attributes of materials. Without such certification, it can be difficult to determine whether a company or product is truly 'green' or merely attempting to greenwash their target audience. As a valuable service to their clients, designers should commit themselves to becoming familiar with the certification organizations that provide a level of accuracy in reporting sustainable attributes.

'First-party certification' organizations are most often internal branches of a company charged with overseeing certain initiatives. This kind of certification can be misleading, as it endorses a way of thinking – a corporate mission statement, for instance – rather than any concrete action.

'Second-party certification' organizations are run by industry–trade groups. Because trade groups are organized with the goal of furthering the agenda of the industry, they can only offer a limited degree of assurance as to the veracity of sustainability claims.

'Third-party certification' organizations are basically oversight groups; organizations that don't have a vested interest in the success of the industry they are monitoring. These may be governmental bodies, independent groups or combinations thereof. Third-party organizations have a clear set of criteria that must be met before they award use of their name and graphic mark. Applying the graphic symbols that most third-party organizations provide to their members can be beneficial in two ways: it builds consumer trust in the product; and it provides an educational service to consumers.

As with any other discipline, mastering the realm of sustainable package design is not necessarily achieved through knowing all of the answers, as much as through knowing the right questions to ask, and knowing where the answers to those questions might be found.

As with any other discipline, mastering the realm of sustainable package design is not necessarily achieved through knowing all of the answers, as much as through knowing the right questions to ask, and knowing where the answers to those questions might be found.

At the beginning of chapter two, we discussed how lawyers begin each case without any preconceived notions, and that package designers should not begin with any assumptions either. Lawyers provide another helpful analogy here. They do not attempt to remember every precedent on the books with the idea that when they begin a new case they can instantly remember exactly which precedents will prove helpful to their arguments. Instead, they are trained to know where and how to look for relevant precedents at the beginning of a new case.

If, as a means of shirking those important research responsibilities, they claim that they 'forget' where to look, or that they were 'too busy' with the task at hand to engage in research, they will invariably lose their case. Lawyers understand that the task at hand is the research, and that without the necessary research, any case they do attempt to build will fall under the weight of ignorance.

Designers must embrace a similar methodology in that, while retaining as much actionable information as possible, they must above all possess a firm understanding of the range of information available, as well as the resources that will provide them with access to that information.

The intention of this book is to provide one such source of information. It aspires as much to being a portal for further information as it does to being a warehouse for present information. Especially in the dynamic atmosphere of present developments in packaging technologies and materials, a designer must develop instinctive habits of purveying the scope of available means.

What about energy?

After considering the many available points of action for designers in the realm of sustainable packaging design, perhaps the best place to conclude the discussion is in the area that quite literally fuels them all: energy consumption. Extraction of raw materials for plastics and pulp; processing these natural resources into viable materials; converting the materials to packages; printing the packages; filling the packages; warehousing the packages; disposing of the packages. Combine all of these with the shipping that occurs between each stage, and you can see that it requires vast amounts of energy consumption.

The fact that each stage in the packaging process requires energy consumption suggests that reductions in energy consumption are easily attainable. As already discussed, rightsizing and lightweighting (making packages smaller and lighter) have positive impacts that compound as they move throughout the lifecycle of package development. Increasing recycled content and using local materials and packaging suppliers rather than geographically distant ones are two other ways to reduce energy usage. Yet, despite the best efforts to reduce energy inputs, no packaging endeavour can reach zero-energy needs. Because this is so, two other factors can dramatically help reduce ecological impact: using renewable energies and purchasing carbon offsets to attain 'carbon neutrality'.

Working with suppliers who purchase renewable energy not only reduces toxic and greenhouse gas emissions and drives future costs lower by increasing demand, it also provides your client with marketing opportunities. The climate change debate has changed the climate (if you will) of consumer attitudes towards corporate stewardship. Announcements of greenhouse gas reductions in the packaging development stage can be an effective advertising strategy. Including a 'scorecard' of results on the package itself can result in increased loyalty to the brand. Luckily, many commercial printing facilities and paper suppliers have committed to renewable energies to fuel their own operations, and graphic designers don't have to search too far for these kinds of savings.

Reducing a company's carbon footprint by 'offsetting' their carbon emissions, while not as beneficial as renewable energy use, is still a helpful step. Offsets can be 'purchased' through many organizations, and are realized through various carbon-reduction strategies, including things such as tree-planting programmes and methane-capture programmes.

Reclaiming the concept of package-as-product

In his book *The Green Imperative*, Victor Papanek coined the phrase 'package as product' to critique consumer infatuation with the outward appearance of packages. This tendency to accept a package's physical extravagance as a trustworthy sign of the product's quality was considered by Papanek as a dangerous form of 'semiotic convenience' that enabled manufacturers to justify excessive packaging. Semiotic convenience was number ten on Papanek's list of 'ten convenience traps' that have fed consumer obsessions with unrealistic notions of having it all by sheer force of consumption.

Unfortunately, the seductive allure of Papanek's semiotic convenience is still alive and well. While his use of the phrase 'package as product' originally aimed to define a corrosive social phenomenon, however, we will use it here as a way to suggest a seachange in packaging priorities. Rather than use 'package as product' as a sarcastic condemnation, we will use the phrase here in its most literal sense: as a way to define a package that is a product in its own right. Once the product has been dispensed from the package intended to hold it, who says the package cannot transform into an after-market product with a function all of its own? This 'new' objective can be seen to treat packaging material in more efficient ways by doubling its functionality.

There are potential pitfalls with such an approach, of course. If the secondary function of the package is too transient – limited to a single use, for instance – then it is merely postponing the inevitable disposal. Also, such an endeavour must be attempted only if it is determined that the product requires a package at all. Similarly, designers must not become so enamoured with the idea of a package performing as a product that they lose sight of the fact that more material is being used than in the original package. There is also the importance of choosing sustainable materials, in that secondary functions that require toxic additives are no great step forward in sustainable package design.

A primary objective of this book is to reinvigorate the debate regarding the end of a package's so-called utility. Some of the earliest packages ever made, if not designed explicitly for reusability, were reimagined by consumers in unexpected ways to serve a purpose once their initial job was done. Tin, glass and wood – all materials commonly used in early packages – all but solicited secondary usage from those who purchased the products contained within them.

Ingrained reuse: wood has provided packaging throughout the ages, and is given to natural recycling – here packaging crates find a new use as bookshelves.

Some tin old, some tin new: adaptive reuse of packages can be inspiring and intensely creative. Here, a common container for breath mints is empowered to make music its designers could never have imagined.

Our present form of consumption has limitations that have become abundantly clear, and this realization has brought us to a point in history where we must strive to devise materials that provide us with long-lasting service. The functionality of a service economy, in fact, may soon replace our idea of personal products. In their book Natural Capitalism, Hawken, Lovins and Lovins discuss the value of 'service and flow', their third principle of natural capitalism. The basic argument is that materials which require extensive capital input to extract, produce and manufacture have value in their own right. Because of this value, a company should want their products back from the consumer in order to harvest the materials within them. Hawken, Lovins and Lovins go on to explain that customers don't actually want the products they buy; they simply want the services that the products provide them. Their proposal (which is a core tenet of all sustainable philosophies) is to create a service economy, where consumers are paid to return products to the manufacturer once they tire of them, thus creating a flow of material that cycles from manufacturer, to consumer then back to manufacturer, in a perpetual loop. This basic idea is nothing new (a simple form of it is leasing), but the triple bottom line benefits that would result in an economy that returned products to their original material flows in order to feed the newer generation of products would positively affect everyone involved.

While the above discussion focuses on products, the same principle can be applied to packages; their materials are valuable in their own right in that they represent a significant investment in time, money and energy. In this light, a secondary use for a package provides the first 'afterlife' service directly to the consumer. At the end of this functional afterlife, the package can be returned to the material flow.

'Value-added packaging' is another useful definition, because it provides the consumer with a product above and beyond the contained product.

Secondary function for a package may manifest itself in many ways, but three general categories can be delineated: 'reuse by default' defines an obvious form of reuse that is closely related to the package's initial function of holding something (like the wooden box on the opposite page); 'reuse by innovation' can be defined as a creative act that transforms the original package in surprising ways (like the thumb piano above); and 'reuse by prescription' describes a clearly defined function for the package by the package manufacturer.

This last designation of reuse begins at the earliest design planning stage, and is perhaps the most exciting arena for designers to consider. The last two sections in this book present innovative thinking in creating packages as products; that, from the outset, were designed to keep the package out of the garbage, and provide a valuable secondary use once the consumer has extracted the product it holds.

Designers must not become so enamoured with the idea of a package performing as a product that they lose sight of the fact that more material is being used than in the original package.

Chapter 2: Package Design and Sustainability

Interview: John Habraken
Creator of the WOBO (world bottle)

John Habraken is an architect and retired professor of architecture at MIT. In the early 1960s he was approached by Alfred Heineken to create a beer bottle that could perform as an architectural building block as a secondary use in developing countries.

An early wood model for the WOBO nested the neck of one bottle between the concave bodies of two others. The weight distribution on this design was very beneficial, but it was rejected in part due to its association with a liqueur bottle.

Q: How did an architect end up designing a beer bottle?

Alfred Heineken conceived of the idea of making beer bottles that could be bricks for people to build houses with. Heineken Company brewed all beer under that name in the Netherlands to make sure quality was guaranteed. The result was that beer for Latin America and Africa was shipped from the Netherlands, and returning empty bottles for refill or reuse of the glass made no economic sense. He saw the heaps of discarded bottles when visiting those countries and, realizing people needed building materials, the idea came to him.

At lunch with a well-known lawyer who was interested in arts and architecture, he asked if he knew someone who might design the bottle for him. His visitor happened to be a cousin of mine, and at the time I had just published my book, *Supports: An alternate to mass housing*, which did not help me to get work as an architect. 'Ask John Habraken,' was the suggestion, 'he is crazy enough to like the idea.'

Q; What is your opinion of the recent spurt in sustainable thinking in design?

I do believe sustainability in general is here to stay in the production of things. But to make the transition from a fashion towards a knowledge base, a serious study of the combination of the use-life of things, the physical lifespan of things and the cyclic nature of material transformations will eventually produce a knowledge base of use to all design and production. We are only scratching the surface so far. As long as money can be made without new knowledge, new knowledge is not welcome. Applying new knowledge tends to be disruptive of processes and conventions, and makes people feel ignorant and vulnerable.

Q: Is interdisciplinary exploration in the fields of design important?

I believe interdisciplinary interest and training can only come after one is master in one chosen field. In the education of such a field, however, there should be emphasis on the general principles that drive it. It is these principles that most likely will make a shift to another field of design easier. The question as to what general design principles may apply to all design fields is of interest to philosophers and theorists, but will eventually only be answered from a comparison of well grounded knowledge in specific fields. We need to first work on those principles in our own field. The more we know there, the easier it will become for the good practitioner to move into other fields as well, by his or her own initiative, or by invitation.

Q: How did the WOBO project develop?

From the beginning the focus of Heineken was on a bottle that could be a brick. Beer was exported in glass and no other material was considered. Heineken had personally been involved in the design of the beer bottle label and was proud of it. He was extremely ambitious about it and once confided that he wanted his face on the cover of *Time Magazine* as the inventor of the WOBO bottle. Everyone else hated the idea. The company that produced the beer bottles had to cooperate because Heineken Company was such an important customer, but did so reluctantly.

To make a trial run for another bottle design was extremely disruptive and costly for them as it would interrupt the 24-hour melting and pouring of glass. Eventually, the company salespeople – although Heineken actually owned the company – killed the scheme, arguing that it would destroy the beer's reputation.

Right – Fifteen years after the WOBO was created, architect Rinus Berg-van-den designed this house, to be built with all reused materials, including recovered waste sulfur for mortar, vehicle parts for roof and wall sections, oil drums for columns and 60,000 WOBO bottles.

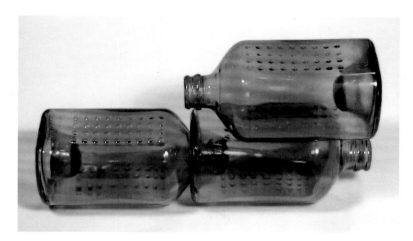

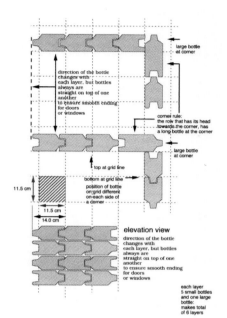

I toured the bottle production plant and learned that the greatest force the bottle gets to sustain is when the metal cap is slammed on the filled bottle. I also learned that total weight of glass for a single bottle is very important. Initially, I designed an entirely different kind of bottle (see picture of wooden model, opposite). These bottles would be placed vertically, upright and bottom up, the neck of each bottle filling the void between two curved bottle volumes. It was an elegant bottle that aimed to minimize the thickness of the glass by guiding the flow of weight downwards. It was rightly vetoed as too 'feminine' or even 'erotic' for a beer bottle, looking more like a container for a liqueur. This was my learning curve about the image of a packaging form.

I believe that Heineken was right in hiring an architect and not a packaging designer or designer of glass containers. It seemed easier for an architect to learn about the bottle manufacturing process than for a glass container designer to learn about brick wall systems.

For me the question of making wall openings and corners without cutting bottles (real bricks can easily be cut) and still avoid continuous vertical joints, was the most interesting problem. I think I solved it in an elegant way. Few architects to whom I show the bottle grasp this problem before they are told about it. Today, there are young architects who are keenly interested in the systemic properties of buildings. In my time the very idea of systems in building was yet to be taken seriously (other than prefab 'systems' that were no true systems at all). But my generation did learn how one makes brick buildings, an art that is very old, and which used to be very sophisticated.

Q: In this world of increasing populations and declining natural resources, is there a future for the WOBO?
I do not think there is a future for the WOBO bottle. We may end up drinking beer from cartons or plastic containers as we already drink it from aluminium containers. (Which, by the way, find much easier second usage in third-world countries, but are still relatively expensive.) Heineken is now pushing the sales of mini casks from which one can fill glasses at home.

Above – This drawing of how the bottles fit together to create walls was developed for the 2003 Alehop! exhibition in Barcelona. A major consideration was how exposed edges could function effectively as window and door openings.

The WOBO was designed to offer building materials to third-world countries. In 1963, 60,000 WOBOs were manufactured, although few were ever put to use. It's estimated that 1,000 bottles could construct a 3 x 3 metre (10 x 10 foot) structure.

Chapter 2: Package Design and Sustainability

56

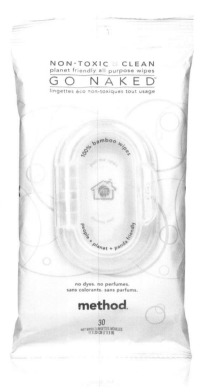

3 | Sustainability in the professional realm

Cleaning up the packaging industry

This chapter features different players in the sustainable package design movement, beginning with larger and more far-reaching organizations that are driving change through their systems-thinking services. While these organizations look at packaging through the broader lens of corporate behaviour, and so see it as a single piece of a larger puzzle, the Sustainable Packaging Coalition (SPC) was created expressly to drive change within the packaging industry. After looking at the SPC, we'll look at an impressive collection of established corporations, upstart companies, design firms and material suppliers that are all making sustainable ideas reality. These entrepreneurs are changing the way businesses' relationship to humanity and nature are defined, and applauding their efforts is a certain first step towards spreading their innovative spirit.

The hope in presenting such a sweeping look at how various participants in the package design industry interact is that graphic designers feel empowered, with a deeper understanding of the variables they must contend with as they approach a package-design project, and understand that all segments of the industry are in the process of embracing real and quantifiable sustainable change.

There's clean, and then there's clean. The number of companies that are started with sustainable thinking as a core philosophy is quickly rising. Many young entrepreneurs dedicated to sustainable package design aspire to be role models for the next generation. Method's sustainable packages contain sustainable products, and in an industry where toxic chemicals are all too common, truly natural cleaning products are badly needed.

then...

Package design is a discipline that services every imaginable consumer market. Understanding this, one can sense the great challenges in reforming the packaging industry as a whole, yet at the same time envision the multitudes of opportunities to affect change. Looking at the way a single niche market has slowly changed can help us understand how the various players in any one industry behave and interact. It can also provide evidence of how corporations are themselves now driving change, rather than dragging their feet as they had been up until recently.

The important steps that the music industry has taken over a 15-year period reveal a markedly different business attitude. The recent attention that the business sector has placed on the 'triple bottom line' must be viewed as a factor that will, once and for all, open the door to sustainable creativity for graphic designers.

In the early 1990s, at a time when the shift from 12-inch vinyl records had gone mainstream, some large retail music stores and record companies insisted on packaging CDs in tall boxes that matched the height of a traditional record sleeve. The CD was placed in a petroleum-based 'jewel case', which was fitted into a paperboard box twice its size, then wrapped in cellophane. Despite the waste of raw materials, the inefficiency of shipping (with half of the package empty), and the increased energy burden that resulted from this packaging scheme, the music industry resisted smaller packages. They did so in order to prolong the use of the in-store rack systems that had been developed for record sleeves.

In an inspiring act of industry activism, David Byrne, former singer with Talking Heads, teamed with the legendary graphic designer Tibor Kalman and his New York studio M&Co, to emblazon his 1991 CD 'Uh-Oh, Love Comes to Town' with calls for reform in the dysfunctional packaging system. The front cover of the paperboard box (left) contained a label that stated: *'THIS IS GARBAGE. (This box, that is.) The American record business insists on it, though. If you agree that it's wasteful, let your store management know how you feel.'* The music industry eventually eliminated the paperboard carton. But, while its elimination made a tremendous difference to the ecological impacts of the music industry, it didn't change the fact that jewel cases – the reigning package form for CDs since then – were petroleum-based products that were environmentally caustic in both their origins and their end-life disposal.

In an ingenious example of planning a secondary usage for a package, the back of the paperboard box was printed with a cut-out postcard containing a letter of protest that could be sent to the consumer's senator.

THIS IS GARBAGE. (This box, that is.) The American record business insists on it, though. If you agree that it's wasteful, let your store management know how you feel.

... and now

Approximately 1.8 billion jewel cases are manufactured each year, and every single one of these is derived from petrochemicals. A better packaging alternative has been sorely needed. The Natural Resources Defense Council (NRDC), a remarkably effective environmental action organization, has teamed with Warner Music Group and Cinram, the world's largest producer of CDs, to phase out petro-based CD and DVD jewel cases. In what Dr Allen Hershkowitz, Senior Scientist at NRDC has described as *'the most progressive set of procurement standards of any music company on Earth'*, Warner has committed to packaging all of their CD and DVD products in 30 per cent post-consumer waste paperboard, that is uncoated and FSC-certified. The sustainable paper stock is being supplied by StoraEnso, a Scandinavian paper, packaging and forest-product company that has long been committed to sustainable business practices. The clear plastic wrap so common to these commercial products will be replaced with a biopolymer wrap. A biopolymer jewel case is also under development as a possible future alternative.

Many alternatives to the jewel case have been available for years, and connoisseurs of music have seen their fair share of innovative paperboard CD cases. One company dedicated to providing sustainable cases for anyone using CDs or DVDs for any purpose is the Sustainable Group. One of their many sustainable products is the RESLEEVE, a 16-pt bending chipboard case that is made from 100 per cent recycled content (56 per cent post-consumer recycled).

As music, and digital information of all kinds, becomes more compact, the need for physical packaging is reduced, and many people now get their music directly from the internet. Still, the phasing out of CDs and DVDs as digital storage devices will not occur any time soon, so shifting packaging (even for products that might become obsolete in the next decade) to more ecologically friendly systems represents a tremendous step forward.

The CD and DVD industry is a huge market, yet when viewed from the perspective of the packaging industry it is one product in a sea of products. However, if each consumer product market could benefit from similar forms of inter-industry activism, tremendous gains could be realized. But, as we've seen, with the inter-related nature of sustainable practices, a change in one industry often informs positive change in others, so that each has a compounding effect. On the following pages we will see numerous examples of business innovations that, along with changing the specific industry the companies belong to, provide inspiration and knowhow to any other industry willing to improve their own environmental footprint.

Goodbye jewel case, hello sustainability. The Sustainable Group's RESLEEVE is made from 100 per cent recycled content with 56 per cent post-consumer material.

Organizations helping organizations

Featured on these pages are three of the most visionary and influential organizations that provide an exhaustive list of services to any business that is serious about positive change. Their frameworks all derive from what is called 'industrial ecology', a philosophy that uses ecological systems as its role model and primary metaphor.

Rocky Mountain Institute

'Abundance by Design'

In their seminal book, Natural Capitalism: Creating the Next Industrial Revolution, Amory, Lovins and L Hunter Lovins of the Rocky Mountain Institute (RMI), together with Paul Hawken of Smith & Hawken, have set an ambitious agenda for deep and lasting changes in the way in which we conduct business in this world. But before (and since) the publication of this book, RMI has engaged in groundbreaking research, development and implementation of powerful sustainable projects. 'Natural Capitalism' can be explained as the belief that the planet's resources are the only available means of human survival and advancement, and they should be managed, consumed and cared for as the precious materials they are.

A nonprofit organization that began in 1982 to explore alternatives to inefficient and destructive energy habits, RMI works with governments, corporations and communities to use technological advances to enhance energy strategies. The thrust of their philosophy is that our present methods of material consumption are inefficient, uninspired, misguided and not in the least bit sustainable. In response, they have proposed four principles of Natural Capitalism: 1) radically increase the productivity of natural resources; 2) shift to biologically inspired production models and materials; 3) move to a 'service-and-flow' business model; and 4) reinvest in natural capital.

Natural Capitalism is a book that everyone should read. It is inspiring and insightful, and filled with more actionable information regarding sustainability than any one person could ever desire. A visit to their website will provide the same. www.rmi.org

The Natural Step

'Inspire. Innovate. Lead'

Founded in 1988 in Sweden, the primary objective of The Natural Step (TNS) is to facilitate a 'global shift to ecological and social sustainability'. Their strategy is 'To develop scientifically valid principles for sustainability; to foster system-wide implementation of these principles, and to develop new tools in association with leading scientists; to support the use of the TNS Framework in companies and organizations through direct training and consultation; to provide a forum for dialogue, particularly for decision-makers capable of influencing ideas and becoming leading role models of sustainable development, and to make sustainability knowledge and best practices easily understood and accessible.' Their strategy of cross-sector cooperation between large business sectors aims to break down barriers between companies and industries in order to create a common language of sustainable innovation.

The system developed by TNS is being implemented by companies such as McDonald's, Scandic Hotels, The Home Depot, BP, Interface Inc., Nike, Woolworths and the US Environmental Protection Agency. Below is a diagram used by The Natural Step and others to define the need for a change in the way natural resources are presently being consumed. www.naturalstep.org

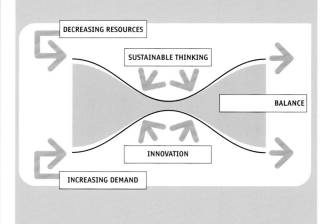

DECREASING RESOURCES

SUSTAINABLE THINKING

BALANCE

INNOVATION

INCREASING DEMAND

William McDonough and Michael Braungart

'Cradle to Cradle'

These two individuals – American architect William McDonough, and German chemist Michael Braungart – have been working together since 1991, when they co-authored The Hannover Principles, an ecological design framework devised for the 1992 Earth Summit. While their best-known collaborative text is *Cradle to Cradle: Remaking the Way We Make Things*, many offshoot initiatives have developed as a result of their partnership.

A) McDonough Braungart Design Chemistry (MBDC) is their umbrella organization that provides sustainable consultation across a tremendously wide array of industries. Their cradle-to-cradle design paradigm is *'powering the next Industrial Revolution, in which products and services are designed based on patterns found in nature, eliminating the concept of waste entirely and creating an abundance that is healthy and sustaining'*. Their philosophy rejects the 'take-make-waste' model of material consumption for the sake of a system that takes advantage of two closed loops – one that continually cycles biological nutrients and one that continually cycles technological nutrients. The term 'nutrient' is used to clarify the fact that waste should not exist, but instead 'used' materials should be used again and again to feed the respective systems.

MBDC provides sustainable design services, manufacturing and chemical protocols, training and many other things. Their clients include BASF, Designtex, Ford Motor Company, Herman Miller, Nike, Seventh Generation, Steelcase and the US Postal Service. MBDC offers stringent guidelines for their third-party 'Cradle to Cradle' certification, including Gold, Silver, Platinum and Basic designations, depending on the sustainable attributes of the products. www.mdbc.com

B) GreenBlue is a nonprofit offshoot of MBDC that *'stimulates the creative redesign of industry by focusing the expertise of professional communities to create practical solutions, resources, and opportunities for implementing sustainability.'* Their initiatives include Green2Green (green building materials), CleanGredients (online database of cleaning product ingredients), Sustainable Textile Services, the eDesign Idea Competition (a partnership with the EPA to develop cradle-to-cradle principles for the design of electronic products) and the Sustainable Packaging Coalition, explained in greater detail over the next few pages. www.greenblue.org

C) William McDonough & Partners is an architecture and community design firm engaged in developing sustainable architecture around the world, from factories and college buildings to city planning in China. www.mcdonoughpartners.com

D) The Environmental Protection Encouragement Agency (EPEA) in Germany emphasizes *'cooperation across every sector, from green organizations to industry and government'*. www.epea.com

The Sustainable Packaging Coalition (SPC) (nonprofit industry workgroup)

With the burgeoning growth of interest in sustainable package design, nonprofit industry workgroups have developed in different geographic regions of the world.

The European Organization for Packaging and the Environment (EUROPEN), for instance, has brought together industry leaders throughout Europe with the common goal of reducing environmental impacts of packaging. With a focus on the triple bottom line of social, environmental and economic vitality, EUROPEN offers a framework that embraces cradle-to-cradle material management, and provides leadership in helping companies meet the goals set by the European Union's Sustainable Development Strategy. Once such initiative is the European Shopping Baskets (ESB) Programme, an ambitious agenda designed to assess the market dynamics behind the 100 most commonly used products in the European Union, as a means of defining efficient packaging systems. A comprehensive assessment of the industry is also available through EUROPEN, which has divided the information into three helpful categories: packaging, used packaging and EU policies.

Another example of concerted industry efforts to reform packaging is the US-based Sustainable Packaging Coalition (SPC), a nonprofit offshoot of GreenBlue that provides guidance on matters related to sustainable packaging to its members. Their services include a forum for supply-chain collaboration; sharing best practices and design guidelines; supporting innovation and effective new technologies; and providing education, resources and tools.

The SPC's criteria (right) blend important objectives of sustainability with private-sector considerations and strategies that address environmental concerns related to the lifecycle of packaging. Their methodologies reflect a deep respect for the cradle-to-cradle material-flow philosophies that were first developed by William McDonough and Michael Braungart, with a goal of transforming a comprehensive packaging system *'that is economically robust and provides benefit throughout the lifecycle – a sustainable packaging system'*. The SPC was founded in 2004 by nine member companies, and now has over 130 member companies.

SPC's criteria for sustainable packaging

01:
is beneficial, safe and healthy for individuals and communities throughout its lifecycle

02:
meets market criteria for performance and cost

03:
is sourced, manufactured, transported and recycled using renewable energy

04:
maximizes the use of renewable or recycled source materials

05:
is manufactured using clean production technologies and best practices

06:
is made from materials healthy in all probable end-life scenarios

07:
is physically designed to optimize materials and energy

08:
is effectively recovered and utilized in biological and/or industrial cradle-to-cradle cycles

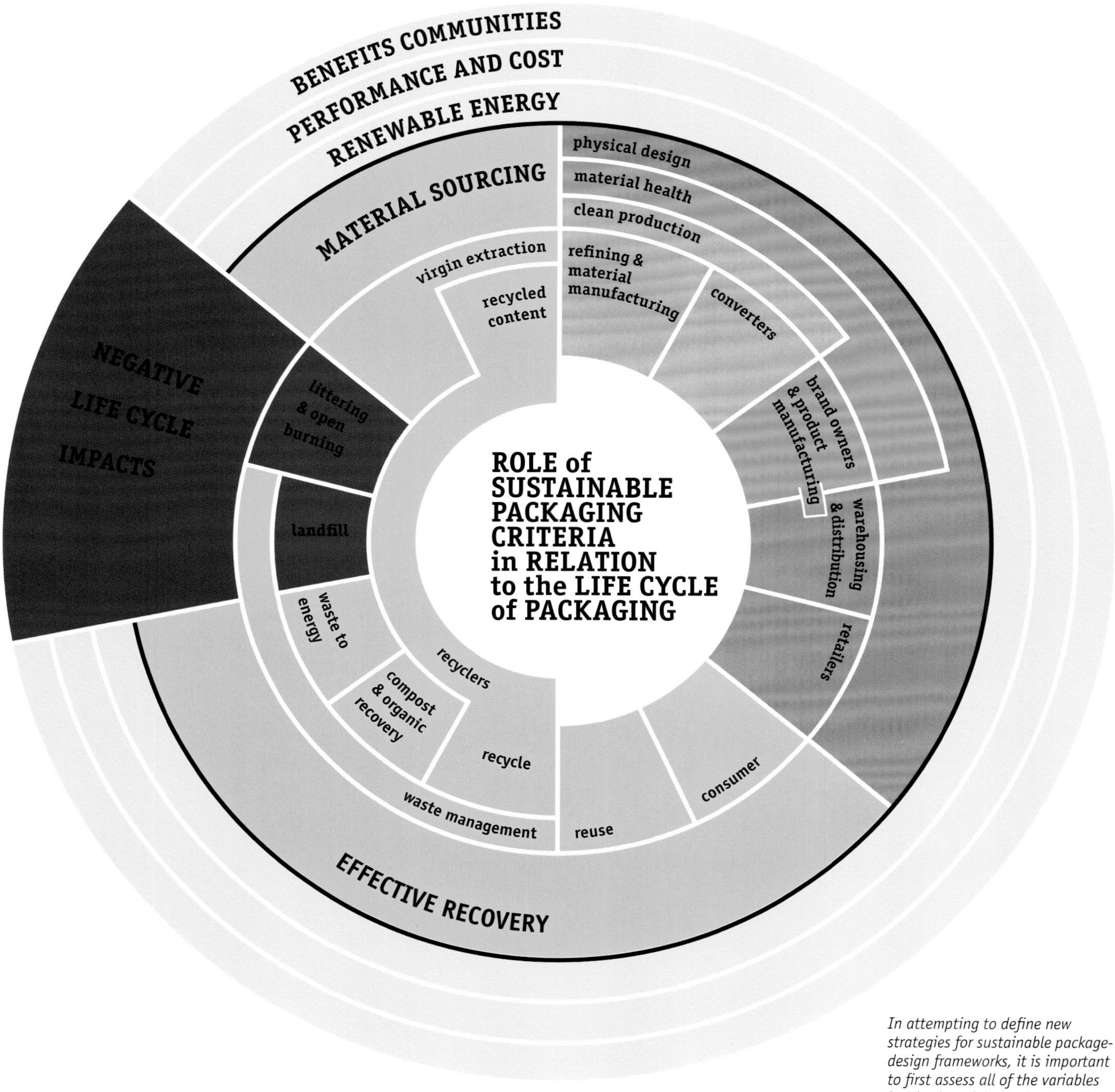
BENEFITS COMMUNITIES
PERFORMANCE AND COST
RENEWABLE ENERGY
MATERIAL SOURCING
physical design
material health
clean production
virgin extraction
recycled content
refining & material manufacturing
converters
brand owners & product manufacturing
warehousing & distribution
retailers
consumer
reuse
NEGATIVE LIFE CYCLE IMPACTS
littering & open burning
landfill
waste to energy
compost & organic recovery
recyclers
recycle
waste management
EFFECTIVE RECOVERY
ROLE of SUSTAINABLE PACKAGING CRITERIA in RELATION to the LIFE CYCLE of PACKAGING

In attempting to define new strategies for sustainable package-design frameworks, it is important to first assess all of the variables involved, and determine how they define the whole. The SPC uses a version of the above diagram to define a working method for thorough lifecycle analysis of the packaging supply-chain. While this graphic defines the broad framework of the packaging lifecyle, the graphic on page 67 pays special attention to the linear nature of the flow between individual components.

Interview: Anne Johnson
Director of the Sustainable Packaging Coalition

Q: Now that large segments of the packaging industry are embracing sustainable packaging, what do you see as the main hurdles remaining?

One can design the most environmentally sensitive packaging on the planet, but if there's no system to collect and recover it at the end of its useful life, it isn't sustainable. Design-for-Environment (DfE) is beginning to take root as consumer goods companies and retailers are increasingly requiring their supply chains to report on different environmental metrics, asking for better packaging. Those companies that traditionally participate in the production end of the packaging supply chain, however, have distanced themselves from any end-of-life responsibility. We're beginning to see signs of change.

Awareness is building that end-of-life issues need to be addressed before we can reach the point where any packaging is considered truly sustainable. Sustainable packaging is all about systems thinking; it's not just the packaging but also about the materials systems that relate to the package. In the US, we don't have any political leadership on the issue of recycling and the creation of a sustainable materials economy. An effective national recycling infrastructure requires vision, leadership and commitment at all levels, from federal and state governments to community leaders and consumers. I'm hopeful that the increased interest in sustainable packaging, which

is driving growth in using recycled and compostable materials, may begin to bring some much-needed attention and movement to this issue.

Q: What are the primary motivators in the recent increase in sustainable packaging?

In Europe, there's been significant focus on addressing environmental issues since the EU Packaging Directive of 1994. Driven by limited landfill space and greater awareness of resource conservation, the EU has taken a regulatory route through producer responsibility and other mechanisms to drive environmental responsibility in packaging. In the US, landfill space and resources are plentiful. The interest in sustainable packaging has been driven primarily by industries that are required to comply with a global patchwork of regulatory packaging requirements and address increasing demands from brand owners and retailers. Consumers have been a minimal influence. Interest in corporate social responsibility, a growing realization that sustainability has real business benefits, and the sharp rise in energy prices have all contributed to a growing industry awareness around packaging.

When the SPC presented its Definition of Sustainable Packaging in 2005, it coincided with Wal-Mart's announcement that they would initiate a sustainable packaging effort. The SPC Definition helped to focus the industry on what was important while

the Wal-Mart announcement catalyzed their supply chain of more than 60,000 suppliers. Since then, many retailers and consumer-product goods retailers have begun implementing programmes around sustainable packaging.

One of the primary objectives of the SPC is to create the tools and resources to inform industry about sustainable design practices, providing the science and facts to help with decision-making. GreenBlue, as the convener of the SPC, is focused on ensuring that this awareness translates to a permanent shift in practice. With the growing urgency of environmental considerations, the business imperative for these practices is becoming self-evident.

Q: With the advancements in biopolymers, can we expect a reduction in the use of toxic, nonbiodegradeable plastics?

The current focus on climate change will actually drive further use of traditional packaging and nonrecyclable flexible packaging, at least for the time being. The consumption of fossil fuels is currently the primary source of greenhouse gas emissions, and lightweight packages typically reduce greenhouse gas impacts. Unfortunately, we will likely be looking at the accumulation of persistent polymers in the environment far beyond the next five years. Based on current trends, however, we may soon see the gradual elimination of PVC in packaging. It's important to note that most polymers

'Sustainable packaging is all about systems thinking; it's not just the packaging but also about the materials systems that relate to the package.'

Anne Johnson

are not toxic, but some rely on problematic additives. Yet all traditional polymers are physically persistent in the environment.

The research and development of biopolymers is growing exponentially. They present an incredible opportunity to displace the use of nonrenewable resources in the creation of technical polymeric materials with renewable resources. Most of them don't yet have the performance characteristics necessary to replace petroleum-based polymers. However, it's incorrect to assume that because a biopolymer is made from a renewable material, it's also biodegradable or necessarily more sustainable. Some

biopolymers are readily biodegradable and some are not. Some will act just like petroleum-based polymers if released in the environment. There's a long way to go in creating a composting infrastructure in the US for anything other than garden waste and grass clippings.

With the focus on sustainability there's an unprecedented expectation that the introduction of new materials should come along with a fully developed end-of-life strategy. Clearly, this wasn't the case when polymer materials were introduced in the past. Biopolymers represent a hope that we can develop more sustainable, locally

sourced packaging materials and effective recovery systems, but there's still more work to be done.

Q: What advice do you have for graphic designers with no background in the technological aspects of package design, but who are nonetheless developing packaging for businesses, and who are interested in contributing to sustainable change?
The SPC has developed 'Design Guidelines for Sustainable Packaging' for the packaging design community. This document presents, in an accessible form, background on

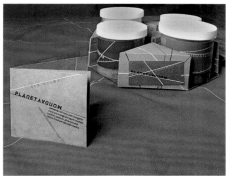

Designers can imagine packaging as delivery systems that create an opportunity for conscientious consumers to participate in the 'closed-loop' cycles. This package system allows consumers to visit a ready-made takeout food service and leave with a meal. The modular system includes a furoshiki wrap (a traditional Japanese wrapping cloth) that doubles as a blanket, reusable triangular cartons and containers, and a base composed of two eating mats. The plastic cartons accrue stock so the organic food company is not reliant on constantly purchasing expensive replacements. All labels are removable, allowing different foods to be placed in them.

'For example, what is the energy and greenhouse gas impact of increasing the amount of recycled content in a carton?'

Anne Johnson

sustainable packaging together with a framework for considering sustainable design and DfE strategies for packaging. Sustainable design is discussed in the context of an expanded definition of quality. We have added optimize resources, responsible sourcing, material health and resource recovery to the traditional design objectives of cost, performance, aesthetic and regulatory compliance. The document presents a series of DfE strategies, and under each we ask a standard set of questions: What is it? Why is it important? How do you do it? What questions should you ask? What regulations apply? And what resources are available? Our goal was to incorporate lifecycle thinking into many of the standard design objectives. We want this to be a living document, and invite designers to contribute ideas on how the guidelines might be improved, and what resources might be added.

Q: How can graphic designers stay abreast of advancements in sustainable packaging?

There are now a number of sustainable packaging newsletters offered by the mainstream packaging trade press. *Packaging Strategies*, *Packaging Digest* and *Packaging World* all have sustainable packaging newsletters or portions of their magazines dedicated to the topic. As the discussion moves beyond the direct supply-chain, I suspect you'll increasingly see the topic discussed in the inks and adhesives industries. The academic press has been lagging on this issue, but I'm aware of several texts that are currently in process.

Q: What are the ways in which graphic designers can contribute to a change in client mentality?

Businesses are most likely to shift their thinking if there's a provocative business case to support it. It's getting clearer every day that sustainability and sustainable packaging touch on core business issues, client relations and marketing opportunities. Beyond business, helping to convey the importance of lifecycle thinking will help create the mental infrastructure for longer-term thinking about how we design solutions between our consumptive and shortsighted present and the sustainable future we need for our children.

Q: Can you explain the MERGE system in a way that could be understood by laymen?

MERGE is a screening tool for designers that will calculate comparative environmental profiles for designs based on metrics such as energy consumption, resource consumption and greenhouse gas emissions. Originally developed by Dr Richard Denison at Environmental Defense in the 1990s with support from SC Johnson, it was intended to evaluate environmental metrics for chemical product formulation and packaging design. We received an exclusive license from the Environmental Defense Fund in 2006 for the packaging portion of the MERGE tool. This design-phase tool will provide ready feedback to the designer on a series of seven environmental metrics for a particular package design.

Information on a package design is entered and used to calculate a series of metrics, and these results are used as a baseline. A designer then can compare the environmental impacts of modifications to the design. For example, what is the energy and greenhouse gas impact of increasing the amount of recycled content in a carton? MERGE will allow the designer to compare the environmental performance of the modified design to the baseline design, and see what environmental trade-offs exist in one design versus another. As practitioners of DfE know, there are no silver bullets, and often what we seek to optimize are these environmental trade-offs.

We're currently in the process of redeveloping MERGE, and anticipate that the new version will use a significantly expanded set of metrics, but from a functional point of view it should be very similar to the original program in that it will be design-focused, and allow for design comparisons. We plan on making it a web-based tool with an improved user interface and graphical capabilities in order to increase usability.

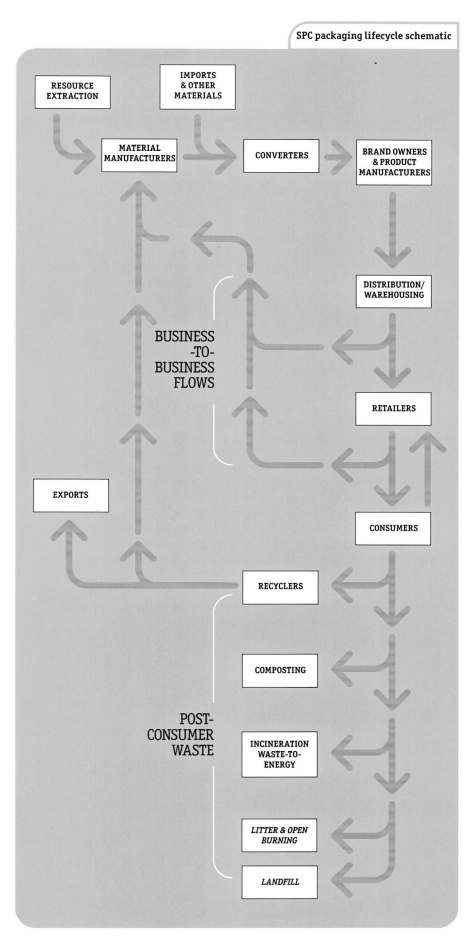

SPC packaging lifecycle schematic

RESOURCE EXTRACTION

IMPORTS & OTHER MATERIALS

MATERIAL MANUFACTURERS

CONVERTERS

BRAND OWNERS & PRODUCT MANUFACTURERS

DISTRIBUTION/ WAREHOUSING

BUSINESS -TO- BUSINESS FLOWS

RETAILERS

EXPORTS

CONSUMERS

RECYCLERS

COMPOSTING

POST- CONSUMER WASTE

INCINERATION WASTE-TO- ENERGY

LITTER & OPEN BURNING

LANDFILL

This packaging schematic is used by SPC and its members in order to track material lifecycle flows. By visualizing these flows, designers can better remember potential points of intervention as they plan packaging schemes and material use. The two categories at the bottom of the schematic represent negative termination points.

67

Case Study:
Starbucks Coffee Company

Starbucks Coffee Company has been committed to minimizing the environmental impacts of its business practice since its inception. With over 10,000 stores internationally, Starbucks clearly understands the importance of operating sustainably. *'We have a responsibility to sustainably source and manage our materials, but it's very difficult for one company to address this issue alone',* states Margaret Papadakis, Senior Buyer for Starbucks' Packaging division. *'Our involvement with the SPC has aimed to educate and align with other major packaging buyers and our suppliers to promote more sustainable practices.'* And because the company's sustainability objectives coincide with the SPC's mission, Starbucks was eager to provide an informative case study for other companies in the organization to learn from.

The details of the case study provide a clear picture of how creative thinking can lead to substantial environmental improvements in a package, even as it positively affects the bottom line.

The products under consideration are Starbucks staples: bite-sized, chocolate-covered nuts, espresso beans and dried fruit, along with chocolate-covered graham crackers. The packaging system for these had been slated for an aesthetic overhaul in order to cosmetically coordinate it with other design developments in the Starbucks line. A primary objective in the sustainable redesign process was material reduction, because the multiple layers in the old package weren't necessary for protecting the product, and the resulting source reduction would translate into savings in materials, shipping volumes and shipping weights.

Papadakis, who is on the Executive Committee of the SPC, understood that coordinating the dynamics between the various divisions within the company (including the marketing team, the packaging procurement team and the food packaging team) was one of the more serious challenges to surmount. *'As with any cross-functional group, there are competing priorities. The challenge is the larger we get, the more difficult it is to communicate the mission and come to a consensus on projects.'* This consensus must also conform to the needs of the outside confectioners and material suppliers. While time-consuming, this coordination between departments assured a comprehensive and well thought-out strategy. *'The key is thinking about the total lifecycle of the material during the design phase to make it possible for recovery.'*

The design phase in this case study included two sizes for each product; an 85g (3oz) package and a 285g (10oz) package. Because the larger package provided the greatest opportunity for sustainable improvement, the comparative details of that box are presented here.

The lightweight process began with using thinner paperboard, and continued with the elimination of the interior tray and the reduction of the outside sleeve from one that fully enclosed the product to one that covered only as much of the bottom of the bag as necessary to provide the package with vertical stability. These source reduction efforts are substantial enough, but the design team at Starbucks continued its 'greening' process by

The Starbucks design team continued its 'greening' process by using 100 per cent post-consumer waste paper from domestic sources, and eliminating pulp bleaching.

old sleeve	old tray	updated sleeve	updated tray
— 16pt paperboard	— Sourced overseas	— 14pt paperboard	— Eliminated completely
— Virgin paper	— Coated with petrochemical,	— 100 per cent post-consumer waste paper	
— Bleached paper	nonrecyclable polylaminate	— Nonbleached paper	
— Covers entire product	— Virgin paper	— Covers less than half the product	
	— Bleached paper		

procuring 100 per cent post-consumer waste paper from domestic sources, and eliminating pulp bleaching. Each of these steps, while appearing to be a minor alteration, represented tremendous improvements in environmental standards across the entire range of sustainable opportunities. The results were a 50 to 60 per cent reduction in materials, which reduced the negative effects of material extraction (for paper, inks and adhesives), the energy used in production, the fuel consumed in shipping (upstream and downstream) and the post-consumer waste impacts, since the new package can be recycled.

Finally, as an added value, the new package makes the tasty chocolates – what Starbucks calls the 'hero', clearly visible on the shelf, unlike the old system, which shrouded the chocolate in layers of materials.

Papadakis understands that there are some compromises necessary for creating more sustainable

packaging. *'When designing for recycling, foil-stamping is highly discouraged because it cannot be stripped off the paper during the recycling process. It does force our creative group to be more innovative with their designs so they are engaging without having to depend on traditional methods of execution.'*

But she is certain that Starbucks will continue, despite the challenges. *'We are working towards applying our education and research through involvement in the SPC and other organizations to develop Starbucks Sustainable Packaging Guidelines. This will be a list of guidelines which will assist designers and developers in making better choices when evaluating packaging solutions'*, Papadakis states. *'We also plan to utilize evaluation tools such as the Environmental Paper Assessment Tool (EPAT), SPC's Sustainable Packaging Guidelines and Packaging Material Assessment Tool.'*

A side-by-side comparison of the old and new packages shows that the total volume has not changed. By simply changing the materials and reconsidering the package structure, substantial improvements in sustainability can be realized.

Chapter 3: Sustainability in the Professional Realm

Case Study:
Hewlett Packard

No corporate initiative will succeed without full support from the top, and HP's sustainable packaging operation is very much managed with a sweeping vision for change. With business enterprises in 178 countries and a plethora of autonomous product divisions disbursed worldwide, there are as many points of potential miscommunication and inefficiency at HP as there are points of innovative collaboration. Understanding this, and understanding that there is no single 'silver bullet' to enhance packaging sustainability, HP's Package Engineering Programme Manager, Randy Boeller, oversees a corporation-wide competition that awards the most impressive sustainable packaging innovations, then disseminates the details of those winning entries to the rest of the HP community. In this way, the PEAC (Packaging Environmental Advisory Council) Awards provide incentive for further innovation at the same time it serves as a database of best practices.

While there are fundamental corporate commitments regarding such things as the elimination of old-growth paper pulp, the elimination of heavy metals in inks, the elimination of PVC packing, and minimizing packaging material use, the PEAC is flexible enough to provide each division with the freedom to determine which sustainable approaches are most appropriate to their needs, and how they will attain those improvements. An application for awards requires extensive documentation and proof of successful implementation, and stresses the need for innovations that improve the impact of the entire supply-chain.

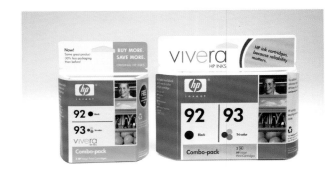

Above – The smaller box on the left in these images represent HPs new inkjet cartridges, replacing the larger package that came before it (on the right). This reduction in material was accompanied by a 40 per cent decrease in weight, and the introduction of recycled paperboard. Because the boxes are smaller and fit the products more snugly, a dramatic reduction of interior components was also realized.

Opposite – Size reductions in packaging can be combined with increased stability to make even larger reductions in secondary packaging, which in this case also happens to be a display box (below). The package to the right was the original, and because it possessed a thin top, it required secondary packaging to protect the top edges. The image to the left is the new package, and because it has a flat and strong top, a much smaller secondary box is needed to store the packages.

The PEAC Awards provide incentives for employees to improve environmental standards, and perform as a tool for corporate-wide knowledge-sharing. The programme also signals to employees that waste reduction is a core principle of the organization.

INCENTIVIZING CONSUMER PARTICIPATION

Beginning in 2004, HP has included prepaid, pre-addressed envelopes in ink cartridge packages so consumers can send used cartridges back without having to hunt for their own envelope and pay their own shipping fees. This simple step increased the amount of consumer participation in the recycling campaign so that, in the programme's first year alone, HP received as many cartridges in a single day as it had received in a month with its previous, web-based campaign. This recycling effort has kept an estimated 45 tonnes (50 tons) of waste out of landfills every year it has run.

GRAPHIC EVOLUTION

An innovative graphic design programme initiated by HP called Graphic Evolution takes into account the consumer dynamic of brand loyalty. When any new product is first introduced into the market, HP designers pull out all the stops on their design presentation, creating rich and eye-catching graphics for them. As the product establishes its performance credentials in the eyes of the consumer, however, the packaging for these 'proven' products becomes progressively less flashy, moving towards fewer colours, less ink coverage and less high-quality paper stock. The sequence runs from the expensive roll-out package (which requires more energy and materials) to mid-range design solutions, once the product is selling, to basic design solutions that are significantly less environmentally damaging.

MULTIFACETED IMPROVEMENTS

HP has changed carton materials for their ink cartridge packages from plastics such as PP and HPDE to paperboard, while reducing the package size and eliminating a thermoform tray. They also designed a booklet that was half the size of the original. The size changes alone allowed for 90 per cent more product per pallet, which, among other things, eliminated the need for almost 800 tractor trailers in a single year. The weight of the package was reduced by a total of 40 per cent, which has had a tremendous impact on fuel consumption. This project alone eliminated 662 tons of packaging landfill waste in 2006, and saved HP approximately £4 million ($6.2 million) in the process, showing once again that sustainability – because it aims to optimize material use, and reduce energy loads – is often a close partner to profitability. Also, it should be noted that the larger and older package is a significant improvement on the previous package, which was nearly twice its size and made from plastics rather than paperboard. This shows that sustainability is a process of continual innovation which, in this case, began in 2001 and in that time period witnessed not one, but two substantial 'jumps' in sustainable packaging improvements.

THE SMALLER THE PRIMARY PACKAGE, THE SMALLER THE SECONDARY PACKAGE...

Working within the constraints defined by large container stores can be difficult. As a means of simplifying the processing and reducing theft, these large container stores have historically demanded difficult-to-open, excessively large and toxin-laden 'clamshells' of any product supplier they work with. HP has dramatically reduced its ecological footprint recently by banning PVC (resin 3) in any packaging and replacing it with recycled plastics such as RPET. As seen below, those material changes have accompanied a dramatic reduction in package size. This has repercussions throughout the supply-chain. The illustrations show how dramatically fewer materials are required for secondary packaging which translates to similar reductions through the entire range of bulk packaging.

The PEAC Awards provide incentives for employees to improve environmental standards, and perform as a tool for corporate-wide knowledge-sharing. The programme also signals to employees that waste reduction is a core principle of the organization.

These illustrations show how secondary packaging can be reduced by designing more compact primary packaging.

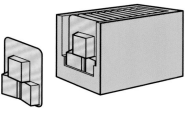

Hewlett Packard:
packaging the packaging

By this point in the book, it should be clear that any sustainable improvements in packaging can occur only with a keen eye on the packaging systems that bring the retail package to market. Because this is a book intended primarily for graphic designers, the images throughout feature the design of these retail packages – what is called the primary packaging. In the interest of providing some insight into the positive changes that are occurring in the secondary and tertiary packaging – the mailer packaging, and the bulk packaging that provides safe transit to the retail market – some of HP's ambitious bulk packaging initiatives are featured here. These examples are astounding, not only for their combined level of material reduction, but for their simplicity and common sense.

It's often said that big change occurs in small steps. Take, for example, the modest proposal to eliminate small cardboard inserts within an Inkjet Cartridge 'Bundle Pack' (a combination of several small products in one package). When approximately 25 million of these products are sold each year in North America, a seemingly small per-unit weight – 4.4g (0.6oz) – results in a total shipping-weight reduction of 110 tonnes (121 tons). Instituted in 2006, this simple move eliminated the need for the insert, which reduced material usage, saving the company £250,000 ($385,000) a year in the process.

In another example (below left), a padded paper envelope was used to replace a corrugated carton as a mailer for 33 different accessory products (polyurethane 'bricks' were used on the top and bottom of the carton), resulting in a reduction of 142 cubic metres (5,000 cubic feet) of polyurethane in the first 6 months alone. This small step reduced shipping weight, shipping volume, build time (by 20 to 30 seconds) and warehouse space. It also saved HP approximately £25,000 ($38,500) in material costs alone over those first 6 months.

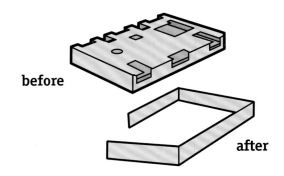

before

after

While the previous examples dealt with changes in small packages, the Fox Scanner Sub-Assembly (SSA) example, while requiring a small action (above), parlayed into larger improvements in the bulk packaging system. The SAA, which does not have a flat bottom, requires a bottom-holder. Before 2004, the bottom-holder was a complicated construction that mimicked the inconsistencies of the scanner bottom. These bottom inserts were material-intensive and required hand building. The upgraded version used a single strip of corrugated board that stood on its side so that it was strong enough to hold the scanners in their appropriate, horizontal position, even as it accommodated their uneven bottoms. This simple redesign reduced packing materials by 40 tonnes (44 tons) in a single year. This reduction affects both upstream (extraction, production and so on) and downstream (waste disposal) impacts, and led to other HP divisions implementing similar changes. The lighter-bulk pack-weight also reduced the amount of fuel required for shipping, and the European disposal fees associated with packing materials.

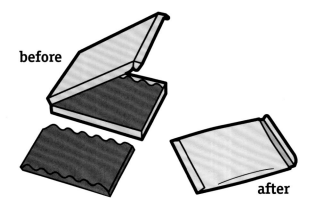

before

after

old bulk package

— each computer packed in individual cartons
— 12 computers fit on a single shipping pallet
— large amounts of plastic, styrofoam and corrugate
— time-intensive to unwrap and inventory each individually
— substantial shipping volume dedicated to packaging alone

new bulk package

— 8 computers packed in larger carton
— 32 computers fit on a single shipping pallet
— 75 per cent less packing waste
— 73 per cent time allotted to receiving, inventory and deployment
— significantly increased product-to-shipping volume ratio

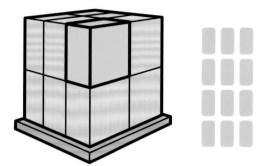
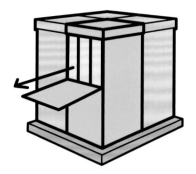
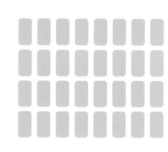

The SLED Desktop Bulk Packaging System represents one of the more substantial steps in minimizing bulk packaging at HP (above). This innovation, which was originally designed for one specific desktop model, has a patent pending and is being configured to work with most HP desktop computers.

Rather than individually package each CPU, a new eight-unit carton has been designed, and with this simple move 75 per cent of the packaging waste has been eliminated. Within its original format, 12 units could be shipped on a standard pallet. The new system allows for 32 units on the same pallet.

The larger, eight-unit carton possesses other efficiency features once the product has reached the customer warehouse. In the past, each computer had to be unpacked from its own carton, shrinkwrapped with other units, then placed into inventory, resulting in the need for material disposal and new material usage (shrinkwrap). The new eight-unit carton possess its own resealable locking lid, which allows for convenient warehouse storage in its shipped form. Individual computers can be taken from the cartons as needed – they also have an easy-access door –

and the carton can then be safely and securely resealed until the next unit is sold. A tray insert at the top of each eight-unit carton holds the accessories such as keyboard, mouse and wires, and so is removed and easily stored with others of its kind. These simple features result in a 73 per cent reduction in receiving, inventory and deployment process time.

Finally, as an example of finding innovative ways to deal with packaging waste that does result, an HP division that sent 200 tractor-trailer-loads of EPS foam (expanded polystyrene) to landfill every year researched organizations that require such materials for their own operations. They found companies that made products such as carnival toys and beanbags stuffing from virgin styrofoam. By transferring their 'waste' material to these manufacturers, this division eliminated a tractor-trailer-load of styrofoam waste every day and a half, and in the process eliminated the need for the same amount of virgin plastic. Eliminating packaging waste at the beginning of the design process eliminates the need for post-consumer innovations such as these.

75% reduction in shipping materials = ship the product, not the packaging!

Case Study: Method

Adam Lowry, co-founder of Method, likes to say that the company did not grow into greenness – it was born with environmental sustainability as its foundation. The concept of commercial environmentalism is at the core of the Method philosophy. *'We believe the best way to effect positive environmental change is to provide consumers with a better product through design, and create mass appeal, rather than merely creating a "green" brand that speaks only to environmentalists'*, says Lowry. *'Method is hip, not hippie.'*

'Regardless of whether a consumer buys Method because of its performance, its great fragrance or just because they like how the bottle looks on their countertop, they are purchasing the greenest brand on the market. It is in this way that real positive change is being created – those not necessarily environmentally concerned to start with are brought into the brand through its mass appeal and become loyal. We call this "moving the needle".'

Method has a goal of becoming a 100 per cent sustainable business by 2020, and measures everything it does from an environmental perspective, using six fundamental concepts:

1) Eliminate the concept of waste. Eliminate waste from all aspects of the business.
2) Eliminate toxic chemicals. All Method products are nontoxic in application and biodegradable.
3) Renewable energy: production processes, transport and so on use 100 per cent renewable energy.
4) Close the loop. Design all materials for recovery either through biological systems or through technological systems.
5) Inform and educate. Sensitize stakeholders to the Method mission, and why it's important.
6) Reinvent commerce. Offer products in a paradigm-shifting way to achieve environmental sustainability.

Method's approach is endorsed by the US EPA's Design for the Environment (DfE) programme. 'DfE has validated our product development process, and has recognized over 50 of our products in terms of safety for people and the environment.' Method works on an ongoing basis with the EPEA, the environmental research institute led by Dr Michael Braungart, author of *Cradle to Cradle*, to provide in-depth assessments of the ingredients and packaging materials they are considering for use in their products

Method employs Environmental Design Guidelines for each new product or packaging change. *'These guidelines are a list of challenging musts and wants that include a "dirty list" of ingredients, materials and processes which we do not allow'*, says Lowry. *'We also use something called a* GreenCard *which helps us qualitatively and quantitatively determine the sustainability footprint of a product, package or material. It includes such factors as recyclability, recycled content, proximity of manufacturing to consumption, package-to-product weight ratio and many others.'*

Above – The distinctive approach to form exhibited in Method's bottle designs is echoed here in their paperboard carton boxes, which are made from 75 to 85 per cent post-consumer material.

Left – It's not the materials of this bottle, but the materials within it that make all the difference. A triple-concentrated formula allows for a package that is three times lighter and three times smaller, thus reducing packaging material, shipping weight and volume. Such significant reductions in the extraction and use of raw materials is the result of a company that is fully invested in innovation for sustainability.
This design (made from HDPE 2 plastic) was awarded a Silver Medal by Business Week's IDEA awards for shifting the laundry industry to a 3X format, which could save over two billion kilos (five billion pounds) of water, plastic, and fuel annually.

Interview: Rudiger Becker
Packaging Manager, Homecare

What are the largest hurdles to overcome when attempting to create a more sustainable package and/or packaging system?

I think one of the biggest hurdles is the due diligence necessary to understand whether you truly have a more sustainable packaging option that still delivers on the functional necessities of the application. The development of these materials often takes significantly more resources and time and typically costs more when compared to traditional offerings. I do believe, however, consumers are going to demand more sustainable solutions which will build scale and ultimately drive down costs.

What are the worst habits or trends that need to be addressed in order for the industry to significantly reduce its negative environmental impact?

The use of 'flexible packaging' brings up some interesting issues. While the flexible package can dramatically reduce the amount of material used to package a product, it can have a potentially negative impact on the package's recyclability. Typical flexible film is made up of multiple layers of different polymers that are laminated together making the structures difficult to separate and recycle.

Recent developments have seen the emergence of mono-material films that are composed of laminated layers of polypropylene (PP), which can be readily recycled in facilities equipped to handle PP. Unfortunately, the bulk of MRF's in the US are not currently able to handle the recovery of PP. The challenge is to have MRF's equipped to handle a wider array of materials and for package designers to incorporate these materials into their products, so that there is enough scale to warrant the investment by the MRF's. It is a classic 'Chicken or the Egg' dilemma.

Could you explain how bottles that have necks and pumps are shipped from the manufacturer to the stores?

Packages that include a pump or trigger are typically more susceptible to damage during shipment than a typical cap. When designing a standard corrugated case for a non-trigger/pump package, you can actually use the primary package to share some of the compression force the case experiences during transit and storage. In certain situations the primary package can support up to 40% of the load placed on the case, meaning less material is need for the corrugated case. The problem that triggers and pumps pose is that they cannot support any significant load placed upon them. To avoid any damage to the pump or trigger additional head space can be added to the case, board strength could be increased or dividers can be added to the case to provide additional support.

This design by Karim Rasheed shows that a package can be both 'good' in the environmental sense, and 'good' in the design sense of the word, as the bottle is made from 100% recycled plastic.

What kind of advice would you give to a young package designer who was really trying to contribute to sustainability, but wasn't sure where to start?

I would always start with the end in mind. If you can understand the true lifecycle of a package then you can design a package in such a way as to give it the best chance of being reclaimed and used again. Designers should avoid materials that negatively impact the quality of recycle streams that we have in place today. Ideally, a bottle that is made today can be used by the consumer, recovered after use, recycled and remade into that very same bottle tomorrow.

> *'... the best way to effect positive environmental change is to provide consumers with a better product through design, and create mass appeal, rather than merely creating a "green" brand that speaks only to environmentalists.'*

Adam Lowry

Case Study: Pangea Organics

Joshua Onysko's journey into sustainable entrepreneurship began with the humble act of making soap in his mother's kitchen, but the seed of his own personal venture was not fully planted until he used that same soap during his travels in India. *'Eighty-seven per cent of the world's food is grown by women,'* Onysko explains, *'yet they own only about one per cent of the world's land. I see an imbalance there, and within that imbalance I see a solution.'*

Onysko's personal philosophy includes using the *'negative as a lesson, and the power of the positive as a source for moving forward'*. A goal of empowering women from around the world to own their own land and grow their own products helped drive Onysko to create a skincare company that now purchases hundreds of ingredients from women's cooperatives around world on over 16,000 hectares (40,000 acres) of organic agricultural land in 52 different countries.

Onysko was further motivated by his concern that corporations dictate governmental policies, while nonprofit organizations are too often inefficient, and squander funds due to mismanagement. By creating a company that combines the ethical and sustainable motivations of a nonprofit with the operating efficiency of a corporation, Onysko hopes to provide a role-model for the next generation of business owners where the economic, social and environmental considerations affecting the global communities involved with every facet of his business operation weigh as heavily on the decision-making process as his company's financial success.

What Pangea has termed 'ecocentric bodycare' is embodied in a comprehensive business model with sustainability at its heart. None of their products contain petroleum-based ingredients, genetically modified ingredients or other synthetic ingredients. While many

All product boxes are made from 100 per cent post-consumer paper that has been seeded with herbs such as basil and amaranth.

Pangea's Zero Waste pulping process is responsible for the 100 per cent post-consumer newsprint boxes used for all of their products. The boxes contain seeds from different herbs, so they can be soaked with water and planted in the backyard.

When confronted with obstacles in experimental production techniques, many companies revert to old and familiar methods, resulting in a lack of new ideas. In an excellent example of using obstacles to fuel creativity, Pangea's insistence on using pulp paper for folding boxes resulted in a further innovation. The thicker material and coarse surface of the pulp fibre (two attributes that would have discouraged many other companies) created physical resistance that negated the need for adhesives; thus the glueless box was created. The former glue flap was enlarged for more drag, and a belly band holds all of the graphics and necessary information.

None of the bottles in the Pangea product line make use of adhesive labels. Instead, the graphics are screened directly onto the glass or plastic. While screening the delicate details of the design directly onto the dark brown bottles represented a considerable production challenge, the final results avoid the excessive waste that is normally associated with label cutting and gluing.

chemical foaming agents found in other brands can take up to 200 years to break down in the natural environment, all of Pangea's ingredients begin biodegrading within 48 hours after use. Furthermore, the company's soap factory, a 930-square metre (10,000-square foot) facility, is a model of energy efficiency and powered by 100 per cent renewable energy.

The company motto, *Always Beneficial, Never Artificial*, also manifests itself in their revolutionary packaging model, where all product boxes are made from 100 per cent post-consumer newsprint paper that has been seeded with herbs such as basil and amaranth, so consumers can literally plant the package in their backyard, and get fresh herbs in return. Bottle labels and their toxic adhesives have been eliminated altogether by screening the designs directly onto the bottles. Even for their secondary packaging (or packaging used for wholesale shipping), Pangea is exploring a stacking system that uses small dots of adhesive to hold the boxes temporarily together, rather than wrapping palettes of them in large sheets of plastic, potentially reducing petroleum usage by 80 per cent.

Interview: Joshua Onysko
Founder and CEO of Pangea Organics

Q: How did you go from making responsible products to making responsible packaging?

We originally sold raw bars without any packaging. A lot of people wanted to know where to get more, so I used hemp twine to attach a hemp card that had the company name, URL and phone number on it. Stores that started buying it in bulk loved that it was minimal packaging and eco-friendly, but customers were damaging it, so I designed a box from a craft paper with 30 per cent recycled paper. It had die-cut bubbles all over it so people could see the soap, and then we wrapped a label around it.

I eventually went to the box factory to observe the manufacturing process – the die-cutting and the gluing – and it occurred to me that I just couldn't make die-cut boxes anymore – it was simply too wasteful.

I think about 40 per cent of the paper that Americans recycle actually goes back into the waste stream because we don't have the system in place to deal with it. So, we ended up teaming with an egg-carton company because they were made from 100 per cent post-consumer newsprint. The newspapers are shipped in, shredded, pulped in water, then put into a mould which is pressed into the box-shape. All the scraps go onto a conveyer belt and right back into the process; zero waste and minimal energy consumption. And there's no glue necessary for a clamshell box. We used the clamshell for the soapboxes, but not everything can go in a clamshell.

The whole paper-making process was of great interest to me. How much energy is spent taking this hard tree and making it so soft and pliable? Imagine the energy it takes to make a two-by-four into a pair of panties – that's how much energy is required. We considered using hip and trendy bamboo, but learned that fabrics and papers made from it are extremely unsustainable; it takes four times the amount of petrochemicals to turn bamboo into paper. The world already had too much waste paper, so we asked a company to make sheets of the 100 per cent post-consumer waste newsprint we were using for the clamshells. Any material cut from the die-cut was put right back into the next batch. And instead of using glue, we had the designer create an origami fold for the closure, so there's no glue on this box either. There's a spot of glue on the label, but we're trying to get rid of that too.

Q: Any stumbling blocks when developing seeded packaging?

Most seeds are either too small or too large to go into packaging, so we had a limited range of choices. Another issue was avoiding invasive species; you don't want to end up creating a botanical crisis. But the main problem occurred during the pulp-drying process because it was actually killing the seeds; the germination rates were about 10 per cent. In the end we had to make cold-process packaging, which is funny because our product line is already cold-process. Once we resolved that problem, we ran into international distribution problems. We're sold in 20 countries and all of a sudden people claim you're trying to smuggle seeds! We had to go through regulatory approval.

Q: How can graphic designers help make a difference in the packaging industry?

There's an ad that shows a family having all kinds of problems in their lives, and at the end it states that they don't need a therapist, they need an architect. When you start looking at the world around you, you realize how many problems could be solved with simple tweaks in design. There are two things that cause most of the problems in the world. One is information (or lack thereof) and the other is miscommunication. Usually both of these things can be solved with good design. And designers need to understand how powerful their minds are. Design will solve the problems of the world. I tell designers to never think that what they're designing isn't important. If it's being designed, after all, it means somebody's going to use it.

Q: What do you see as the main hurdles on the way to a sustainable future?

Consumer education. The bamboo fabric is a perfect example of that. People get a warm

'How much energy is spent taking this hard tree and making it so soft and pliable? Imagine the energy it takes to make a two-by-four into a pair of panties – that's how much energy is required.'

Joshua Onysko

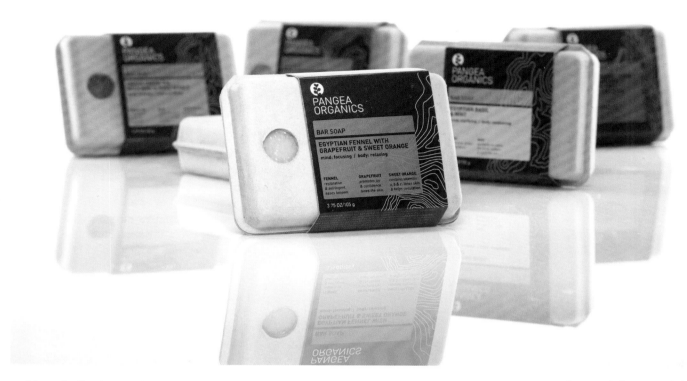

and fuzzy feeling because bamboo makes great flooring, but making clothes or sheets out of the same material is not necessarily sustainable.

We have to start thinking and educating beyond how we presently behave, and eliminate our simplistic understanding of the world. I would say that two per cent of designers strive to design above and beyond what they think their consumers want.

Q: Can you discuss the design process and your collaboration with IDEO?
I walked in and said 'everything must be brown', and they said 'well... we don't know about brown', and I said 'it needs to be brown.' You want to connect the people to the earth immediately. Brown grounds, right? And in a sea of white bottles with blue letters, I want to be the brown bottle; when people see brown bottles, they're

going to think Pangea every time.

The labels were a big issue. Label manufacturers fill up about 20 dumpsters a day with scraps from label cutting, and all that gets landfilled. So, we screen-printed our bodycare bottles instead. And that was our next hurdle because when you design intricate labels like ours, screen-printing is very complex, especially on a brown bottle! But in the end we're saving thousands of pounds of plastic garbage a month, not to mention adhesives.

And cosmetic tubes? We've been working with a manufacturer in China who supplies us with LDPE number 4, which is easily recycled. But finally, after 12 months of research, we found a supplier in the US who can provide us with HDPE number 2 tubes, with up to 70 per cent post-consumer content. Not only is it recycled, it's also already given something a second chance.

Just unpack the soap, and plant the package. A fully biodegradable, moulded-pulp box contains seeds of various herbs so that it can be planted in the backyard.

Case Study: Innocent

The name of this beverage company that makes 'tasty little drinks' is no accident. While guilt can be associated with many forms of human behaviour, enjoying a fruit drink shouldn't be one of them. Innocent, which began with three college friends making smoothies at a London music festival, has strived to act ethically in every area of business. Because drinks are nothing more than spills without packaging, Innocent has been determined to fold sustainability into their packaging practices from the beginning.

Over the course of the eight years they've been in business, Innocent has kept abreast of the latest plastic recycling advancements, adding higher and higher percentages of post-consumer recycled (PCR) plastic as technology improved. In the fourth year of business, they achieved 25 per cent PCR, then in 2005 they attained 50 per cent PCR. Finally, as of September 2007, Innocent was the first company in the world to reach the goal of a 100 per cent PCR drinks bottle (PET). The significance of this achievement cannot be overstated. With the development of 100 per cent PCR plastics that possess optimal clarity and strength, and that be used safely to contain food, plastic litter has suddenly become that much more valuable, and enhanced recycling systems will result, not to mention that this development eliminates the need for the extraction of petroleum for virgin plastics.

This marks a high point in closed-loop maximization of plastic as the bottles themselves are fully recyclable and their production results in a 20 per cent reduction in plastic. And because the energy-use for recycling a plastic bottle is eight times less than making a bottle from virgin materials, a 50 per cent carbon reduction has resulted from the process, with another 5 per cent being realized through lightweighting.

In 2007, Innocent experimented with PLA (Polylactic Acid), a biopolymer derived from corn, for their breakfast thickies, but after committing to an innovative trial with the material, they decided that their 100 per cent PCR bottles were more sustainable. Innocent's Head of Sustainability, Jessica Sansom, explains that there were concerns 'about the use of food crops to produce plastics and fuels, in that they can take land that is needed for food crops, and push up the prices of food, so it is really important to make sure that we use what would have otherwise been waste materials where we can.'

Innocent was also concerned about the viability of composting without proper systems in place, commenting that 'composting is not yet a mainstream end-of-life option here in the UK, with only 5 per cent of households having any sort of collection of food waste. We have also received feedback from plastics recyclers that PLA bottles

innocent® pure fruit smoothie
blackberries & blueberries

innocent® pure fruit smoothie
cranberries & raspberries

innocent® pure fruit smoothie
strawberries & bananas

Left – As a result of concerted effort from the very beginning of Innocent's business enterprise to use sustainable packaging, all Innocent beverage bottles are made from 100 per cent recycled plastic.

Opposite – The Big Knit campaign encourages individuals to knit small caps that can fit onto the top of Innocent bottles. The caps are sent to Sainsburys, where they are placed onto bottles, and for each bottle with a cap sold, Sainsburys and Innocent will jointly donate money to a charity that helps feed and tend to the elderly during the cold winter months.

can add costs into their recycling operations and in some cases prevent recycling of conventional plastics. So, at the end of 2007, we introduced our new 100 per cent recycled bottle for all of our smoothie recipes instead. This bottle only uses material that would have otherwise gone to landfill, and the bottle can itself be recycled again, with the majority of UK households having a plastics recycling collection.'

Innocent's secondary packaging – boxes used for shipping product to retail centres – are all made from 100 per cent post-consumer recycled content.

The bottle's distinctive graphics attempt to keep the conversation about environmental and social stewardship from getting too heavy, and instead they opt for an optimistic and cheerful celebration of responsible consumption. Pearlfisher, the world-renowned design and branding agency responsible for Innocent's whimsical bottle designs, has supported other mindful business pursuits such as Green and Black's Organic Chocolates, and Union Hand-Roasted coffee.

Even as they make sure to 'do good' while manufacturing bottles for their product, Innocent has found a way to make money for charities quite literally on those bottles. Ever since 2003, their annual Big Knit campaign encourages individuals to contribute to a fund raising effort to benefit Age Concern, a charity that cares for the elderly in the United Kingdom, by knitting small hats that can be placed onto Innocent bottles that are on sale at Sainsbury's, the well-known supermarket. In 2006 alone, 230,000 hats were knitted, raising over £100,000 ($154,000).

In order to support the communities that provide Innocent with their raw food products, the company requires that all suppliers meet a clear set of minimum social and environmental standards defined by Innocent. Furthermore, 10 per cent of Innocent's annual profits are donated to charities in countries that supply the fruit for Innocent's drinks.

While guilt can be associated with many forms of human behaviour, enjoying a fruit drink shouldn't be one of them.

Case Study: Tresdon/ Icon Development Group

In answering the age-old question of the chicken and the egg, perhaps one of the least convincing answers would be that they arrived at the exact same time. That answer, however, seems appropriate when considering the question as to whether the packaging function of the Tresdon wine system came before its storage function, or vice versa.

'The three R's (reduce, reuse and recycle) are still great governing principles that we use in our package design today', states Jason Ivey, Principal of Icon Development Group (IDG). *'The Tresdon packaging incorporates all of these principles – it reduces the material required to package and ship the wine bottles, it gives the consumer an option to keep the packaging and repurpose it in multiple ways and the packaging can easily be made from any pressed, recycled material.'*

The 'package' phase of this product comes in a variety of sizes, holding anything from one to 12 bottles of wine. Once any of these packages arrives home, it can be used individually to hold wine bottles or glasses, or combined with other Tresdon racks to create a larger wine rack. As a part of its functional DNA, the wine-rack system is designed to allow for continual expansion.

Assembly of these racks does not require hardware or adhesives of any kind, but instead relies on a system of carefully placed, friction-fit slots. The patented nesting system can be made from recycled pressboard.

While still in the store, the package provides ample view of the front and back labels on most wine bottles. And during shipping – whether in large quantities from distribution centres to retailers, or in smaller cartons that can be delivered from wholesalers to consumers, the Tresdon system requires no extra protective packaging material – the edges of the rack push out at the corners and can nestle into a shipping carton while protecting its cargo. This eliminates the need for styrofoam pellets, plastic bubble-wrap or any other form of filler.

While primarily a product design firm servicing the electronics industry, IDG aims for a more interdisciplinary model of design. *'Design isn't just about aesthetics; design is an entire problem-solving discipline. Design is also very much on the forefront of pop culture, giving us a voice that other industries may not have.'* Jason Ivey is hopeful that designers of all specialities can contribute to sustainable change. *'Finding new and better ways to make packaging smaller, more reusable or multifunctional should be right up our alley.'*

The two-bottle package (above) and the three-bottle package (opposite page) can attach to other Tresdon racks to create an expandable system of wine racks.

The smallest Tresdon package holds a single bottle of wine and, once home, can convert into several customizable racks.

Interview: Jason Ivey
Principal, Icon Development Group

What are the most common misconceptions of clients regarding sustainable design?

Many automatically assume that sustainable packaging will cost a great deal more. They also think the packaging will look like a brown paper sack. This look may be all right for the purveyors of organic foods, but what about the tech company that wants to package external hard drives? These companies need to see that sustainable packaging doesn't have to look 'earthy' – it can be made to look high-tech or edgy.

What are the worst trends in the package-design industry that need to be addressed?

The amount of gratuitous material that goes into packaging a product is shameful. Take a computer mouse as an example: the plastic moulded packaging around the product is easily three or four times larger. It's mainly there to house flashy graphic panels and give the product a greater visual presence on the shelf, or to deter theft. But there are certainly other ways to achieve those goals besides the size of the packaging! Once the whole thing is brought home and the product – the mouse – is removed, the rest of the packaging – graphic inserts, instructions, warranty cards and so on, go straight in the bin.

Wasteful means of producing packaging are so ingrained into the daily design and production methods of companies today that it will take time to turn this big ship around. Many companies have existing relationships with packaging designers or manufacturers because these relationships have proved to be quick and cost-effective, albeit wasteful. The fact of the matter is that

it does cost an initial investment of time and money to explore greener options, and there is a learning curve – and companies with budgets and deadlines just don't want to invest that.

How can a designer effectively advocate for more sustainable package design without alienating the client?

Designers have been educating their clients for years – about things like aesthetics, target markets and production. Now, we just need to add sustainability to our list. We need to learn about it ourselves then pass that knowledge onto our clients.

Designers need to first educate themselves. What other alternatives are out there? Which local printers carry low-VOC inks? Get in touch with companies that use cornstarch-based plastic, for example, and get samples of their product so you can show

your clients. Show your clients that all their needs to sell product, protect product, give visibility to product, and so on, can still be met through more sustainable methods. The client shouldn't be made to feel like their needs are compromised through this process, and it's the designers job to educate them and sell them on the idea.

What do companies stand to lose by dragging their feet in this arena?

A lot of future business opportunities lie in supporting green design and production methods. More and more people are becoming aware that there are alternatives to wasteful packaging, and if companies don't get on this train and present themselves as a proponent of change, sooner or later they will lose some of their market. Public perceptions of backward companies will also be damaged.

Case Study: Twist

Maintaining a clean kitchen shouldn't require polluting the rest of the world, yet with the present over-reliance on single-use paper towels and toxin-laden sponges, this has too often been the case. The sponge company Twist began with making products derived from fully sustainable resources, and completed the cycle by wrapping their products in equally sustainable packaging. *'We believe in a clean world'*, says Twist co-founder Brian Ross. *'And that means more than sparkling countertops. It means paying attention to what goes into our products, and what happens to them when they're tossed away.'* Ross and co-founder Egil Wigart began the company in 2006, intent on combining good design with environmental responsibility as a means of creating *'functional, beautiful and responsible alternatives'* to standard kitchen cleaning products. For the sponges themselves, the cellulose is sourced from renewable pine-tree farms in Norway and the loofah is sourced from renewable loofah farms in Mexico. 100 per cent biodegradable, one of their sponges will completely disappear after seven weeks if buried in the soil.

Ross likes to point out that the choice of using a sponge in the first place represents an environmentally friendly gesture. *'With the absorbency of a paper towel and the reusability of a sponge, one of our Euro Cloths is equivalent to 17 rolls of paper towels and lasts 25 times as long as a traditional terrycloth rag.'* Considering, too, that over 99 per cent of all industrial waste is reused in the production cycle, significant waste reduction is achieved in both the home and the factory environment.

The company is committed to continually improving their production processes to further minimize their effects on the environment. Each of the three sponge products has been designed from production to packaging to be as functionally effective and ecologically sound as possible.

Beyond the sustainable materials, Twist wanted to offer some sort of reusability for the package. Relatively certain

The entire line of products is packaged in post-consumer waste paper with soy-based inks. As the dishes dry, consumers are invited to transform the package into a birdfeeder.

The company was created with sustainability as a guiding force, so that the entire product line is made from sustainable resources, and the packaging for each of the sponges is made from post-consumer waste paper.

The interior of each box provides a clear set of directions to help transform the package into a birdfeeder.

that there wasn't a viable secondary use closely tied to the product performance arena, they decided to encourage an activity that connected the user with nature. By making a birdfeeder that could be hung directly outside the kitchen window, Twist has envisioned a way to invite nature a little bit closer.

Teresa Forrester, the designer in charge of the Twist packages believes designers have amazing opportunities to change the way companies view their packaging systems. *'It's not about trying to change the client's mentality, but about better understanding the end goal for their particular product or idea',* she insists. *'Then being able to take that information and produce a better, more ecological solution than what currently exists for that particular market.'*

Finally, in the interest of providing as much cultural and social sustainability as environmental sustainability, Twist is committed to providing educational support to the community in Tetla, Tlaxcala, in Mexico, where all of their products are made and assembled.

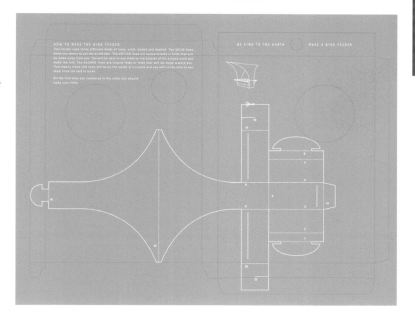

By making a birdfeeder that could be hung directly outside the kitchen window, Twist has envisioned a way to invite nature a little bit closer.

Case Study:
Sandstrom Partners

Sandstrom Partners is no stranger to sustainably oriented package design. In 1994, Steve Sandstrom, principal of Sandstrom Partners, created the graphic identity and packaging system for Tazo Tea, a brand that has not only retained its distinctive style, but has embraced package sustainability and reusability from the beginning.

Taking inspiration from a lifelong infatuation that one of the company founders had with old stainless-steel camping kits, a primary packaging directive for Tazo was a canister lid that could also serve as an infuser – a product that any drinker of full-leaf tea would have need of. 'We developed a patented metal tea canister for full-leaf teas that had an infuser designed into the lid both for convenience and reuse,' says Sandstrom, 'That was the first really sustainable thing we did for the brand. We created packaging that did more than provide shelf-appeal and product information. We created a compact expression of the brand with every inch considered.'

Despite the predicted surge in consumer interest with sustainability, package design still has a few consumer hurdles to overcome as Sandstrom sees it. 'Consumer perceptions and beliefs regarding product safety have led to their fair share of overpackaging', says Sandstrom. 'Plastic seals, for instance, build confidence that the product is as pure as the day it was manufactured.' And overpackaged goods can fill certain consumers with a sense of security.

Sandstrom believes that devising sustainable packaging alternatives is a simple matter of picking the lesser evils, understanding that sustainability is a process and not a product, and that any reduction in environmental impacts is a step in the right direction. He also has another term for material reduction in packaging: 'value engineering'. 'Cutting the size of a package down to its most functional size shouldn't be seen as the result of miraculous insight. Less packaging means less material, and less material means less expense, less shipping cost and less warehousing costs.'

A recently completed package design project for gDiapers, a company that makes flushable nappies,

Left – Tazo Tea set out to use their packaging as a functional product in its own right, designing infusers into the tops of their tin canisters.

Opposite – The gDiaper Starter Kit provides a handle to eliminate the need for shopping bags and encourage secondary usage. Other sustainable touches include a belly band that serves as a post-purchase informational brochure, recycled-content paper, soy inks and the use of small stickers and die-cuts to eliminate the need for repetitive production runs.

provided Sandstrom Partners with a fresh opportunity to create sustainable packaging. The gDiapers are made of all-natural fibre and are 100 per cent biodegradable, and offer a more environmentally friendly product than petroleum-based disposable nappies. Considering that 38,000 disposable nappies are landfilled every minute in the US alone, an alternative is desperately needed. The flushable interior of the gDiaper uses elemental chlorine-free tree-farmed fluff pulp and super absorbing poly-acrylate to absorb wetness. gDiapers are the first consumer packaged good to receive official Cradle to Cradle certification as a 'biological nutrient'. This designation certifies that the entire product formulation is safe for human and environmental health throughout its lifecycle, is easily recycled or composted and meets strict standards for energy-use, water-use and ethical conduct in the workplace of the company and its suppliers.

gDiapers' goal of turning waste into a resource carries over into the product's package design, which was created at Sandstrom Partners. The exterior package of the gDiaper Starter Kit is printed on 95 per cent recycled paperboard (35 per cent post-consumer), and is also printed with soy-based inks.

A belly band that wraps around the package serves a secondary function as a user's guide and informational brochure. Because designations for nappy size and product colour are not printed directly on the package, there is no need for multiple production runs. Small stickers affixed at the time of packing clarify nappy size, while circular die-cuts allow the consumer to identify the colour of the reusable shell. This die-cut also streamlined the packing process, saving time and energy in the process. 'A built-in handle prevents the need for shopping bags', says Sally Morrow, the creative director for the account, 'even as it suggests post-purchase functionality.'

While some companies prefer packages that do not wear their 'green' attributes too loudly, a main objective of this package was to signal the uniquely sustainable attributes of the product as a way to stand out from the competition – plastic, disposable nappies, which are well-known to be an environmental problem.

The packs of refill gDiapers are presently made from plastic in order to provide a moisture-seal that prevents the materials in the nappy from prematurely biodegrading. Due to budget constraints familiar to any young company, biopolymers were not an option, so LDPE (one of the preferable plastics) was used so that the material could be easily recycled.

From start to flush.

Insert flushable by pressing it into the 'little g' pants snap-in liner.

Close Velcro™ tabs at the back away from little hands.

To flush, tear flushable at notch from top to bottom.

Pull open completely. Make sure all contents fall into toilet.

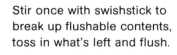

Stir once with swishstick to break up flushable contents, toss in what's left and flush.

Case Study: Celery Design Collaborative

Started in 1997, the Celery Design Collaborative began supporting sustainable businesses with their design skills almost immediately, designing the logo and various collateral material for The Natural Step soon after the international sustainable development organization opened its US office. More recently, Celery was selected as one of *I.D.* (International Design) magazine's '*I.D.* 40', and nominated for a biennial design award from the Cooper-Hewitt National Design Museum, both in 2007.

With the motto of *Smart, Fresh and Healthy*, Celery has worked with large corporations such as HP and Sun MicroSytems, as well as advocacy groups, nonprofits and small, sustainably minded start-up companies such as CleanFish, a sustainably-harvested fish company.

Along with providing for their own clients, this six-person studio has compiled a set of ecological design tools that they've made available online as a way of helping designers searching for sustainable paper products and materials. The introduction states: '*Through your paper choices, you are directly connected to the preservation or the degradation of land, water, air and the creatures that dwell therein.*'

Their latest packaging project is an innovative secondary-use package for Lemnis Lighting, a Dutch company that has helped revolutionize the lighting industry by developing LED technology which may soon replace the grossly inefficient incandescent lightbulb. Estimating that lighting accounts for a full 19 per cent

Above – The packages are printed with muted colours on the interior, and the bottoms are detachable so that the carton can open into a lampshade. Die-cut holes on the gussets allow light to beam outwards. This image shows two packages nested face-to-face inside one another, since the lightbulbs will often be sold in twos.

Left – New package designs for the ultra-efficient Lemnis LED bulb feature a triangular form for minimal shipping volume and maximum reusability as a lampshade. Colour-coding that takes advantage of the package form helps identify the different bulb wattages.

of global energy consumption, Lemnis has created the Pharox LED bulb, which is 90 per cent more efficient than incandescents and last 50 times longer. With a lifespan of 25 years, and a 10 watt bulb emitting the same amount of light as a traditional 60 watt bulb, the Pharox is also both more efficient and longer lasting than CFLs (Compact Fluorescent Lightbulbs).

The package has been specified with 100 per cent post-consumer paper, and designed for assembly without adhesives. The carton can be converted into a lampshade in a few easy steps (see opposite, top image). The bottom of the carton is detachable, and die-cut holes that allow the bulb to create beams of patterned light along walls, ceilings and other surfaces are cut into large gussets that fold inwards from the exterior of the box. These gussets provide protective padding for the lightbulbs while the package is in transit, and aid in securing the closures of the package. Die-cutting the gussets only ensures that the exterior package is free from holes.

Celery partner Brian Dougherty believes that packaging is about telling an interesting story, and creating an experiential opportunity for consumers. The collaborative's new package design for Lemnis reimagines the standard rectangular shape that has been associated with lightbulbs for decades with an eye-catching form that relates more directly to the three-dimensional shape of the product. A colour-coding system to clearly designate different bulb wattages becomes a major design element in its own right, covering the entire top and bottom of the package, and coating the interior of the carton so that, when converted into a lampshade, the colours provide a vibrant and modern aesthetic.

Other projects the Celery Design Collaborative has developed include the website for the Sundance Summit in 2007, an event focused on bringing the mayors of America's cities together in an effort to curb global warming, recycling awareness campaigns for municipal governments and ecological printing guides for paper companies invested in sustainable paper development, as well as a host of other environmentally and socially conscious endeavours. Their business is literally built upon nurturing social, cultural and environmental wellbeing.

Celery's 80% design solution

Celery Design Collaborative has developed a set of ecological design tools to aid their clients in their decision-making process. The tools, available online at www.celerydesign.com, have been compiled with the help of AIGA San Francisco and the Alameda County Waste Management Authority and Recycling Board. Among them is what they define as the '80% Design Solution', a highly functional tool due to its categorization of colour through the Pantone Matching System® (PMS). Approximately 20 per cent of the PMS colours should be avoided to prevent heavy metals from entering into the packaging project, which leaves 80 per cent of the PMS colour spectrum still available. These colours are listed as such by the US Environmental protection Agency's Sections 313 of Title III of the Superfunds Amendment and Reauthorization Act.

PMS colours to avoid:

regular/warm reds	metallics
123–126	8001-8005
136–140	8521
1365–1405	8540–8541
150–154	8560–8561
1555–1615	8580–8582
163–168	8600–8601
1625–1685	8640–8641
170–181	8660–8662
1765–1815	8680–8682
183–195	8700–8702
211–216	8720–8722
436–440	8740–8742
455–457	8760
4625–4645	8762
469–472	8780–8781
490–495	8800–8801
497–501	8820–8822
4975–5005	8840–8841
504–509	8860–8862
5185–5215	8881–8882
5535–5565	8900–8902
560–565	8921
567–572	8941–8942
	8961

89

Interview: Brian Dougherty
Partner and co-founder, Celery Design Collaborative

Q: What have been the most frustrating aspects of trying to push for more sustainability in your design practice?
It's been frustrating that downstream vendors in the communication realm have been slow to take sustainability seriously. I wish print vendors were teaching us how to make our production process super-efficient and nontoxic, but the reality is we're usually doing the research ourselves and pushing them to try more sustainable processes. The good news is that it teaches us to think more holistically, and the process gets easier as we go. The bad news is that those research costs are difficult to recoup. It becomes an investment in our studio's knowledge base.

Q: Do you have a set of sustainability criteria that you apply to every job?
Rather than having a checklist at the end of a project, we try to integrate sustainable design decisions into every phase of design. It's an important part of our early strategy work, it's a consideration while we brainstorm, it influences the form factor and materials we choose, and the production processes we specify. Sustainability is not the only factor in any of those decisions, but it is a component throughout the process.

Q: What do you see as the most common myth that clients believe in regards to the 'impractical nature' of sustainable production, and what are effective ways to dispel them?
Many companies simply don't think sustainable design is applicable to them unless they are overtly promoting some environmental benefit. It's fairly easy to convince clients that they need to 'walk the talk' of sustainability on their Environmental Performance Report, for instance, but that doesn't automatically transfer into their other communications. The next phase for many companies is extending green design from some niche or special project within the organization across all parts of a company's designed communications.

Q: What have been the most persistent myths that production and print houses hold, and how do you suggest designers dispel those myths?
Production companies are expected to deliver nearly perfect results every time, so they tend to be wary of materials and processes that are unfamiliar. Most of their customers just care about the finished product, not the production process. As green designers, we do care about the

process. Designers often have a great deal of control over the production process if they choose to exercise it. The trick is to involve printers in the process early and to ask lots of questions. Once you agree upon an environmentally superior process, it's important to make sure that's what really happens on the press floor. You can't assume that something will get done just because you mentioned it to a sales rep. If you are

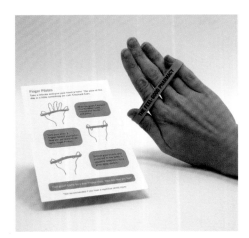

Made from 100 per cent post-consumer recycled paper, this package uses a rubber band to hold it together. Hung from doorknobs with a fresh-cut flower, this 'package' contained 'healthy advice' on how to reuse the rubber band (like finger pilates and the yin/yang spin card shown left).

Elephant Pharm is a small chain of pharmacy stores that provide holistic and natural remedy services alongside the standard pharmacy services. Celery created their first promotional package (opposite) from 100 per cent post-consumer paper stock. While this package design has received a lot of press for its sustainable qualities, Celery took the most recent package design even further.

breaking from a printer's business-as-usual, it's important to make certain that they follow through and do what they agreed to.

Q: What advice would you give to graphic designers just coming into the industry who don't have the luxury of choosing their own clients?
We don't exactly 'choose' our clients, but we do define a vision for our studio and we pursue certain types of work. We build a strong portfolio and a bedrock of experience, and that tends to attract the kind of work we want. If our portfolio or experience don't support the kind of work we want, then we find ways to develop those. We create self-initiated projects, for example, or volunteer for nonprofits, we conduct our own research,

or whatever it takes to gain that experience. This was true when we were just starting out, and it's still true now that we're working for lots of Fortune 500 corporations.

Q: How can graphic designers make the 'right' choices regarding sustainability when they are caught up in the daily struggle of making a living?
I recommend that designers read books such as Paul Hawkens' *Natural Capitalism*, *Biomimicry* by Janine Benyus, and *Cradle to Cradle* by William McDonough. As we learn more about the concepts underlying sustainable business and ecological design, it becomes easier to see through superficial environmental claims and to make well-reasoned decisions.

Above – Sometimes it's a matter of rethinking how a project is 'packaged' altogether. In order to more effectively distribute their Global Citizenship Customer Report in multiple languages, Celery helped the Hewlett-Packard Company develop a single CD-ROM containing the equivalent of 19 printed reports. The foam interior of the packaging is a bio-polymer PaperFoam which can be recycled with the paperboard case.

'Designers often have a great deal of control over the production process if they choose to exercise it. The trick is to involve printers in the process early and to ask lots of questions.'

Brian Dougherty

Case Study:
Chameleon Packaging

Most design agencies rely on external sources for information about materials. As a division of Design & Source Productions, Inc., Chameleon Packaging is dedicated to developing, procuring and distributing all manner of sustainable materials so that they may be more easily found and used by designers and corporate clients alike. And in order to simplify this process, Chameleon has created tools such as their sustainable materials wheel chart (see page 95).

While they provide a diverse array of services, they have recently become most recognized for their 'new stone age' product; the environmentally friendly, tree-less paper, Terraskin®. TerraSkin®, unlike any other sustainable substrate, is made from stone powder – calcium carbonate to be exact. Their unique 'paper'-making process of combining 80 per cent stone powder and 20 per cent nontoxic binding resin results in unique qualities such as a vibrant white surface that requires no bleaching whatsoever, and a high degree of tear-resistance. Because it is not comprised of fibres, it is also water-resistant and, because it is nonabsorbent, requires approximately 20 to 30 per cent less ink during the printing process. Production of TerraSkin® requires no water and no trees, although careful attention must be paid to the mining processes necessary to obtain the minerals that comprise the tree-less paper. After three to nine months in the natural environment, the material will safely biodegrade. Because it is naturally tear- and water-resistant, the need for any lamination is eliminated. Due to these impressive sustainable qualities, TerraSkin® has been awarded a Cradle to Cradle Silver Certification, a third-party certification through MBDC that ensures a product meets standards in the area of closed-loop properties, biodegradability and renewable energy strategies, to name a few.

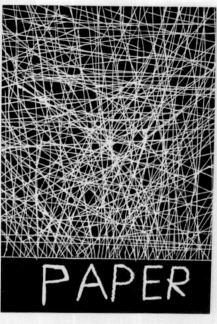

The Museum of Modern Art (MoMA) in New York City developed a gift-packaging line that makes use of TerraSkin®. This particular shopping bag was produced to accompany MoMA's 'Eye on Europe' exhibition, and was recognized with an American Instore Graphic Design Award from Graphic Design USA.

As an example of the trade-offs that are sometimes made in the pursuit of sustainability, Burt's Bees sells all of their products in individually wrapped packages rather than larger, more environmentally friendly bulk sizes, even though they are fully aware of the sustainable benefits of doing so. While bulk packaging is more efficient for packaging materials, the products Burt's Bees makes do not have artificial preservatives, so they must be used in a timely fashion in order to maintain their freshness and their maximum effectiveness – something bulk containers would most likely prohibit.

Burt's Bees was founded with environmental stewardship in mind when a waitress and a honey-maker joined together to sell products like soap and candles out of the beeswax that was harvested from a small one-man operation. The credo of serving 'The Greater Good' has manifested itself in numerous environmental and social programmes, and their packaging has strived for low environmental impact. Many of the company's products are packaged in aluminium, which can either be reused efficiently by consumers or readily (and economically) recycled. Any products that require tubes are produced from recycled plastics, a growing number of their product labels are biodegradable, and most recently they have packaged soap products in TerraSkin® paper (above).

Burt's Bees soap products are wrapped in TerraSkin® paper. Along with possessing a number of important sustainable qualities, TerraSkin® can be made in a wide range of paper weights, from thinner, more flexible weights like these wrappers, to thicker and more rigid weights that can carry significant product mass, like the shopping bag on the opposite page.

Chameleon Packaging's unique 'paper'-making process of combining 80 per cent stone powder and 20 per cent nontoxic binding resin results in unique qualities such as a vibrant white surface that requires no bleaching whatsoever, and a high degree of tear-resistance.

Interview: Nicole F. Smith
Environmental Director, Design & Source Productions, Inc.

Q: What was the motivating force behind Chameleon's pursuit of sustainable practices?

Innovation – this has really been the driver for Design & Source, and specifically Chameleon. We are constantly researching trends, and bringing new materials to our customers. Sustainability is truly innovation, looking at standard applications and using innovative, sustainable, healthy materials.

Q: Can you talk a little about how you find your sustainable materials?

Many ways – some through research, some through research in other fields, some through our manufacturers directly, trade magazines and of course trade shows and expositions around the world, so we know what's happening and where.

Q: How do you verify the sustainable aspects of the materials you use?

Being there. It's definitely not easy, especially when they never seem to be in your backyard, but I travel a lot, and I try to visit every step of the process. For instance, we work with post-consumer recycled PET (soda and water bottles) fabrics, and I personally have been to the recycling facilities in Asia that they collect the raw material from, and then to the mills that are weaving yarns from that same recycled plastic, to the actual facility that makes bags with the finished fabric.

We really need transparency with all of our factories, so that we can trace every step, and hold them accountable, so that we can be accountable for our customers. It's really exciting though, seeing innovation around the world and the many different ways it manifests itself! Another large help in our organization is our overseas offices that help with auditing and quality control – as I can't be there all the time, this is really a lifesaver. Last but not least, testing and certifications: really important.

Q: What are the ways graphic designers can contribute to a change in client mentality?

Well if they are in the role of specifying the substrate and inks – that's the first, best step. Otherwise this would be tough, unless they are reading up on the SPC guidelines and taking an active role by educating themselves, I am not sure how much they can get across. But if they do have that specifying role in their position – then they have the power to suggest more sustainable options. Clients always want you looking out for them, so it's always an added bonus when a designer can bring innovative options to the table.

Renewable

BAMBOO

What is it:
Textiles made of bamboo, rapidly renewable (annually)

Applications:
Make-up bags, handbags, tote bags

Recycled

DOUBLE P

What is it:
100% post-consumer recycled PET (recycled drinks and water bottles)

Applications:
Shopping bags, toiletry bags, tote bags, wine bags

DOUBLE G

What is it:
100% post-consumer recycled grocery bags, using no dyes or inks

Applications:
Boxes, pouches, toiletry bags, tote bags, organizers

REVA

What is it:
100% post-industrial recycled ethylene vinyl acetate (EVA) (like flip flops)

Applications:
Trays, toiletry kits, pencil cases, dishes, bookmarks, key rings

Degradable

TERRASKIN®

What is it:
Tree-free paper, made of stone (tear- and water-resistant)

Applications:
Shopping bags, gift boxes, promo/marketing materials, signage, labels, hang tags

Q: Now that the packaging industry is embracing sustainable packaging, what do you see as the challenges remaining for large-scale change?

Well, there is no perfect solution to anything, so I think the trick is learning the pros and cons of each material, and making sure you have the right application. There are challenges for many of these materials, all slightly different – sometimes it's cost, sometimes it's availability or capacity issues. I think the biggest thing we need to remember though is that there is no perfect solution – diversify and at least start taking the baby steps. You can't hold out for the perfect solution, because then no-one makes progress.

Tools such as this wheel chart of sustainable materials from Chameleon Packaging provide graphic designers with an effective resource. Below are the individual elements listed on this wheel.

Renewable / Compostable

INGEO™
What is it:
Textiles made of 100% annually renewable corn

Applications:
Handbags, tote bags, customized items

BIOPLASTICS
What is it:
100% annually renewable starch (corn, beets, potatoes)

Applications:
Folding boxes, blister-packs, bags, disposable servingware

Recycled / Compostable

PULP
What is it:
100% post-consumer recycled paper pulp

Applications:
Moulded boxes and trays, clamshells, disposable foodware

Renewable / Recyclable / Compostable

SUGAR CANE/ REED PULP
What is it:
100% annually renewable fibre pulp (by-products bagasse, reed and rice straw)

Applications:
Moulded boxes and trays, clamshells, disposable foodware

FALCATA
What is it:
100% rapidly renewable falcata tree (grows in 4–5 years)

Applications:
Folding boxes, trays, disposable foodware

Chapter 3: Sustainability in the Professional Realm

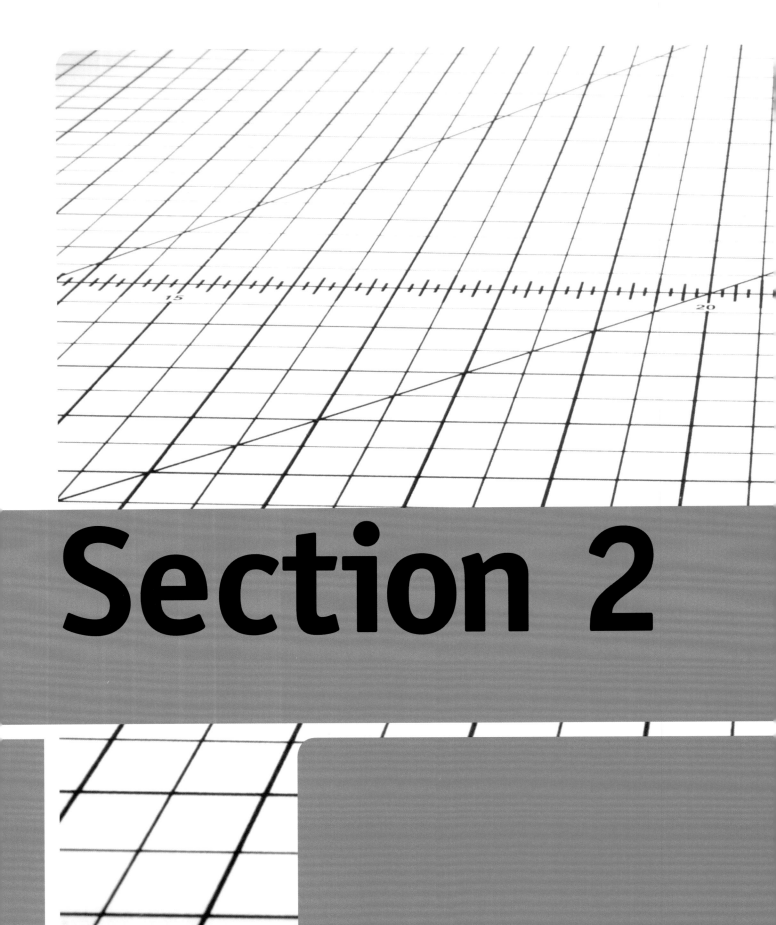

Section 2

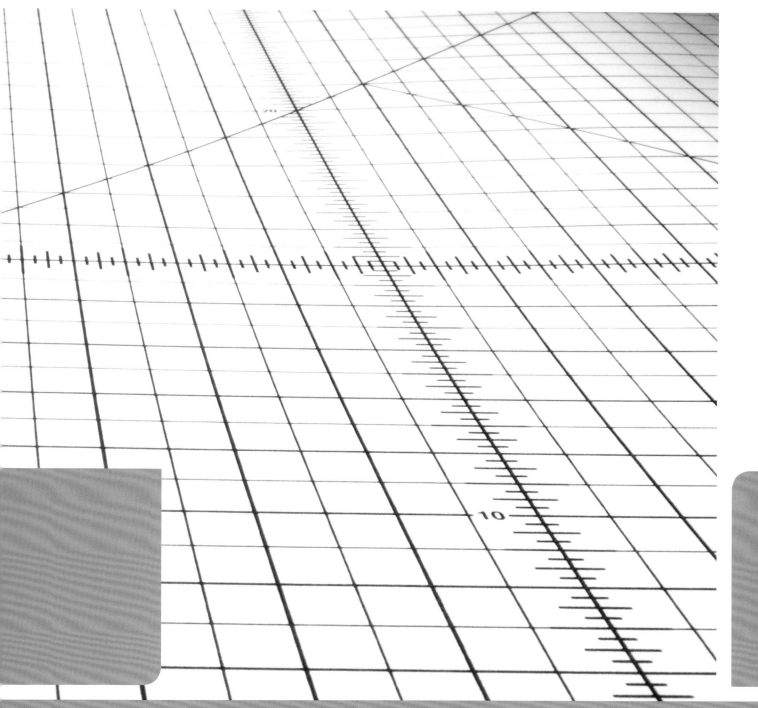

Re:structure

'… paper, in handicraft and industry, is generally used lying flat; the edge is rarely utilized. For this reason we try paper standing upright, or even as a building material; we reinforce it with complicated folding; we use both sides; we emphasize the edge. Paper is usually pasted; instead of pasting it we try to tie it, to pin it, to sew it, to rivet it. In other words, we fasten it in a multitude of different ways. At the same time we learn by experience its properties of flexibility and rigidity, and its potentialities in tension and compression.'

Josef Albers

4: Materials and construction
5: Case studies in building prototypes

Re:structure

The famed artist and Bauhaus teacher, Josef Albers, discussed the need for designers to experiment with the materials available to them (see quotation opposite). It was this kind of dedication to innovation that propelled dramatic change in the field of graphic design nearly a century ago, and it's this kind of dedication to innovation that's required now in order to transform the package design industry so that it can meet the economic, social and environmental needs of the next century.

The second half of this book contains practical information regarding the development of sustainable packaging prototypes. Chapter four introduces some fundamental building practices that will help anyone get the most out of their prototype building experiences. Mastering comping techniques is helpful not only to individuals immersed in the packaging industry, but to any graphic designer. Freelance designers often offer 'one-stop' shopping for clients, and this requires skills across the board, including comping impressive prototypes. Independent studios often develop whimsical self-promotional packages that are intended for a relatively small group of clients or potential clients. Such short-run projects are cost-effective only when they are comped. Recent graduates of graphic design courses, meanwhile, need perfectly constructed packages for use in their portfolios. So, these techniques will prove extremely helpful to many individuals in the design field.

Chapter five features a wide range of package-as-product prototype explorations. Graduate students at the Savannah College of Art and Design in the US were assigned with the task of developing viable secondary-use packages for common products. With a firm understanding of sustainable materials and resources, a package designer can aim to devise packages that do not need to be discarded once they've done their 'first' job of delivering the contents to the consumer. As discussed at the end of the first section, a secondary use that exacerbates other environmental impacts is not worthy of development. Successfully creating a truly functional secondary use, however, can be quite beneficial, in that it prevents material – even sustainable material – from entering the waste stream too quickly (if at all).

Many of the examples that follow are made from various papers, which implies that a secondary use simply postpones the inevitable. Yet, slowing the cycle of reuse has its own ecological benefits, and those benefits should not be dismissed. While cradle-to-cradle (C2C) principles apply to materials that are reused in perpetuity, these package-as-product ideas can prevent the C2C loops from constricting too tightly. The goal, then, is not to make a package that converts into a product that lasts a lifetime – what product, after all, lasts that long? – as much as to increase the functionality of the package beyond present boundaries. Simply put, we can reduce waste by increasing function.

While some of these solutions have production limitations, their intentions are worth noting. Prototypes are models that lead to more highly refined models; the objective here is to inspire new ways of thinking about the package. In this context, the examples aim to serve as mnemonic devices for further innovation to come.

The structure of this package does not change, only its orientation and the placement of some of its lateral supports. The second image, which shows the package as a focal point for the products' home use, demonstrates just one way in which it could be utilized. Natural materials, some from found sources, create a clear aesthetic statement.

Section 2 – Re:structure

The most important word in the subtitle of this chapter is the one you probably skipped over – **with**. Paperboard constructions must work with the inherent potentials and shortcomings of the actual material. In this section you will find that paperboard can do some surprising things. You will also find that it has clear limitations. The package designer must wrestle with the material frequently enough to discover the limits and the unexpected dexterity of paperboard's range of accommodation.

It is important to remember that limitations provide their own set of creative possibilities. In *Six Memos For The Next Millennium*, author Italo Calvino dedicated a series of lectures to the creative potentials inherent in self-imposed constraints. *'In order to escape the arbitrary nature of existence, (he) is forced to impose rigorous rules and regulations on himself… But the miracle is that the system of poetics, which might seem artificial and mechanical, produces inexhaustible freedom and wealth of invention.'*

Calvino's focused commitment to the exploration of lightness in fiction, for instance, allowed him to uncover the elusive meaning of weight in our lives.

The best professional designers will also acknowledge how a client's insistence on constraining the parameters of a project will often lead to unexpected and ingenious solutions. Giles Calvert, in his book *What Is Packaging Design?* offers two quotes that may be helpful here – the Chinese proverb *'Every kite needs a string'*, and the scientist Douglas R. Hofstadter's observation that *'… the welcoming of constraints is, at bottom, the deepest secret of creativity'* – both of which allude to the necessity of constraint as a guiding force.

So as you wrestle with paperboard – as you cut, fold, curve and twist this material – listen to what it is telling you about its own nature. It is that nature, more so than the nature of your own expectations, that will provide a path to success.

4 Materials and construction

101

Working with three-dimensional forms

The limitations of paperboard should be seen more as potential opportunities to explore the unique attributes of the material. Embracing the tendencies of paperboard as it attempts to define its own curves can open the doors to myriad new possibilities.

The folding art of origami

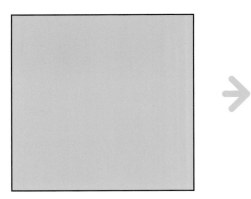

This section begins with a look at an ancient art that is similar in many ways to contemporary paperboard construction. Origami, the art of paper folding, is derived from two Japanese words: oru means 'to fold', and kami means... you guessed it... 'paper'. The evolution of the art generally follows the origins of paper, from ancient China during the second century AD to its highest degree of accomplishment in Japan, starting around 1,000AD. There is a magical aspect to creating myriad ornate three-dimensional objects from a flat piece of paper.

Friedrich Froebel, the inventor of Kindergarten, recommended paper-folding as a means of developing a child's critical thinking abilities as early as 1835. He saw it as one of many symbolic activities that could further an individual's appreciation of the connection between thinking and doing, and between humans and nature. Great three-dimensional revolutionaries such as Frank Lloyd Wright and Buckminster Fuller have suggested that their early Kindergarten experiences played a role in their visionary thinking.

The famed Bauhaus teachers Josef Albers, Walter Gropius Johannes Itten and Paul Klee all embraced Froebel's philosophy that play and experimentation provide fertile ground for learning. Albers' Preliminary Course challenged students to explore methods of manipulating materials in ways that had not previously been considered. His students engaged in a multitude of paper explorations, origami being one of them.

Of course, origami results in a product rather than a package – with some exceptions, origami sculptures do not hold anything. And, within the framework for this book, this is an important distinction. Origami exists for its own sake, and so each fold is intended for intrinsic needs. Packaging, on the other hand, exists to serve something entirely beyond its own form (or, more accurately, something within its own form). The shape and function of any package is derived from the needs of the product it is designed to hold.

Even so, origami provides us with dual inspiration. It shows us what paper can do, and it provides us with

'... the ability to construct inventively and to learn through observation is developed... by undisturbed and unprejudiced experiment, in other words, by a free handling of materials without practical aims.'

Josef Albers

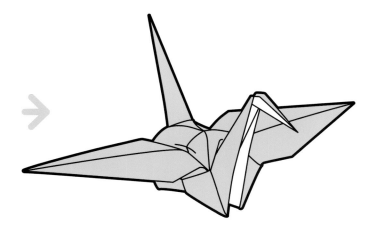

a glimpse into the potentials for secondary usage. Once our paperboard package is freed from its primary purpose of holding, protecting and marketing a product, it could return in essence to whence it began – a flat piece of paper. Of course, a piece of paper with a distinct and unshakable past – that of its former three-dimensional self – but no longer burdened with the obligation to contain anything. Its second life may be purely ornamental, much like the primary purpose of origami.

Origami requires patience, exactitude and a firm exertion of control. Working with paperboard will require more than this. Because packaging must be firm enough to hold its product, the lightweight paper used in origami will simply not work. Thicker and more rigid paper is required and because of this, scoring and cutting tools are required. The most common of these are the bone folder and the scoring tool and, of course, the #11 Xacto blade and holder.

Some excellent books on origami have been written and compiled by the renowned paper-sculptor Paul Jackson, and this divergence from the practical needs of packaging

– even if only temporary – can provide great inspiration and insight into material properties. Another very helpful reference when designing paperboard packages is literature on pop-up mechanisms such as the book *The Elements of Pop-Up* by David A. Carter and James Diaz. Much like origami, these pop-up techniques are immensely varied and provide insight into the impressive possibilities of paper construction. Like origami, many pop-up structures are for ornamental use, so while much can be learned from studying them, the package designer must be able to adapt these ideas so they perform in more functional environs.

Traditional origami paper is white on one side and coloured on the other. This has decorative purposes, of course. For us here, it also allows you to follow the illustrated directions on the following pages. If you don't buy origami paper, then a regular piece of copy paper will be fine, providing, of course that you cut it down to a square – approximately 15 x 15cm (6 x 6in).

An exercise in folding: Origami crane

A

B

A

B

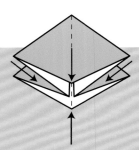

1 *Beginning with the coloured side of the square facing upwards, fold the paper diagonally in half (a). Unfold, and then repeat across the other diagonal (b).*

2 *Unfold the paper and turn the white side up. Fold the paper vertically in half, then unfold (a). Fold the paper horizontally in half, then unfold (b).*

3 *Bring all four corners together, making sure that the extra flaps collapse inwards. The resulting shape should be a square. Make sure the open corner points downwards.*

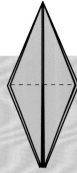
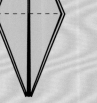

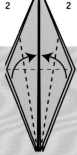
2 2

1

7 *Turn the entire piece over and repeat the same step, so the resulting form looks like this.*

8 *Peel the top left and then the top right corners inwards along the diagonals defined by numbers 1 and 2.*

Turn the piece over and repeat these steps.

9 *Now, stop to compare your bird with this illustration. Do they look anything alike?*

Good.

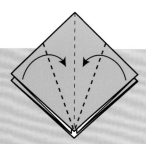
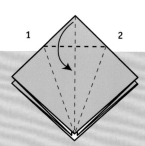
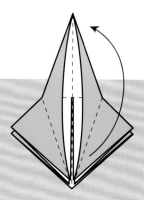

4 Fold the flaps on the top surface inwards to align with the centre fold.

5 Fold the top point downwards along a horizontal defined by points 1 and 2.

Turn the entire piece over and repeat.

6 Peel the top-most corner upwards, and flatten all the folds so that it lies flat.

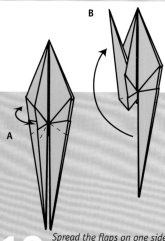
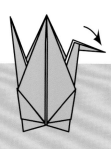

10 Spread the flaps on one side (a), then tuck the bottom 'point' upwards into the opening (b). Then close the flaps again.

Repeat this on the other side.

11 Fold the point of one of the newly formed upward flaps to make the head of the crane.

12 As you pull the points of the wings (a and b), blow gently into the hole at the bottom of the crane (c).

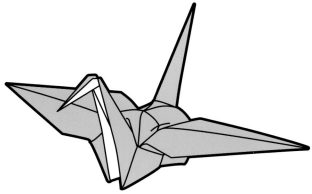

Tweet, tweet.

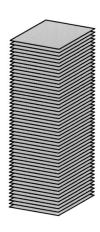

Make 999 more*

*Optional.
(It's said that making 1,000 origami cranes in one year will grant you good luck for the rest of your life.)

This is genius

not this   this

Below – Notice just how efficient the die-strike is – no paper is wasted.

Basic building blocks and terminology

The package on the left is as brilliant as its product is luminous. The light bulb is one of the most fragile products available on the market today, yet its packaging is as minimal as a package can be. This simple wrap represents the epitome of sensible packaging – it protects, it provides a distribution-friendly form, it provides a decorative surface for information and persuasion and it uses only as much material as is needed. Furthermore, the cost of its production is commensurate with the cost of the product; both are inexpensive.

Paperboard is one of the most common kinds of packaging. Over 275kg (600lb) of it are consumed by every person in the US each year, representing approximately half of all packaging by value and weight. It is relatively cheap, it's an excellent substrate for printing and it provides an invaluable service to commerce; its ability to flatten completely for shipping to the product manufacturer. This is called 'flat-packing', 'knock-down construction' or 'collapsibility'. Whatever term you use, this property allows a paper construction to remain flat until it reaches the product manufacturing facility, to pop open in order to accommodate the product, and then to remain rigid and protective for the remainder of its service.

Ironically, while the package for a standard light bulb is remarkably efficient, the actual bulb it holds is anything but. It is estimated that more than 90 per cent of the electricity consumed by a regular incandescent light bulb – like the one in the photo on the left – is wasted; not on light, its primary function, but on escaping heat. While we have significantly reduced wasted energy with the advent of compact fluorescent light bulbs (which generate 70 per cent less heat), the packaging for these (often a plastic clamshell) is less environmentally sound than the old package. The packaging must keep pace with the product!

107

Basic anatomy

An important fact to remember is that any paperboard box – no matter how many sides, angles or curves – can be constructed in any number of ways. Even in a situation where the size and shape of a box cannot be altered due to product specifications, the relative position of any panel on the die-strike can be changed (as shown on the opposite page). These illustrations provide some insight into the value of innovative problem-solving when approaching such structural dilemmas. The shifting of functional panels is a key factor to remember as you explore structural possibilities in your own package designs. With a keen and unrelenting eye for exploration, even the most challenging structures can be resolved.

There are two basic forms of rectangular box structure: the 'aeroplane tuck' which, in both its built form and its die-strike resembles its namesake; and the 'reverse tuck', which places the score of one opening directly opposite the score of the other. Generally speaking, package designers do what they can to get any open seams away from the front of the package. That's why most glue flaps are placed as shown in these illustrations – on the back of the box. If they were placed on a side panel towards the back, they would interfere with the closing of the box. An aeroplane tuck allows the designers to place both open seams on the reverse side, whereas a reverse tuck results in a box that has a top seam on one side and a bottom seam on the other. There is no hard-and-fast rule as to which of these two variations should be used in any given situation, but generally speaking, the reverse tuck provides a little more strength and durability to a box.

Along with these two variations (which don't alter the basic function of the package), there are four other layouts to consider when building this simple box, each of which allows for a different type of access to the contents. Accessibility of the product is always important, whether it be in the form of a one-time entry where the product is permanently removed after purchase, or continual access where the package is used for product storage.

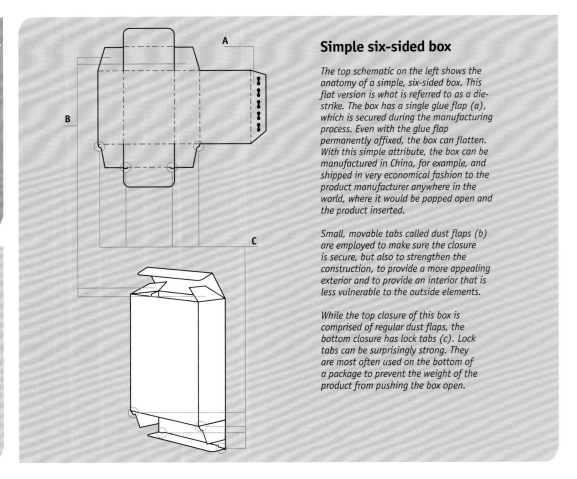

Simple six-sided box

The top schematic on the left shows the anatomy of a simple, six-sided box. This flat version is what is referred to as a die-strike. The box has a single glue flap (a), which is secured during the manufacturing process. Even with the glue flap permanently affixed, the box can flatten. With this simple attribute, the box can be manufactured in China, for example, and shipped in very economical fashion to the product manufacturer anywhere in the world, where it would be popped open and the product inserted.

Small, movable tabs called dust flaps (b) are employed to make sure the closure is secure, but also to strengthen the construction, to provide a more appealing exterior and to provide an interior that is less vulnerable to the outside elements.

While the top closure of this box is comprised of regular dust flaps, the bottom closure has lock tabs (c). Lock tabs can be surprisingly strong. They are most often used on the bottom of a package to prevent the weight of the product from pushing the box open.

Aeroplane tucks

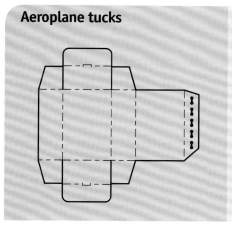

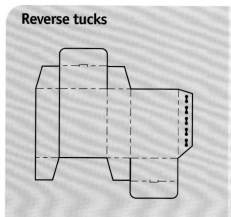

Reverse tucks

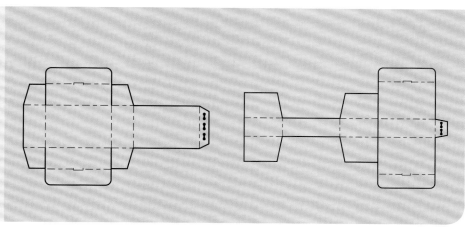

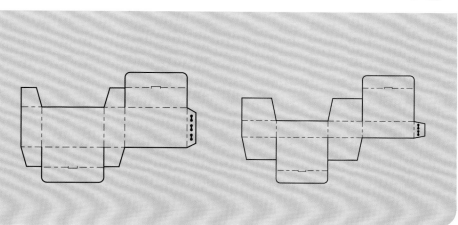

Notice how less and less glue is used for both the aeroplane and the reverse tucks (from left to right). The non-glued sides also get larger as a percentage of the whole. This combination (shorter glued panels plus longer non-glued panels) must always be paid attention to. All things being equal, the shorter the glue panels, the less stable the box becomes, and the less weight it can carry.

The small rectangular tabs on these boxes are a simple mechanism you can add to make the box a little easier to open. Notice on the die-strikes that the cut should traverse the score (a little on both sides of the score), and that the actual score line does not run through the tab.

Locking it up

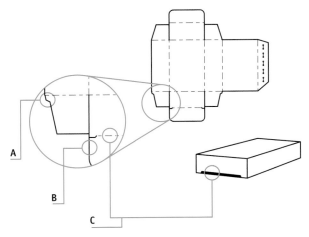

Lock tabs come in many shapes and sizes. The preceding page presented full lock tabs (also called full tuck flaps), which extend across the entire dimension of a carton closure. They are shown here in more detail to highlight the small, yet essential, elements of such a closure. Elements 'a' and 'c' in the illustration on the top right work in tandem to insure a secure lock. Without the proper placement of the full-panel score (c), the locks will not hold. The score itself does not represent the full height of the panel in question, but is usually 1–2mm ($^1/_{16}$ in) shorter. This results in the small horizontal slot opening shown in the three-dimensional illustration. Without that shorter score, the locks do not work. Notice the straight edge on the tuck flap before the rounded corner. This straight edge creates stability for the box when it is closed, and enough friction to make sure it stays closed.

The image on the right shows a partial lock tab, which holds the centre of a closure rather than its entire length. The key holding mechanisms for the partial lock tabs (a and b) are the same as for the full lock tab; the score for the tab is actually shorter than the height of the panel. Partial lock tabs work well with longer openings since they make use of a centred lock, whereas the full lock tabs can begin to droop in the middle of a long panel if it is too long or if the weight of the product is too much. Some cartons with longer openings make use of two partial lock tabs for a sure closure.

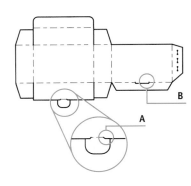

Above – While smaller than full lock tabs, partial lock tabs work well on longer carton openings as they add strength to the middle of the closure.

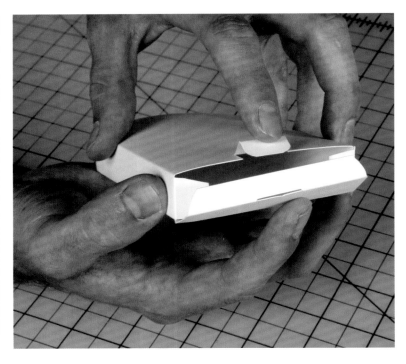

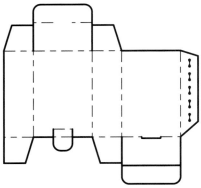

A hybrid of the two above locks is called the 'tuck-and-tongue'. This combination allows the user to grasp the small tab and effectively pull it backwards.

110

Totally glueless

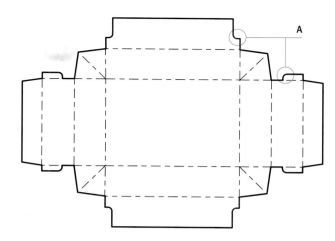

Finding ways to eliminate the need for adhesives can lower production costs and enhance the sustainable attributes of a carton. Two examples of self-locking mechanisms are featured here, with the hope that an understanding of their basic function will provide a springboard for exploring other resistance-based closures.

Along with eliminating the need for glue, self-locking cartons can be helpful in other situations. For example, all cartons must lie flat after the glue flaps have been adhered; this allows them to be shipped efficiently from the carton manufacturer to the product manufacturer. This important restriction exerts great control over carton forms. If no glue is necessary, the carton can be popped open at the product manufacturer no matter what the final form of the package.

QUICKSET LOCKS (above and right)
The images above show a common non-adhesive locking system. It can be called a system because the strength of this closure owes itself not just to the 'ears' that tuck into the small die-cut notches (a), but also to the doubling of the paper as it folds back on itself and the gussets (or bellows) that securely seal the corners. By becoming intimate with how these simple mechanisms work in tandem to create the secure closure seen here, it's possible devise your own innovative, non-adhesive closures.

SLOT LOCKS (left and below)
Shown here is perhaps the simplest and most effective form of a dimensional locking mechanism. This particular example was chosen not only for its simple locking mechanism, but as a segue into the next demonstration. The die-strike reveals the two important relationships to pay special attention to when designing the package form to the desired proportions and angles. First, any increase or decrease in the angle and height of the package must be measured in two areas (a). Second, the 'real' height (or vertical distance from top to bottom) must also be measured in two different areas (b). As seen in this example, it is usually best to hide the lock for cosmetic reasons.

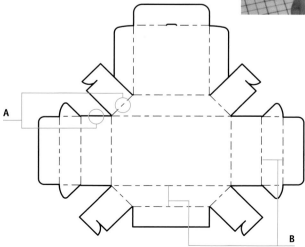

Approaching paperboard at the right... umm, proper, angle

Right angles are easy to work with when designing paperboard cartons. There are many carton structures that break from that simple mould, however. Over the next few pages, angles and curves are studied for their inherent properties.

ANGLE COMBINATIONS AND CHANGING VOLUMES (below)

Using an existing die-cut of an angular carton as a template for a new carton with a different set of angles requires more diligence than many expect. The images below show the 'ripple' effect of altering an angle as little as three degrees; when one angle changes, all angles change. The only angles that do not change are those on the very bottom since both boxes have bottoms that define right angles. All other angles, however, must change according to the needs of the new measurements.

Another important factor to keep in mind is the quickly changing volume of the new box. The minor change in angle will significantly impact on the available interior volume, the shape that the volume defines and even the amount of paper necessary to build the carton.

PARALLELOGRAMS (opposite)

Parallelograms and trapezoids with top and bottom closures are the simplest form of angular carton, in that only the top and bottom shapes vary from a normal rectangular box. There are no significant changes in function or structure in this shape of carton, with the exception of the top and bottom panels and the nature of the dust flaps. A single glue flap is still used, and providing that opposite sides are of equal measurements, the carton will lie flat with the glue flap adhered. Pay careful attention to the angles on the dust flaps (a), especially if there are lock tabs involved.

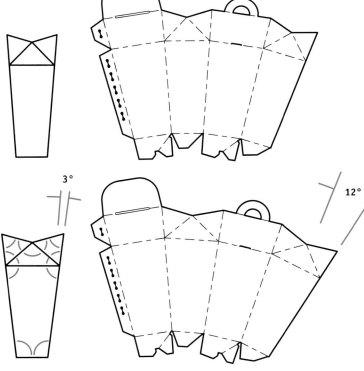

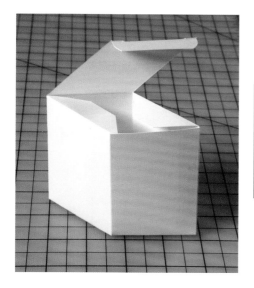

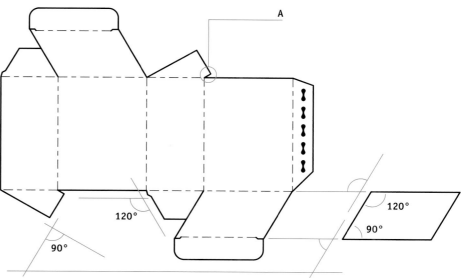

FLATTENING CARTONS WITH TROUBLESOME ANGLES (right)

Angles and curves in a carton can be problematic to the packing system, in that if a carton cannot be collapsed when its glue flaps are adhered, there is no efficient way to ship it from the factory it was built in to the product manufacturer (unless the carton and the product were manufactured in the same place, which is not common).

Featured here are two typical ways to enable a carton with non-aligning angles to be practical for shipping needs. In the first example, an extra score is added to the carton (a). This score is traditionally only used once in the carton's life – in that journey from carton manufacturer to product manufacturer. Careful attention must be paid to avoid placing this score on the front of the carton, as seen in the image on the right. The examples for curved packages on the following page also shows how this can be is handled.

Another method is to replace any glue flaps with lock tabs, as is seen in the second example (b).

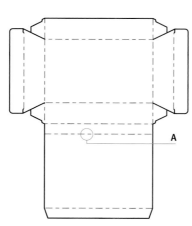

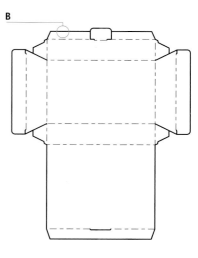

Curves and countercurves

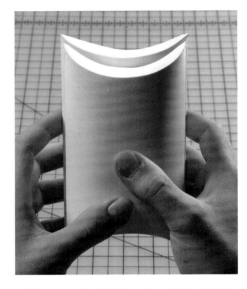

Playing with curves will reveal the limitations of paperboard pliability. You can hold a flat piece of paperboard in your hand and manipulate it into all kinds of curvature, but as soon as you introduce a curve into a multisided carton, you'll discover the inevitable reality; for every curve, there must be a counter-curve on the opposite side of the score. The best curved cartons use this physical certainty as the basis of their success. On these pages there are several important points to consider as you investigate the role of curves in your carton.

CURVES EQUAL CURVES
The pillow pack is perhaps the purest example of taking advantage of paperboard's natural tendencies. The tension that results from pinching the scored edges together provides the necessary pressure to keep the package closed.

The images on this page intend to show how the severity of one curve dictates the severity of the opposing curve, and that the more extreme the curve, the more likely that structural problems will occur. There is a comfort zone in any tension closure. Anything with too little tension (curves that are too flat) will result in a box that does not close securely, while anything with too much tension (exaggerated curves), will bind the paper

and compromise its integrity. A close look at the bottom left-hand image reveals crimps in the paper – this is a sure sign that you've reached the boundaries of the paper's comfort zone.

One of the most functional attributes of the pillow pack is that it flattens easily. In fact, it only opens into its dimensional form with the help of the aforementioned tension created when the curves are pushed into themselves.

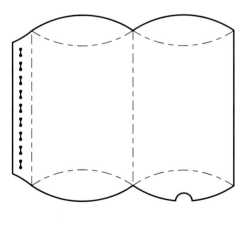

Increasing the intensity of any curve on a carton increases the likelihood that the paper will respond negatively to the severe manipulation.

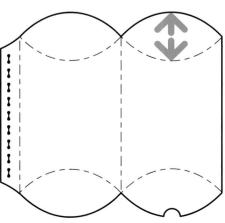

COLLAPSING A CURVE (right)

While the pillow pack naturally collapses once tension is released, curves that are bound by the folding of more than one score will prevent a carton from flattening. (This is a bad thing, because the carton should be able to flatten for efficient shipping from the package manufacturer to the product manufacturer.)

There are two ways to work with a curve that cannot attach to an outer panel on a carton. The first is to replace any glue flaps with lock tabs, as seen on the previous pages. This allows a carton to be flattened easily, no matter what kind of curve it has on it. The second option, and usually the more pragmatic in the eyes of the product-packer (the company responsible for getting the manufactured product into the carton), is shown on the right. Notice how the extra score along the two sides of the carton allow it to flatten. While this may seem like a substantial cosmetic fault, as long as such scores are on the sides of a box, they remain concealed once surface graphics are applied.

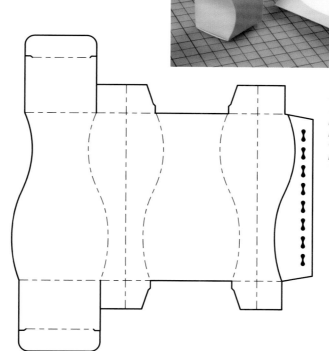

Notice in this photograph how the constructed box on the left does not have scores. When building prototypes for a photoshoot or presentation, it's not uncommon to omit scores for cosmetic purposes, providing it's understood that they will be necessary for production.

CURVES ON AN OTHERWISE ANGULAR CARTON (right and below)

This photograph and diagram show one example of the successful integration of a curved corner into an otherwise straight box. When exploring this method, pay special attention to the distance available that will allow the paperboard to transform from a curve to a straight edge. In this example, the height of the carton allows the paper the structural leeway to adapt. The force of the gussets pushing outwards also provides a tension that is beneficial to the form of the carton.

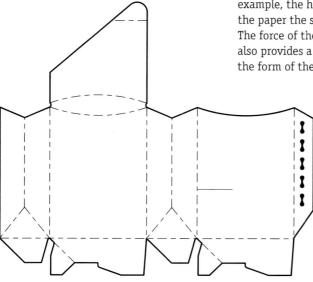

Tutorial one | Scoring and folding

The next few pages provide a closer look at techniques that will help you to build comps to a standard worthy of presentations and photoshoots. The case studies in the next chapter provide further guidance.

This first example looks at the fundamentals of handling paperboard in box-building. The right amount of preparation will make the building go smoothly. All measurements should be double- and triple-checked, and you should build a dummy beforehand to ensure that all is as it should be.

There are simply too many paper products available to specify brands or weights for comping, although .014 and .016 SBS board or boxboard are common for production, and can be purchased for comping purposes. For example, new printing papers for home colour printers come in weights that approximate the necessary paperboard thicknesses – while some print beautifully, others do not. Even variables such as box-size and the severity of the angles within the box are important factors to consider.

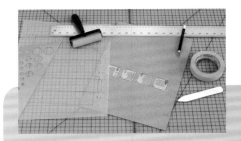

The straight edged tools shown here are metal – plastic set-squares and T-squares can quickly lose their pure edges. The bone folder is a fine tool for scoring boxes, while the brayer ensures that any gluing between surfaces is burnished extremely well. Keep a piece of tracing paper between the brayer and the artwork to prevent smudging or smearing. Notice that the output has no lines denoting scores or crops – instead a series of crop and score marks has been printed which will be cut away as the box is made.

Turn the cardstock over and, using a T-square to make sure the work is square, tape it down again and then take the time to 'join the dots'.

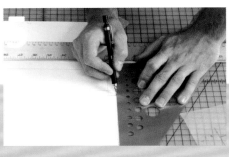

Use a hard lead for faint and thin lines. While seasoned individuals often skip this part, don't fall prey to the temptation; making a mistake at this point will prove time-consuming and costly.

Use the bone folder and a steel ruler or set-square to firmly score all horizontals and verticals.

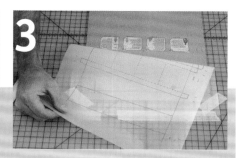

1 Align a vellum output of the die-strike (or an accurately rendered 'tissue') with the crop marks on the output. In this example, the output was printed directly onto heavyweight cardstock, but if you are gluing a thinner output onto thin cardstock, adhere them together very well, and use the brayer to ensure they do not eventually peel.

2 Once the tissue is aligned and taped securely, use a pushpin to mark each intersection on the die-strike. Push just hard enough to penetrate through the paperboard.

3 While the tissue is still taped along one edge, peel it back to make sure that you've push-pinned all the necessary corners. It's not possible to print light colours onto chipboard when creating a comp, because the paper is already a rich brown and there is no white ink available in composite printers. In this example, the texture of the chipboard was scanned in, then the work was designed over the scanned texture.

7 Notice that the set-square is used to accurately score the verticals – this provides a high degree of accuracy, and prevents any deviation from the precise nature of the die-strike.

8 Once you have made all the scores, follow the same sequence when cutting the box. Notice how the straight edge is used to protect the important parts of the output; if the blade cuts away from the straight edge, only the scrap paper will be affected.

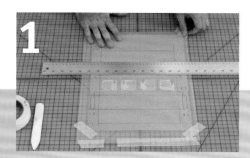

9 The bone folder can be helpful in making sure that all scores fold along a straight edge. Consider pushing the corners beyond the angle they are intended to define in order to prevent the paper from insisting on its memory. Only do this, however, after you've established that the paper can be bent without feathering on the outside of the fold.

Tip: Adhesives

Rubber cement, if mixed to the proper consistency and 'painted' smoothly onto both surfaces, works very well. It also has more lateral 'give' than spray adhesives, which prevents any feathering of the outputs on corners that bend further than 90 degrees. Make sure the glue is fully dry before putting the pieces together.

There are several kinds of adhesive papers, but do test them because, while a few work extremely well – they don't pull off the surface – there are many other kinds that lack the sufficient 'tack' for the strenuous needs of comping a package. Unfortunately, the best spray adhesives also happen to be the most toxic.

Remember that adhesives only work as well as the surfaces to which they are applied. More absorbent papers and boards require more glue, or glue that is inherently stronger. The later case studies of the creative process provide more insight into materials and appropriate adhesives.

Comping set boxes

While comping paperboard boxes requires a clear and comprehensive understanding of the qualities inherent within the materials, and the final comp must reflect the functional parameters of the production specifications, comping a set-box requires only that you make the prototype appear as if it were a production example. This kind of comping takes advantage of the fact that the materials for the underlying structure of the prototype do not have to be the same as the final production package. Most production set-boxes make use of a vacuum-formed polymer that is either colour-dyed, airbrushed or sprayed with a felt-like substance called flocking. They are hollow and lightweight shells that are designed to address only the visible surfaces of the package.

As will be seen in the upcoming case study chapter, illustration board is not the only material available for such building techniques. It is, however, a very versatile material for set-box packages. For those not capable of working with wood, for instance, scanning wood into the computer so it can be printed onto high-quality paper, then adhered to illustration board substructures, can provide a very convincing facsimile of real wood.

Foam-core might seem to be a better material for this kind of building due to its apparent sturdiness, but it rarely provides the same quality as illustration board. Illustration board provides sharp and easily constructed corners, ample strength for most projects, and a dexterity of form that foam-core lacks. While many industrial design departments and dedicated package design programmes have vac-form machines which enable a designer to make a true prototype of a platform, the methods on these pages provide those without access to such expensive machinery the opportunity to build perfect comps.

The sample platform featured on the next two spreads is intended to explain several issues that arise once something more than a simple rectangular platform is required. Two factors are explored here: 1) dealing with a multilevel platform; and 2) dealing with angles other than 90 degrees.

118

The above images portray the finished platform. They are presented here first to give an idea of why each step in the process is taken.

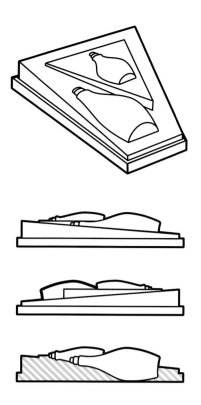

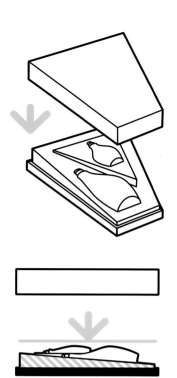

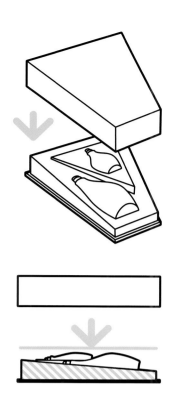

When comping multilevel platforms it is important to get your measurements right. In most cases it is easier to build separate constructions for each individual platform level, as seen above. These illustrations show different views of the platform and product placement. The bottom illustration shows the empty spaces within the platform. The 'unused' volume within a package must be sculpted as deliberately as any other facet. This affects the aesthetics, but can also greatly affect the cost and environmental impact.

These illustrations (above and right), show how two different kinds of exterior box would look. The above illustration is an example of a hatbox-style construction, which has a substantial bottom to meet the tops.

This illustration shows a bottom lip that serves to hold the full top up. Notice how both of these boxes 'top-off' the enclosed products, meaning the top of the box, when in place, can hold all products securely during shipping.

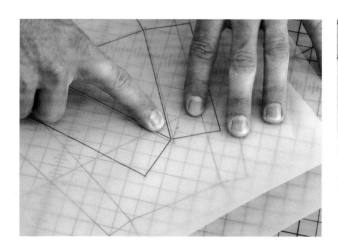

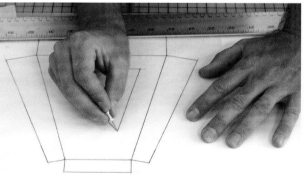

The photograph above shows how the tracing for the smaller platform accommodates the thicknesses of its own sides in order to nest within the larger platform. More space may need to be left, depending on the thickness of the material that the boxes will be wrapped in. If in doubt, leave more space rather than less; if the nesting of the two platforms is a little loose, it is unlikely to be noticed, but if the nesting is too tight, the platforms will not fit together, and one or the other will have to be rebuilt.

Transferring the measurements of the die-strikes to the illustration board is very similar to the method on the previous page for paperboard. But here there is no need to push the holes all the way through the material. Instead, all the cutting is done on this top surface. Hot-press boards are well suited to this kind of construction due to their smooth surfaces. (The rough texture of cold-pressed boards requires more adhesive.)

119

1

Cuts made to define the corners should only go partway into the board so that it folds without the need for force. It is better to cut too far than not far enough. If the cut is not deep enough, and it is forcibly folded, the thin layers within the board will delaminate and the board will be irrevocably damaged.

2

If the board is cut through too far, however – or even cut all the way through – a strip of clear tape adhered to the interior will hold the corner. Once the cuts are deep enough, use the tape to secure the corners.

3

Make sure to pinch the corners securely so that the tape holds the corners square and secure, and cut away any excess tape with a scalpel. The properties of packing tape make it ideally suited for this job – it's very thin and strong. Buy the best tape you can afford, as cheaper products usually tear too easily.

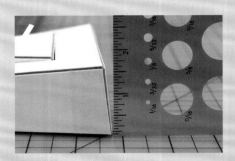

4

Making sure all of the angles in a box are placed properly will prevent unnecessary and time-consuming mistakes. Here, the platform is not completely vertical. The result is an awkward angle that will cause problems once the platform is placed into a hatbox.

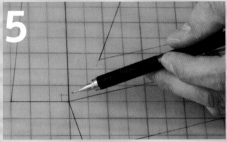

5

The problem occurred because the tracing defines a right angle in the wrong place – where the side surface meets the top surface. Instead, if a true vertical is required, the right angle should be rendered between the base and the vertical edges.

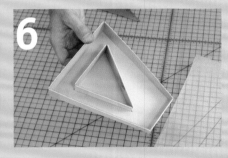

6

A close look at the bottom reveals the snug fit between these two platforms. However, if they were to be wrapped with felt-paper, there would not be enough room, and the interior platform would have to be built slightly smaller. Cutting the smaller platform all the way through to the bottom is often much more sensible than cutting it so that it sits on top of the larger platform. There are two reasons for this: 1) both platforms can be wrapped separately, and so the edge where they meet will be perfectly straight and visually clean; and 2) the weight of whatever object will be placed on the top platform will not forcibly bend the larger platform.

120

Tutorial three | Curved platforms

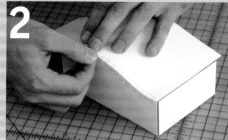

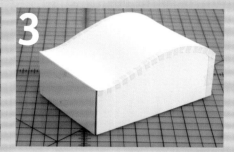

Working with curves on a set-box is not nearly as difficult as it might seem. While the sides of the box should be made from illustration board for the sake of strength and rigidity, the top part can be made from either illustration board (if the curve is gentle enough and the extra strength is required), or from heavy-stock Bristol. The paper for the top in this example is a 100lb Bristol which was produced with 100 per cent wind power. Once proper measurements have been established, begin by cutting thin bands of masking tape, and adhere them along the edge where the two materials meet. Using a scalpel blade makes it easier to cut and pick up the pieces.

The second and third examples show the application of the masking tape by hand. It's important to keep the tape strips narrow and close together. If they are spread too far apart, the hot glue will bubble between the pieces of tape and create an unworkable edge.

The last step is to hot-glue the interior. Make sure to apply the glue liberally because you will want to remove the tape once the glue has dried.

The image to the left shows how, even when using illustration board as the material for a curved top, it is usually beneficial to add extra support. In most cases, comps must be tough enough to make it through several photoshoots; they may be mishandled, so they need to be built well. Finally, the image below shows the interior of a platform (the above images show a box top). Before gluing a platform together, the holes for the products must be cut, as this example shows. Concealed areas may be messier than edges that will be seen when the box is opened.

Tutorial four | Wrapping techniques

There are many ways to cover a platform. This particular sequence works well with all kinds of paper and thin fabrics. It's a very traditional method, and can be done either as a 'blind' or 'registered' wrap. This example is blind, in that there is no need for an exact alignment between the paper and the box. Blind wraps are usually done when a belly band or label will identify the package. When registering your wrap – if there is design work on the paper that you are wrapping or there is a pattern that requires horizontal or vertical alignment with the box – all you need to do is pushpin the top four corners before you put glue on the output so you can see the holes once you turn it upside down and glue it. Then simply align the corners of the actual box with the four pushpin holes.

Adhesives must provide a secure connection between the board and the paper. As mentioned earlier, hot-press boards require less glue due to their sheer surfaces. When dealing with fabrics or feathered papers, fabric glues or binding glues work best.

If the wrapping paper is extremely thin and light, like ricepaper, you might consider spray-painting the box first, or painting the exposed edges of the board to make sure they do not show through the thin paper. Wrapping angular and curved boxes requires more forethought and practice.

This is the first step in the wrapping process. Make sure there is ample paper on all sides, and that all surfaces have enough adhesive.

Using a straight edge held against one side of the box, you should cut outwards from each of the four corners. Do this only on the sides of the box – the front and back of the box need to have enough paper to wrap around to the side, as shown in the next image.

The angle for this second set of cuts should be enough to keep the paper away from the bottom edge so that, when the bottom is folded upwards, there is no awkward crimping of paper. (About ten degrees is sufficient.)

These cuts should now be made on the opposite end of the box.

Making sure that the edge of the box is pressed firmly against the table, push the box onto its side.

Cut excess paper off the sides so that when you fold them inwards there is not too much paper crimped in the interior (use the edge to guard the 'live' area). Leave a little extra rather than trying to make it just right and ending up a little short.

7

Now cut 'ears' from each corner. These should extend from the edge of the board and define its thickness. Cutting a slight flare as you move away from the edge is fine.

8

Cutting the small 'ears' serves two purposes: they cover the corner edges very well; and they prevent the larger pieces that must be folded inwards from overlapping awkwardly. Make sure the paper is firmly rolled onto the side of the box.

9

Gently pull the ears, then press against the longer, interior side of the box.

10

Once both sides have been pressed against the board and then downwards into the interior, and once both ears have been pressed into the side of the box, the longer piece can then be pressed along the interior side securely. The next step is to turn the box around and follow the same process for the other side.

11

Cut inwards and upwards approximately 1.5mm ($^1/_{16}$ in) on the remaining pieces. Make the cut at approximately 45 degrees.

12

Now, using a straight edge, cut away from the box. The reason for making the small inward cut is to prevent the edge of the paper from catching on anything it rubs against.

13

You can cut away any excess paper after you press the box down onto its side.

14

These final stages show the finished box closed and open. Notice the extra paper on the interior of the open box. If a platform were to be placed inside, there would be no need to clean the bottom up any further. However, if the bottom were to remain exposed

15

(as shown here), it would be important to cut a rectangle of paper and glue it over the exposed surface. The examples in the next chapter reveal techniques for wrapping with other materials and other shapes.

Applying a variety of textures to a set-box can provide a rich, tactile experience. As seen here, the exterior wrap, once removed from the box, can be hung as a decoration, while the box itself can be used as a tray to carry and hold the sake. Seen here are two packages from the same designer – a paperboard construction and a set-box.

Now that we've explored some practical issues of constructing packaging prototypes, it's time to take an in-depth look at specific case studies. The individuals responsible for the work seen here – all students on the Graphic Design programme at the Savannah College of Art and Design in the US – developed these projects from scratch. A secondary function for all packages was required, and presented here is a wide range of such secondary uses, from simple containers, to dispensers, to unexpected uses that require transformations of the package's original form.

The first section focuses on building with paperboard. There are several good books that provide an abundance of paperboard diagrammatics, including Lazlo Roth and George Wybenga's *The Packaging Designer's Book Of Patterns*, and *The Paperboard Packaging Council's Ideas and Innovations: A Handbook for Designers, Converters, and Buyers of Paperboard Packaging* (second edition). Any designer interested in exploring the potential of folding cartons should be familiar with these books. But the real challenge is to go further – to explore what happens once you begin diverging from some of these established packaging patterns.

While there were strict limitations in size, materials and structure to the paperboard projects, the set-box has no limitations except those of the imagination. Set-boxes may be built with metal, tin, wood or any other material, or if budget does not allow for such extravagance, paper products that mimic the surface and texture of the aforementioned materials. The incredibly wide range of textured paper products allows the package designer to create rich and evocative packaging without the considerable weight that using the actual material might require.

While these investigations created a fair amount of waste themselves, creative use of scrap material reduced the level of waste in all situations. By using substantial amounts of material upfront, prototypes aim to reduce the amount of production material that will eventually be required.

From paperboard cartons to set-box constructions

5 Case studies in building prototypes

Objectives

Binder clips do what they need to do very well, but while they're waiting around for duty they have a tendency to make a nuisance of themselves. Like loose change, they can be found everywhere until you actually need one, at which point they hide under and behind all manner of things!

The objective for this project was to provide a secondary dispensing function for the retail box without adding too much extra material to the original package. In so doing, the package becomes a valuable product in its own right, keeping elusive binder clips in one, easily accessible place.

Ease of use was the primary concern, which meant not only an easy method of dispensing the product, but a carefree method of reloading it as well. If either process were too cumbersome, the chances were that people would not be interested in using the secondary function. The package was also designed to have two positions from which it could be used; a tabletop position – achieved by pulling back material originally used for a retail closure and locking it into a slot on the back side of the package – and a wall-hanging position, achieved by making use of the die-cut hole on the back panel.

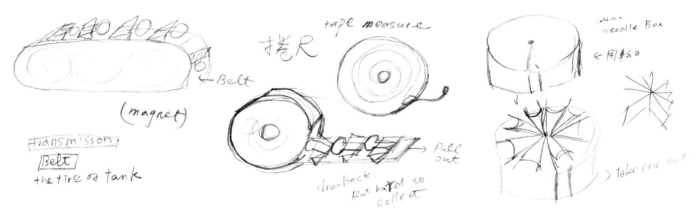

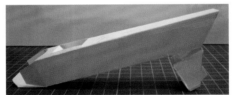

Above – Some early alternative studies found their way from quick sketches to quick, scrap-paper form studies (right and below). A circular, knob-turned dispenser was deemed too complex, and they would have required more paper than was really necessary.

Left – As the package was simplified and dematerialized, a 'kick-stand' top was explored as a means of allowing gravity to play a role in the dispensing process.

Below – The extra material from the die-cut window provides the proper amount of resistance when folded back in on itself. The memory of the fibre allows the interior flap to hold the clips in place until someone pulls on them. What began as a small window grew so that the consumer could estimate the exact number of clips remaining in the box.

126

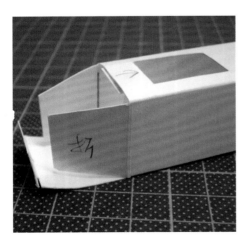

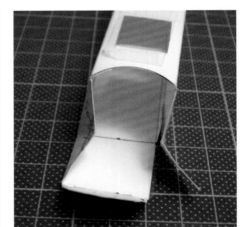

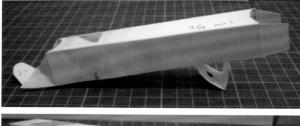

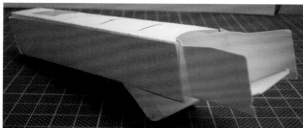

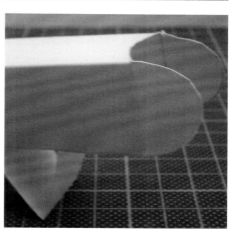

Left and right – An easy-opening top that also allowed for easy reloading was absolutely necessary. Here, the details of the relationship between the internal tray and the external box are refined. The 'roll-back' top provided a simple and cost-effective mechanism for creating the kick-stand, while the dust flaps were eventually rounded in order to provide something that was both aesthetically and functionally pleasing.

Why use glue when it isn't needed? The closure of the internal tray (top right) relies on a simple tab lock that folds up and around two dust flaps for a secure closure.

Right –These images reveal the evolution of the bottom closure responsible for dispensing the product. This closure serves a dual purpose – on the shelf it must lock securely to keep the product in place, but once it is in use, it must perform an integral role in the continual dispensing of the product. The idea was to use the inherent qualities of the paper construction to provide the physical resistance and flexibility required for easy dispensing, while at the same time preventing inadvertent dropping of the product. The final result is a combination of a lock tab and a gusset flange. What results is a dispenser that drops the clips to a point where an individual can comfortably press a finger against the bottom part of the clip, and the clip drops free.

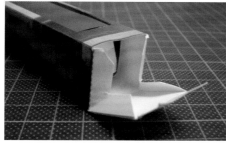

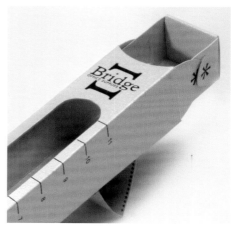

The crescent die-cuts on the sides catch firmly on the rounded dust flaps when the tray is pulled from the box, and what results is a quick-catch system that holds the tray open so that the clips can easily be reloaded.

Chapter 5: Case Studies in Building Prototypes

To make this package more sustainable, the designer could have chosen a nonmetallic ink. As mentioned on page 89, metallic inks contain heavy metals and thus require a more toxic production process, not to mention that such metallics make it impossible for the package to be safely composted. This example can serve as a cautionary tale of how designers can be easily lured into a creating a particular look even as they actively explore the benefits of secondary functions. The challenge to avoid metallics is akin to any other design challenge – exploring other colour options might very well open the door to more effective final results.

Photographic concerns
Products are placed outside the package for scale purposes as well as visual contrast. Two comps were created in order to provide a fuller picture of the package as it exists on the shelf and as a dispenser. Clear acetate has been added to these comps. For sustainability purposes, the acetate could be derived from biopolymers – or the window, which already holds the products securely, could be reduced a little more and the acetate eliminated altogether.

The designer created clear directions with illustrations that provide enough information for any client or consumer to figure out the details of the secondary function.

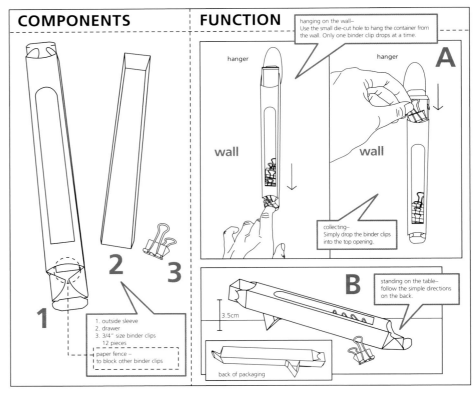

COMPONENTS

1. outside sleeve
2. drawer
3. 3/4" size binder clips
   12 pieces

paper fence –
to block other binder clips

FUNCTION

hanging on the wall–
Use the small die-cut hole to hang the container from the wall. Only one binder clip drops at a time.

hanger

hanger

A

wall

wall

collecting–
Simply drop the binder clips into the top opening.

B

standing on the table–
follow the simple directions on the back.

3.5cm

back of packaging

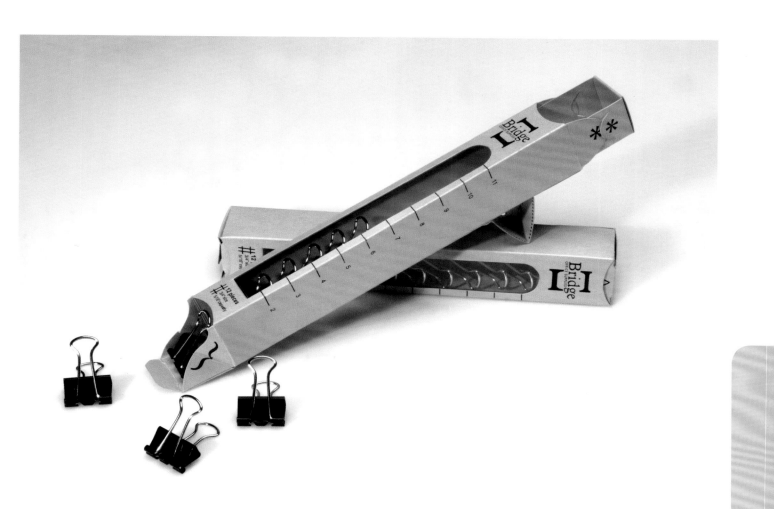

5.1: Yichun Chen | Binder clip dispenser

Objectives

Small products require small packages, but small packages do not confine the package designer to uninspired solutions. Guitar players occasionally drop their picks as they play. While extra picks are traditionally placed between the strings within the headstock, this offhand method only allows for one extra pick, or several picks placed in a precarious manner. This package was designed to provide easy access to numerous picks that are stored securely.

The 'cool' factor invariably informed many details of this solution, from the rough-hewn letterpress typography, to the paper choice, to the formal associations with paperboard match-books. A two-colour solution lowers cost, reduces ink usage, and evokes the smoky, speakeasy past of blues and rock 'n' roll.

Several of the original pick and 'P' letterform ideas were resolved on the computer. While some had graphic potential, they were considered too contemporary and slick for the objectives of creating a more rustic personality for the package.

Early structural studies

The images here represent the very earliest considerations of the package idea. A worn leather wallet was considered briefly, but it was too large merely for the sake of the concept. While basic scale and proportion were clearly dictated by the product and the environment of the secondary function, shape studies began with a basic square format.

A major consideration was making sure the pick holder fit with the headstock of most guitar styles. Research concluded that the style made popular by the Fender Stratocaster had the shortest distance between the nut and the first tuning key. The name 'Pickpocket' takes a literal turn with the introduction of denim texture and the shape of a back pocket from a pair of jeans.

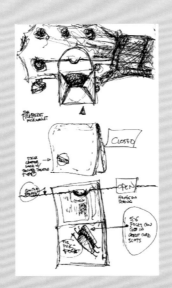

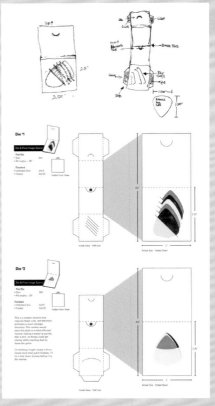

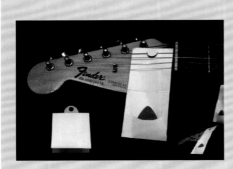

130

Above – A series of letterpress studies were explored to evoke a bygone era of blues and old-time rock 'n' roll. These layouts were composed in the pressbed. The idea was to embrace technical constraints as a means of exploring creatively.

Right – Further letterpress studies were done on various papers. Here, a 100 per cent recycled paper was explored, printed directly onto the paper specimen booklet.

The limited availability of some of the wood-type in the type library was cause for improvisation; rotated lowercase 'd's, for example, were used due to a shortage of lowercase 'p's.

Left – Early comps, including a Photoshop exploration (top middle).

The refinement of the surface graphics reflects two important aspects of designing for small packages:

1) Typographic elements should be enlarged wherever possible. The early solutions (towards the left) reveal a designer's sensibility for respecting the spatial integrity of each element. However, in small

packages generous allocations of negative space can result in compromises in legibility and graphic impact.

2) Notice the increase in visual contrast from left to right. The use of red increases in order to give the package more shelf-presence and more visibility in general. Contrast is pushed even further

in the last two examples with the introduction of a black border. The border acts as a framing device to place more focus on the interior of the package and to ensure that even on an old wooden table, the package will have a visible presence. Other late-stage alterations include a thickening of the spine to better reflect the match-book aesthetic

and to increase the presence of the package, and a tongue-in-cheek comment on the interior flap to enhance the sequential experience of opening the package.

131

Die-strike

This package earned the nickname 'the bomb' due to the shape of its die-strike.

Notice how the slot used for the package closure serves double duty as the guitar clasp.

The punched die-cut serves as a method of placing the package on a point-of-purchase display, but easily folds downwards once the product has been purchased.

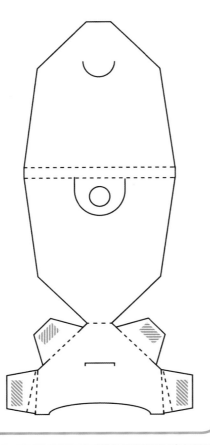

Point of Purchase display

Point of Purchase (POP) displays are an important part of any packaging scheme, and the smaller the package is, the more important the display becomes. In this case, we have an inexpensive product in an inexpensive package, so the POP is a simple glueless box with a backing panel. Guitar picks are a lot like bubblegum, in that they are often used but rarely kept for long durations. Because new guitar picks are always needed, and because the size of the product would make them difficult to locate in the shelving system of a music store, a countertop display is an ideal place to sell such a diminutive necessity.

The vertical graphic immediately reinforces the general theme of the brand, and the slogans on the 'picked' pocket and on the countertop box use wordplay to keep with the irreverence of the packaging. The solid red base picks up on the solid reds of the package to reinforce the brand colour, and the logo is large and along the top of the POP. The POP is a glueless construction to reduce cost and environmental burden.

132

The act of opening a package is a sequential process, and the savvy package designer knows how to take advantage of the 'pacing' that such a sequence provides. From the outside, the words serve a purely informative function. Yet, once opened, the word 'guitar' conveys a completely different kind of linguistic message.

The spine was originally just thick enough to hold the product, but was later widened to give the package more physical presence. The increased thickness also provides the package with proportions that are nearly identical to a standard matchbook. This similarity is not accidental; part of the guitar-player mystique is the cigarette dangling loosely from the mouth.

5.2: Devin O'Bryan | Guitar pick holder 133

5.3: Les Penland | Darts set

Objectives

A friendly game of darts at the local pub can be farcical; infused with a fair degree of swagger and mock-ceremony. Those inclined to own their own set of darts are quite particular as to how they are transported, but newcomers to the game, especially when joining casual darts leagues, care only for showing their competition up.

While many 'beginner' darts sets are packaged either in blister-packs or housed in a cheap carrying case which is then blister-packed, this package is designed as a carrier in its own right. The interior pop-up mechanism, which raises the darts as the cover is lifted, provides a whimsical touch.

The pop-up mechanism was intend to impress team-mates and onlookers, while intimidating the competition in a tongue-in-cheek fashion, as if the simple carton were a high-tech weapons cartridge. The top of the carton, which is scored across the centre, folds back on itself to create an equally impressive stand to rest the darts on while sipping a pint and waiting for the competition to finish their round. The additional material and engineering for the pop-up is minimal, and very little interior space had to be added to the carton. The package was designed so that it could fit into most pockets, and while built here with paperboard, could be made from more a tear-resistant material such as the eco-friendly, tree-less TerraSkin®.

     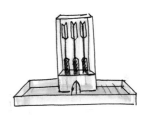

Above – Early sketches explored various ways in which the products might interact with the package. These rough sketches help to work out the form and function of each idea. Both stands and carry-cases were considered for their individual benefits, and in the end the two functions were combined in one package.

Right – An early folding top is explored, which led to a reinforced-edge carton design with self-locking corners, eliminating the need for adhesives. During early prototype development, panels were labelled on the digital file to clarify the placement of graphics.

This paper dummy reveals an early step towards creating a package that serves as both a carrying case and a dart stand. The two-piece carton was abandoned for the sake of an attached lid, and more thought was put into the function of the stand.

Small details like notched openings were explored to find a way to keep the darts more stable while in transit or as they are being displayed.

The basic pop-up mechanism was refined, with an understanding that the back panel would be attached to the exterior carton, then attached to the more complex mechanism that would eventually be housed in the final package. Once the basic mechanism is figured out it is easier and faster to build on it than build a full-blown dummy.

134

Pop-up elements for interactive boxes

One way to make a package more intriguing is to provide more three-dimensional interactivity than expected. With the addition of a few skillfully-placed folds, the mere act of opening a box-top or panel can be designed in a way that literally raises the product to the consumer's waiting hands. Below are a few simple pop-up elements which, when carefully considered, may provide a playful degree of product 'lift'. The goal here is not to show how they are made, as much as to reveal a few structural opportunities that present themselves when opposite sides of scored cardstock open away from each other. These elements can be used alone or combined with other elements in order to form more complex pop-up mechanisms. The pop-ups featured here can be found in *The Elements of Pop-Up* by David Carter and James Diaz, a wonderful book that provides exact details for creating a wide range of pop-up mechanisms.

The '90° angle fold' and the 'Unequal angle fold' are two simple, yet effective, elements. When the cardstock is opened, the pop-up mechanisms rise from the page. These are easy to construct and do not require glue.

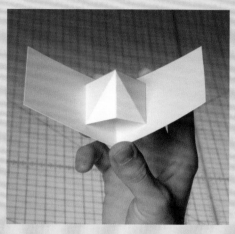

The '180° parallel pyramid' is constructed of four triangular panels. The side panels are scored down the middle, parallel to the gutter of the folded page. This allows for the side panels to fold and lay flat when the page is closed.

The '180° box with a parallel plane' serves as a box with an offset parallel plane jutting out. This extra panel could be adapted to many shapes and sizes so it could hold display graphics.

The '180° angle fold-open box' is constructed of four equal sides. The trick to this one is that the two joining sides are attached to the page at 45° angles. This allows the box to seem as if it is rising upwards from the cardstock.

The '180° cone' pop-up element comprises two triangles attached to the folded page with small glue flaps. When the cardstock is unfolded, the triangles separate in the non-glued area to form a cone.

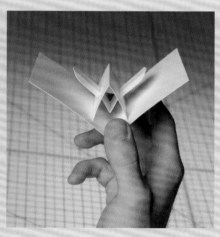

The '180° tent with a tipped-in extension' is formed by attaching a piece of paper to the folded page and scoring it down the middle. The extensions are held in place by sliding the scored paper through slits in the triangular piece adhered to the cardstock.

135

Die-strike

There are four parts to the construction of this package. The top and bottom were constructed and joined, then the pop-up mechanism was built and added to the interior of the package. While adhesives were required to stick the pop-up, none were used for the exterior package.

top

bottom

pop-up mechanism

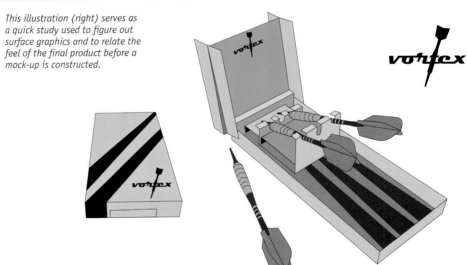

Photographic concerns

The image below presents the package and product at an extreme angle. A sense of proportion, scale and even function are lost in the search for a novel angle to shoot from. While the angles in the image below right are still severe, they offer a familiar perspective, although a product company may resist using an image that does not clearly show the company logo, as is the case here.

This illustration (right) serves as a quick study used to figure out surface graphics and to relate the feel of the final product before a mock-up is constructed.

136

Photographic concerns

Because two comps were used in this photograph, one was able to show the action of the pop-up mechanism, while the other presented the exterior surface graphics. The dynamic angle exaggerates the angular nature of the graphics.

A short focal range adds emphasis to the desired areas of these photographs.

A large-format camera would be needed to correct the extreme perspective occurring in the frames, if the kinetic angularity of these images was not desired.

In all of these images, a black background was used. This might not work in all situations as it might 'swallow' the product. In this case, there is so much contrast that the package colours jump off the dark background. The reflective surface adds another dimension to the photographs.

5.3: *Les Penland | Darts set*

5.4: *Larissa Thut | Candle holder set*

Objectives

Paper and fire! Paper lanterns have a long tradition in Asian cultures, and they have also been used in the West to mark special occasions such as weddings, where they line paths for the bride and groom to enter or leave the reception.

With the goal of creating a set of votive candle holders that also functioned as their own packaging, the challenge was to make them small enough and aesthetically pleasing, while at the same time ensuring that they did not become a fire hazard.

The idea was to create something very simple and versatile, that could be used for any occasion. The market was a younger audience (aged 20 to 35), with expendable income, who appreciated romance. A key objective was to bring together a modern design aesthetic with a traditional form of nuanced lighting.

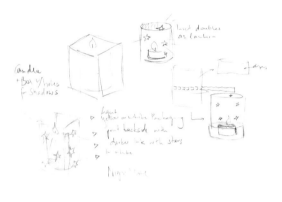

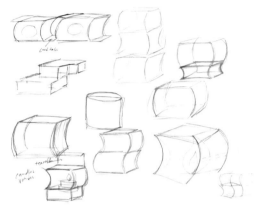

Left – Cylindrical and rectangular boxes and inserts were explored as a way of casting the shadows of painted form on the interior into the dark room.

The early, curved forms were derived from the flickering of a flame. At this early stage, various stacking options were explored. Close attention was paid to the need for the package to keep a safe distance from the heat of the flame.

Left – Early form studies explored the benefits and drawbacks of various curves. The double curve (near left) was selected for its back-and-forth 'flicker', its reference to a yin-yang relationship of curvatures, and its potential for 'nesting' numerous boxes together. This particular box was too narrow, and would have resulted in a fire hazard. The curves were also too extreme. Building three-dimensional comps at an early stage provided the designer with the opportunity to familiarize herself with formal, spatial and material relationships.

Below – Various possibilities for dealing with inserting the candle were explored here, as were ways of creating the die-vinyl for the base, and methods of holding the package together. The bottom right sketch shows a tear-away band.

138

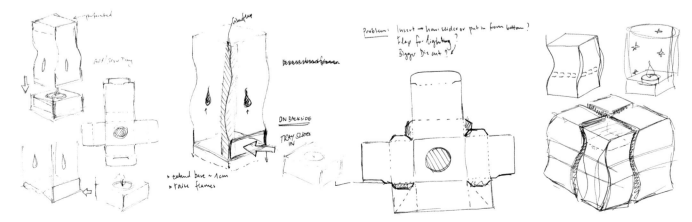

Section 2 – Re:structure

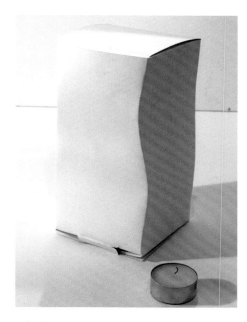

A 'final' form study with refined proportions, and built with a thick vellum to allow for translucence when the votive candles are lit.

As the studies progressed, so did the designer's refinement of the die-vinyl. The schematic (left) shows how this particular project progressed. The dotted lines on the panels on either side of the front represent the score lines that allow this box to collapse flat.

Notice the reverse tuck, and how the insert – the interior box that holds the votive candle – is actually a continuation of the box, and that this does not preclude the use of a lock tab. Later versions made use of a separate insert altogether, so that it could be made from a reflective and more fire-resistant material.

front

The package of four paper lanterns is supported by a base that also acts as a refillable storage container for the votives.

Taking a match to the early studies to observe the behaviour of the flame and the degree of luminosity afforded by the choice of vellum.

Exploring surface graphics through illustration

While it is extremely important to make three-dimensional comps as you develop a package design, early surface graphics studies should be done as two-dimensional illustrations. Here, the designer can see how ideas for die-cuts, colour application and typographic arrangement relate to her three-dimensional forms. Small changes in colour can be explored, as can the graphic treatment of the entire package.

139

Die-strike

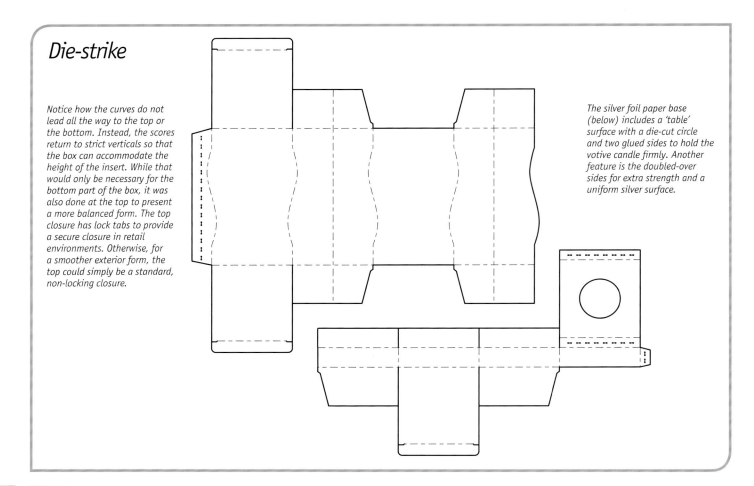

Notice how the curves do not lead all the way to the top or the bottom. Instead, the scores return to strict verticals so that the box can accommodate the height of the insert. While that would only be necessary for the bottom part of the box, it was also done at the top to present a more balanced form. The top closure has lock tabs to provide a secure closure in retail environments. Otherwise, for a smoother exterior form, the top could simply be a standard, non-locking closure.

The silver foil paper base (below) includes a 'table' surface with a die-cut circle and two glued sides to hold the votive candle firmly. Another feature is the doubled-over sides for extra strength and a uniform silver surface.

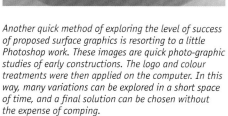

Another quick method of exploring the level of success of proposed surface graphics is resorting to a little Photoshop work. These images are quick photo-graphic studies of early constructions. The logo and colour treatments were then applied on the computer. In this way, many variations can be explored in a short space of time, and a final solution can be chosen without the expense of comping.

As can be seen in the image to the right, a reflective silver paperboard was chosen for the separate insert.

Photographic concerns
Here are a few examples of final product shots. While the top one gives a clear idea of the function, scale and materials of the product, the bottom two represent what are sometimes called 'romance' shots. These provide aesthetic clues to the lifestyle and personal characteristics that the product embodies. Such shots can go a long way towards creating a brand essence when presented on websites or in catalogues.

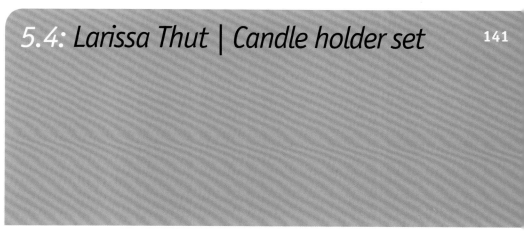

5.4: *Larissa Thut | Candle holder set*

5.5: *Yulien Foo | Tea infuser and wind chime*

Objectives

Designing a package for a simple and inexpensive item can be a challenge, in that there must be a clear rationale for any packaging whatsoever. A tea infuser, for instance, is often sold without packaging. The package featured on these pages becomes a valuable product in its own right, and was conceived originally as package-as-product.

Such 'value-added' approaches to package design can provide more than just an accoutrement to the product itself; they can contribute to consumer experience of the product by suggesting a lifestyle that 'surrounds' the product. Tea is often ceremonially consumed, yet this package-as-product (a wind chime) does not contribute to any one cultural ceremony as much as to the small luxury of idle time in the middle of a busy day.

Early sketches attempted to encase the entire infuser, at times with something as simple as a sleeve. While these ideas proved uninspiring, the fully encased packages required a lot more material, and felt bulky in the hands. Multisided, formfitting packages were also considered.

Early logo studies

Too many designers 'explore' a logo concept by sketching a few formal iterations, then quickly claim 'that idea just doesn't work' if they don't stumble on success immediately. Instead, designers should render forms repeatedly, allowing the mind to fall into a rhythmic and repetitive exercise that loosens the creative flow. Studies should organically grow from exploratory variations and even mistakes, until the designer knows the potential spatial relationships of the forms intimately. These are just a few pages from a more extensive exploration of logo ideas for this project, and do not include either the typographic exploration or the refined logo studies.

Right – These sketches provide a glimpse into the thought process behind this project, once it was established that the package would transform into a wind chime. The earlier studies still show some explorations of packaging the entire product in the round. Colour studies and even logo ideas are spontaneously explored as the designer works through structural ideas. The multislot holder idea is explored early in the process, as are other modular-piece solutions.

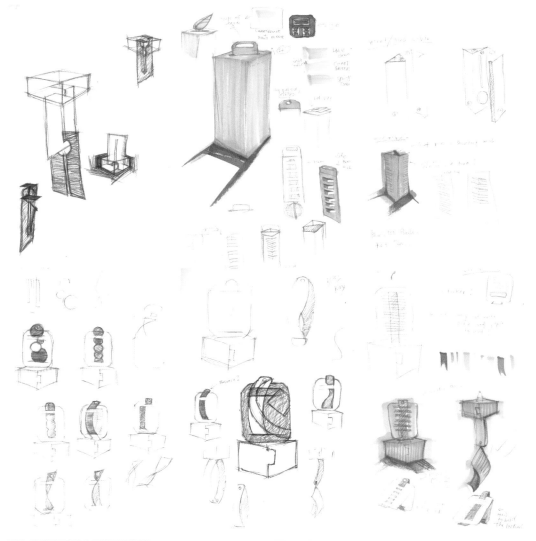

Above – Quick feasibility studies can be helpful when trying to get a sense of scale relationships between the product, the package and the human hand. These studies were done with used laser copy paper, and aimed to assess the structural and aesthetic viability of the form.

Above – A comp to test the structural feasibility of the twirling part of the wind chime.

Above – Numerous surface graphic solutions were investigated. These images show how three-dimensional studies can be explored quickly, and without much expense. These represent a late-stage set of studies that deal with various placements of a small set of textures and patterns. Eventually, colour variations should be explored.

Right and above – Some late-stage explorations of colour variations, and backmatter. Because the rest of the packaging material will become a part of the wind chime, the back panel must contain the necessary sales information, including romance copy, an illustration of the secondary use and a barcode.

143

Die-strike

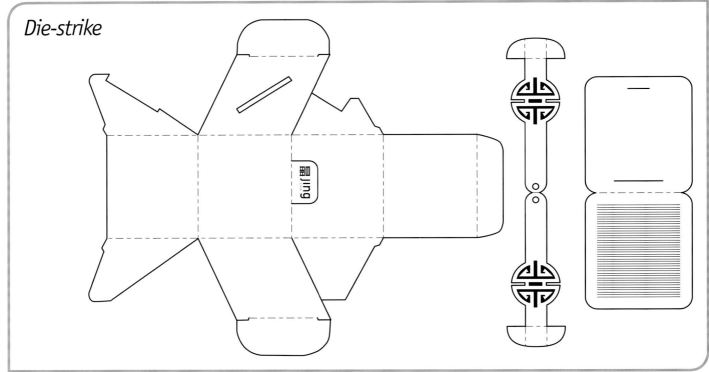

Photographic concerns

These images show different portrayals of the package in its entirety, together with tea-leaves that would be used in the infuser. They are shown together here to provide a comparison between two different modelling choices.

The die-cut tab that features the logo creates a dynamic spatial element for the wind chime, while also defining the stacking scheme for the product while it is on the shelf.

When comping packages for photoshoots, it's important to test a number of papers for colour, surface adhesion of inks and basic durability and flexibility. These examples were comped by gluing two printed sheets back-to-back, so a strong score was necessary to make sure they were sharp.

Notice the lock tabs on the beige band. These are integral to the package's function for both its shelf-life and its secondary use. In both cases, they provide a secure attachment between the trapezoidal box and the upper sandwich card.

The secondary use in all its glory! Die-cut from the beige band is the symbol for 'long-life', a reference to the health benefits of drinking tea.
This symbol is vertically symmetrical, which makes it ideal for a design element that must work upright (as displayed on the shelf), and upside-down (when used as a part of the wind-chime). This versatility is also displayed with the logo placement.

Notice how the form of the band, with the 'long-life' symbol, mimics the shape of the product itself.

Photographic concerns
The image on the right is intended to convey the lifestyle associated with the product rather than to highlight the design of the package.

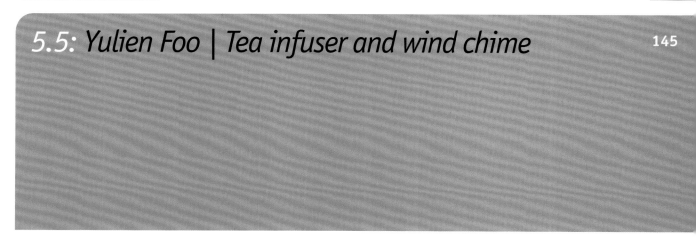

5.5: *Yulien Foo | Tea infuser and wind chime*

5.6: *Clark Delashmet | Aeroplane kit*

Objectives

Go to any toy or hobby store, and you'll find more paper and balsawood aeroplanes than you'll know what to do with. Evoking the 'tinker tendencies' of little boys, the concept here was to design a package for two balsa aeroplanes that could transform itself into two additional paperboard aeroplanes. The perforated package also contains trading cards within its structure. Combining all these elements into one package creates an innovative set of aeroplanes and reduces waste in the process.

This glueless package unfolds itself away from two compartments which house the individual balsa planes, with four trading cards hidden on the middle panel. A belly band that securely holds the carton provides a design surface for retail information on one side, and instructions on how to build the paperboard planes on the other. Two paperboard aeroplanes can then be popped out of the perforated forms in the paperboard to complete the set.

These sketches show the progression of form and function development throughout the project. Along each step of the way, material productivity was enhanced, in that as more paper was eliminated, more and more of the paper's surface area was committed to the secondary usage, and less and less waste paper remained.

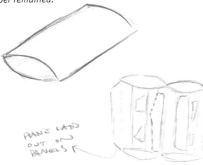

1) At the start, the form held one plane and, when unfolded, revealed a die-cut plane. This version was somewhat paper-intensive.

2) The second form was more dynamic and efficient with material. It also provided the foundation for the final design.

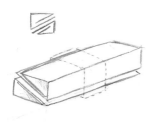

3) The third carton involved doubling up the previous form and wrapping the two together with a belly band. This solution also allowed the product manufacturer to offer a 'squadron' of four planes.

4) The simplification of the form/function relationship continues; what was once two separate cartons becomes a single carton joined by a scored hinge.

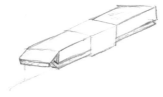

5) The fifth form simplified the closing device by removing the side lock tabs and adding a belly band to hold the form together.

6) The final design was simplified even further by adding a single lock tab on the ends as opposed to the small triangular tabs previously used.

The two images above reveal two end-closure variations. What started out as a crowded end with two triangular tabs was simplified so that only one lock tab was needed. This also keep the carton securely closed.

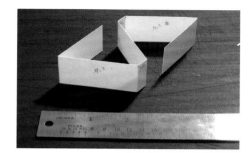

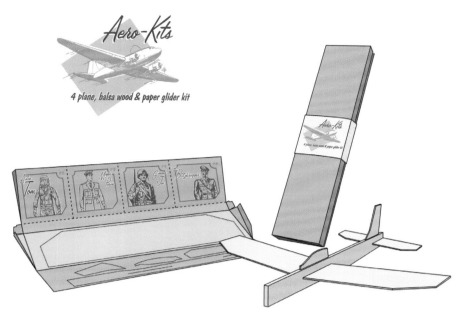

Above – Early paper dummies help to quickly figure out the form of the package and how it would work with all of its folds. It helps to determine the exact measurements as well.

Right – Executing the variations in meticulous fashion is necessary to ensure that the final comp can accommodate the weight and rigidity of the paperboard being used.

Above – Line drawings and illustrations give the client an idea of what the finished product will look like while saving the designer the time and money it takes to provide a full-scale mock up.

Logo refinement: type studies

After the initial research and logo explorations were carried out, and the final logomark was refined, the focus turned to designing an equally successful wordmark treatment. The final version (top right) was arrived at only after numerous 'retro' typefaces were explored for their ability to remain legible, even as they expressed the desired vintage feel.

The final version was ultimately selected for its compatibility with the logomark; along with providing a clear sense of lift, the letterforms accentuate the combination of angles and curves that can be found within the forms of the logomark.

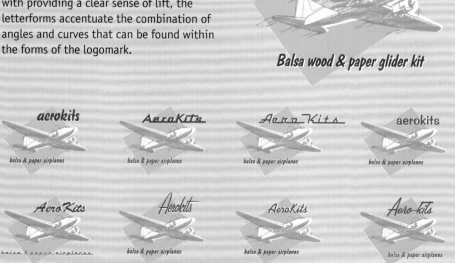

Die-strike

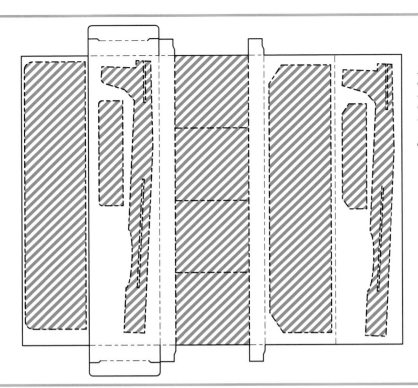

The final die was very simple. It could be constructed from one piece of flat paper, with minimal folds and no glued areas. The striped areas represent the paperboard that is 'reincarnated' into paper aeroplanes.

ASSEMBLY

1. Carefully remove plane from carton.
2. Carefully press plane from die cut carton.
3. Slip stabilizer in tail slot. Slip rudder and canopy in slots in body.
4. Insert end of wing in wing slot and PULL through until centered.

Assembly instructions are printed on the interior of the belly band to aid in the deconstruction of the box.

On the hidden middle panel, trading cards were printed. These cards functioned as collectors' items that could be put away for safekeeping or could be used to give a personality to each of the planes provided in the set. Each card provided a number for cataloguing and on the back it gave a short write-up of the character featured.

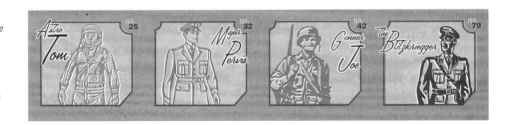

Astro Tom is an astronaut. He likes to fly things that make him feel like he is an astronaut, like jets, fast cars and most important the space shuttle. He flies the space shuttle the best because that is his job. He gets paid to fly up to space and look around. Study hard and you could be an astronaut too!

© 2007 Aero-Kits

Photographic concerns
The white background for the photograph was initially used. While such 'seamless' backgrounds work well with many products, the contrast between the package and the balsa wood product is greater than the contrast between the balsa wood product and the background, thus isolating the package as if it were the primary focus, and not the products.

The final product had little waste. The planes and cards could be used over and over, eliminating the need to buy more planes and create more waste. If desired, the product company could include static adhesive designs to decorate the planes.

Photographic concerns
The final photography was shot on a rich wooden surface to evoke an earlier era. The background also provides contrast and, as a result, the product and package materials are afforded a more substantial presence, and stand out in the photograph. Enough space has been given around the image to allow it to be cropped as necessary.

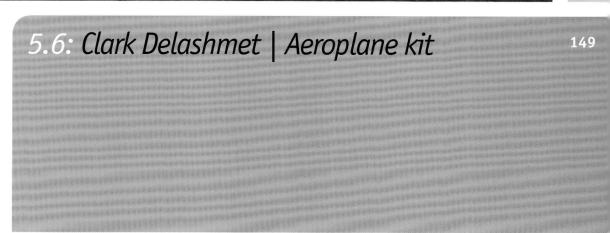

5.6: *Clark Delashmet | Aeroplane kit*

5.7: *Jon Orchin | Torch and lampshade*

Objectives

The product here – a compact torch for outdoor activities – is already versatile in its own right, in that it offers a secondary use as a stand-alone 'candle'. This is achieved by unscrewing the flanged reflective part of the torch, and placing it on the butt-end to create a stand. The idea for this package arose from the desire to further the simple ingenuity of this secondary use by diffusing the light into a softer and more evenly dispersed glow. Market research found that the typical users were not only athletic and outgoing, but also 'intelligent problem-solvers' who embraced simple, yet sophisticated, thinking.

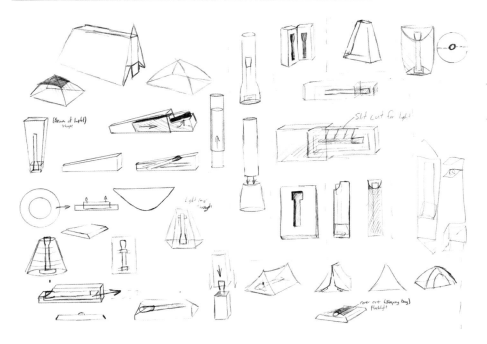

Early form sketches focused on a tent-like package to conjure the outdoor lifestyle common to the product users. While tent ideas were explored purely for their figurative associations, secondary usage ideas revolved primarily around the idea of either a functional stand or a lampshade. Since the torch was designed to stand on its own, the studies for other kinds of stands attempted to give the user holding options beyond the vertical.

Once a lampshade was determined to be the best secondary use, studies with scrap paper were made to determine the actual luminosity that would result. These early form sketches, while exploring the lampshade idea, fail to incorporate the shade with the actual package.

Logotype and colour exploration

With the previous project we considered the need to execute a wide variety of 'quick-response' form studies of logo concepts. Exploring the nuances of the final logo type, once it has been determined, is as important as any other step. Typefaces not only define a spatial and textural flavour, they also evoke emotional reactions. Explore them in black and white and in knock-out (white letterforms on a field of black) to determine their formal qualities.

Studying the psychology of colour is very important. While green might be an obvious colour to enhance a product's nature-friendly aura, there is also a need for product differentiation and deviations from the obvious. A 'contemporary' shade of blue was chosen in this case. Here are some colour attributes that influenced this decision: blue, one of the most popular colours, causes the body to produce calming chemicals; it also suggests security, tranquility, the sky and the ocean. People are more productive in blue rooms. Nothing here contradicts the core values of the nature-loving problem-solver.

Lumineux **Lumineux** **Lumineux** **Lumineux** Lumineux **Lumineux** *Lumineux*

Lumineux Lumineux **Lumineux** **Lumineux** **Lumineux** **Lumineux** **Lumineux**

Lumineux Lumineux Lumineux Lumineux Lumineux Lumineux Lumineux Lumineux Lumineux Lumineux Lumineux Lumineux Lumineux

Quick, scrap-paper explorations were created at an early stage to gain a better sense of spatial relationships, and define optimal volume relationships between product and package.

Above, from left to right:
1) Providing the user with an alternative to the candle-stand option designed into the product. Problems: inefficient use of volume, awkward shelf presence, and secondary use of the package is superfluous.

2) Creating a package that reflects the form of a beam of projected light. Secondary use would include reflective material on the interior of the cone to increase the glow of light. Problems: With a further tapering and reduction of cone-size, which is necessary in order to avoid excessive volume and material usage, the cone becomes unstable. Stacking issues.

3, 4, 5) Variations on a tent form, with number 5 providing a small, multipurpose angular stand (as either a broader base to hold the light or a small lamp shade. Problems: Inefficient use of package volume and materials, and package form is not much more than a formal gimmick.

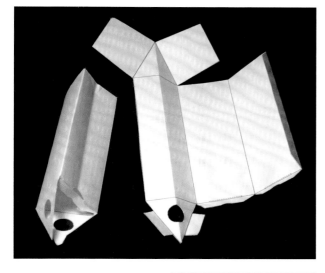

Paperboard boxes should be able to collapse after production to allow for efficient shipping from the box manufacturing site to the product manufacturing site. Studying a triangular box allows us to consider the two most common alternatives when a box cannot collapse along its own scores.

The above composite photograph represents two ways of creating an additional score to a box that is sealed with a glue flap.
The open example results in a score line through the two end pieces. The closed version is a more effective application of this technique since the additional score occurs only on a single panel.

This first alternative technique is common (the Toblerone chocolate box is perhaps the best known example), but it was discarded in this case because the extra score line was deemed an unacceptable detraction from the secondary usage. The score line would be plainly seen once the box was converted into a lampshade. Therefore, the second alternative was chosen; that of using lock tabs to seal the box instead of glue flaps. In this way, the box requires no adhesives at all.

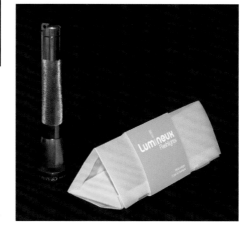

Above – Quick computer illustrations can also help to concretely define a package's potential.

Left – This package is a structural test of the viability of translucent vellum. The paper had to satisfy criteria that could have easily worked against it: it had to be strong enough to withstand the rigours of shipping and store placement; it had to be the right thickness to score yet not tear; and it had to possess enough translucence to allow the light of the candle to shine through even as it satisfactorily diffused it.

151

Die-strike

The large flaps for the top closure were used instead of more lock tabs. While lock tabs work very well in this situation, it was determined that the aesthetic value of the top of the lamp was worth an alternative structural design approach. In this case the large flaps tuck into the box, and the method by which they hold to the corners of the closed box precludes the need for any further lock. They simply prevent the box from opening. The curves at the ends of the panel were designed to mimic the shape of the curves that the emanating light creates.

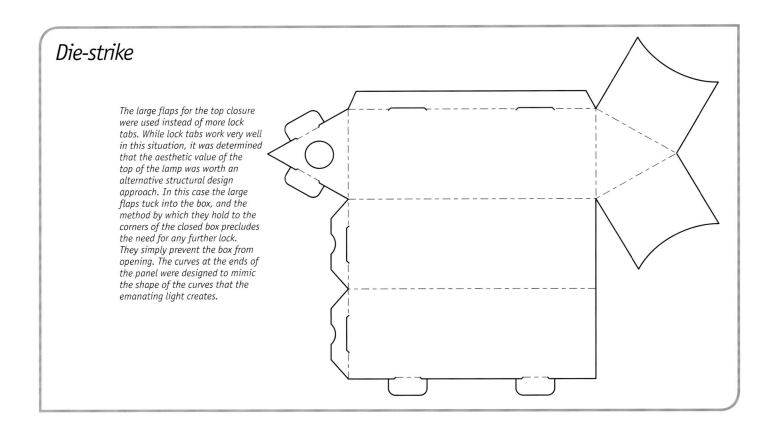

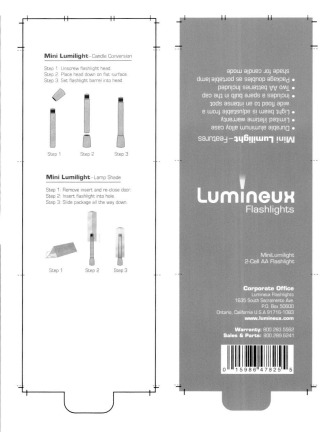

A small belly band is an economical and ecologically friendly method of providing important sales-related information. On the reverse of the band there are easy-to-follow directions to make use of the package's secondary function.

152

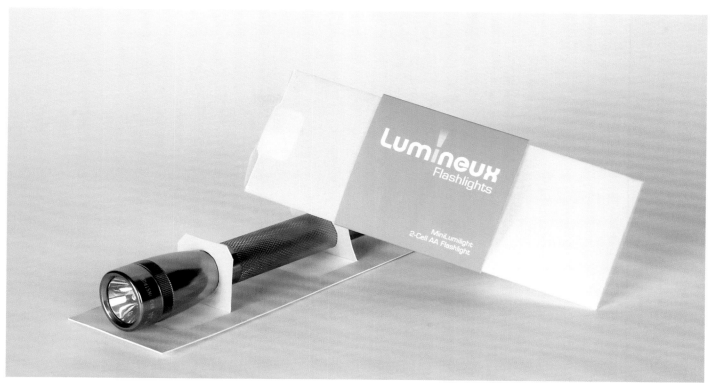

Above – The insert required to hold the product firmly during distribution has been dematerialized as far as possible, and two die-cuts allow for a simple score and fold for secure brackets. The yellow paper picks up on the colour scheme for the brand.

Photographic concerns
Capturing an image of the light being used required careful manual camera adjustment – an automatic flash would take its reading off the bright light and render the image too dark overall.

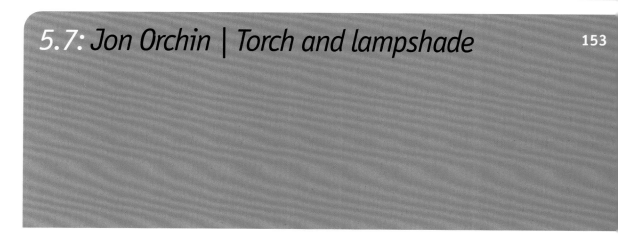

5.7: *Jon Orchin | Torch and lampshade*

5.8: *Jiwon Kim | Chopstick and spoon set*

Objectives

A recent intergovernmental report found that China produced and discarded more than 45 billion pairs of disposable chopsticks every year (which consumes an estimated 25 million trees). Another 25 billion pairs were exported to Japan in 2006, which amounts to 200 sets per person every year (a newly imposed tax on disposable chopsticks has been levied as a means of discouraging their use). This package attempts to encourage long-term use of a single set of chopsticks

(and a spoon), and expands the notion of reuse to the package itself.

This package was conceived as one in a set of high-quality, Asian-inspired utensils that embrace the act of eating as a ceremony worth savouring (the second in the set can be seen on page 165). Chopsticks are often used in conjunction with a small block to keep the sticks off the surface of the table, and a small bowl for soy sauce and other condiments such as wasabi. The objective with this project was to dispense with

the need for either of these tools by taking advantage of the material already required for the retail package.

Of primary concern was to ensure that the paper-based material could withstand the consistent exposure to fluids. While not technically resolved in the comp, a water resistant aqueous varnish could be specified for the area that defines the bowl, or a non-absorbent, eco-friendly substrate like TerraSkin® could be specified.

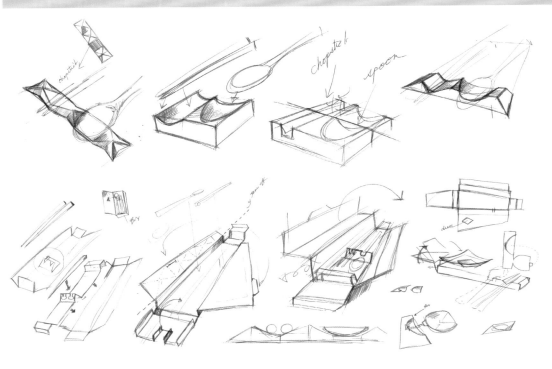

Early sketches were dedicated to exploring utensil-holding structures (left), then soon moved into studying the entire package (below left). Various collapsing structures were considered as a means of utilizing the external package as a functional part of the secondary use.

The detachable forms that were explored above were eventually dismissed due to the extra materials required to make them, and their inability to fit into a functional die-strike. The image on the left shows the evolution of the final concept, of using tension to create a curve in the material that was held in place by a combination of a lock tab (at the top of the bowl) and a slot lock (to hold the cup to the body of the package). An aqueous coating in the bowl area provides an impermeable surface.

Right – Quickly doodled illustrations of various surface graphic ideas allow for an uninterrupted flow of ideas.

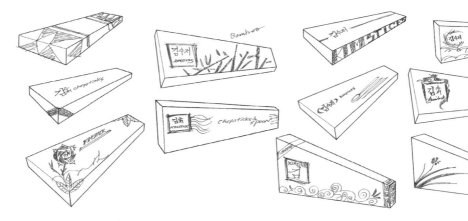

Above – An angled box saved material, but it is also a method of differentiating the package from other chopstick packages, which are traditionally rectangular. The flare also accommodates a larger bowl.
Above right – a detachable cup was explored, and an origami fold insert was made to hold the utensils.

Making sure all of the flaps and locks are where they need to be can be a matter of throwing them together. The Frankenstein method of building: cut, tape, cut again, tape again and so on.

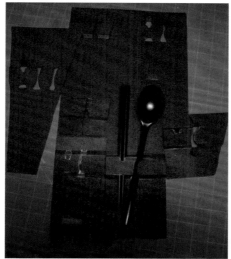

Even the interior holders had to be refined in order to make sure that the paper slots could hold the products firmly, yet release them when necessary.

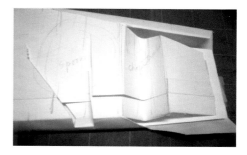

155

Details, details, details. The top picture shows the development of the reverse scores so they can be pushed inwards to create the holding areas for the spoon and chopsticks. The middle picture shows how simple slot locks can hold the sides secure when the box is closed, yet easily disengage when necessary. At the bottom, the details of the double lock tabs were worked out while building with the thicker and more fibrous paper that would be used for the final comps and for production.

Die-strike

While this is a complex schematic, the functionality is straightforward and economical in that it requires no glue (relying instead on several lock tabs), and its 'footprint' is relatively square, ensuring less waste paper.

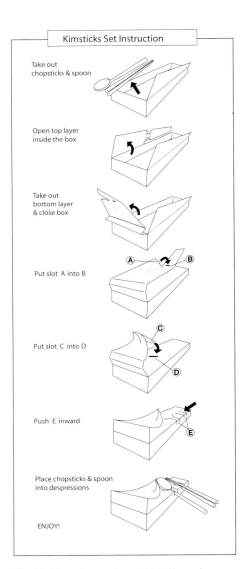

Take out chopsticks & spoon

Open top layer inside the box

Take out bottom layer & close box

Put slot A into B

Put slot C into D

Push E inward

Place chopsticks & spoon into despressions

ENJOY!

The directions above are inserted into the package to help with assembly.

Photographic concerns
Various 'combo shots' comprised of an open and a closed box were explored during the photoshoot. The seamless backdrop places the focus on the relationship between the package and the product, and highlights the contrast between the curves and the angles that exist in both the package and the product itself.

Photographic concerns
Active backgrounds were explored. As is clearly the case here, these can create problems:
1) the distracting sheen of the background material.
2) the high contrast of the white calligraphic poster.
3) the clashing textures, detracting from the tactile qualities of the package itself.

Photographic concerns

Two boxes were constructed for this sequence of images, so the package could be seen as it exists in its 'shelf-life', and then once the soy sauce cup is opened for use.

These pictures show the package in different stages of transformation.

5.8: Jiwon Kim | Chopstick and spoon set

Objectives

Even though it seems that everyone old enough to sit in an aeroplane seat owns a digital camera, disposable cameras can still be found in almost every corner store or tourist location. Digital cameras get broken, after all, or stolen, and even rechargeable batteries can die at the least opportune moment. So, disposable cameras are still bought as impulse purchases by many travellers. Among the many problems with such a scenario, the traveller must keep track of the disposable camera after it is full. Then, once home from the trip, they must drop the camera off and wait until the film is developed.

The project featured here attempts to deal with the inconvenience of carrying a full disposable camera around while still on vacation. The box the camera is sold in is held together with lock tabs so that, once the camera is full, it can easily be turned inside out to create a package to send the camera to the developer. There is pre-paid postage and an address printed on the interior of the carton. Once the film is developed by the company, the camera is brought back into a closed-loop recycling process, and the photographs are sent to the customer – in the original package. For this, the carton is pressed along a different set of pre-scored edges to create a carton that

perfectly hugs the printed photographs.

The entire process is paid for upfront, and, perhaps best of all, if the traveller sends the camera to the developer while still on the trip – thus reducing the weight of luggage and the likelihood that the camera will get broken or lost – the developed pictures will be waiting when the traveller arrives back home.

The packaging delivery system is intended to be designed for large tourist destinations, and the internal packaging for the camera is printed with rail and roadmaps of the specific location. Also included are small booklets that highlight popular restaurants and locations.

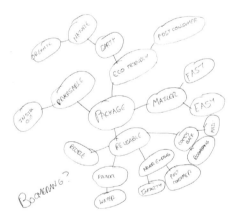

The 'mind map' above allows for spontaneous recording of relevant ideas as they relate to the package, the product and the product name. To the right are a few examples of logo and wordmark studies. While other motifs were explored, these show how the symbol of the boomerang was studied for its formal and symbolic potential.

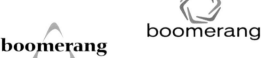

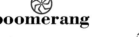

As the project developed, it was determined that a map of the destination city would be a valuable addition. Rather than adding another piece of paper, however, the map was printed on the package insert. A score running across the middle allows the map to be folded neatly in half to fit into most pockets.

An early scrap-paper prototype provides valuable information regarding the necessary relationship between interior package volume and product size and form. The large open area at the top of the box was completely removed in later prototypes so that the camera fit snugly within the interior space.

Below – The multi-use end flaps needed to work for both box structures – the original structure that held the camera, and the final structure that held the processed photographs. Several dust flap variations were explored to ensure that the closures were both secure and easy to use.

Left – The scores for the mail-back photograph package are studied for their function and accuracy.

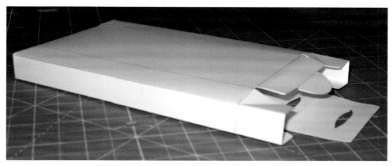

Right – Any package that provides convertibility must also include clear directions for the consumer to quickly and easily perform the conversion. In this case, the insert that was intended to hold the camera in place was printed with a clear set of directions.

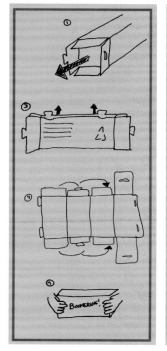

directions

In a few short steps, you can enjoy all the benefits that boomerang has to offer. So, follow these simple instructions to insure that your experience is as quick and easy as possible.

1. Remove camera from box. Do not throw the box away for it is an important part of this process.

2. Enjoy your disposable camera! If you are looking for suggestions for activities consult your map and brochure that came with your camera.

3. After your film is finished, you're going to turn the original packaging that your camera came in, inside out. To do so, gently pull each of the 4 lock tabs away from the box. When finished the box should lie flat.

4. Locate the side of the packaging containing the original graphics and face that side up.

5. Fold the sides of the box together and reconnect the lock tabs. When the box has been placed back together, the package should show the side with the pre-paid stamp.

6. Place your used disposable camera in the box along with the filled out mailing label that was included in your package. This is so we have the address for where you would like your photos sent.

7. Place box in mail.

8. Smile!

boomerang

159

Die-strike

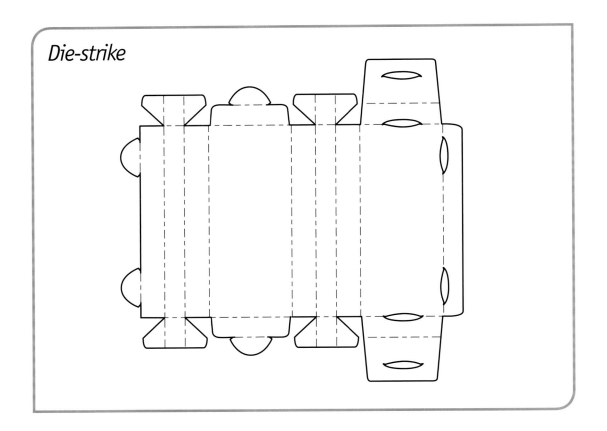

The camera is nested into a small folding insert in order to prevent it from shifting in the box, which is a little longer than the camera to accommodate standard-sized photographs during its later manifestation as a mail-delivery system. In order to optimize the paper-usage for such an insert, directions that clarify the package's sequence of uses are printed on it.

Photographic concerns

The outer package is flattened here to show the interior surface of the pre-consumer carton. The interior is printed with pre-paid postage so that the consumer can send the full camera to the developer. The same carton is then scored along a different set of score lines to provide a mail-friendly envelope to deliver the developed images back to the consumer.

The image above shows the carton in its pre-consumer form (left), and its photo-delivery form (above right). A blank self-adhesive sticker is included in the package so that the home address of the consumer can be written on it, and it can be placed over the original address for the developer. Within the package are maps and guides for any large city that retailers would want to target.

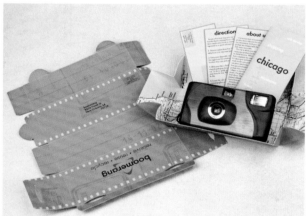

5.9: Kate McElwain | Photo delivery system

5.10: *Jiwon Kim | Multi-use set*

Objectives

This kit was designed as an extension to a smaller spoon and chopstick set featured in the earlier section on paperboard construction (see page 154). This is a more comprehensive set of Asian food utensils, with two spoons, two sets of chopsticks, a pair of sake cups and a sake dispenser.

Due to the nature and size of the products, the outer package had to be rather large. Because of this, considering a secondary use for it was very important – otherwise there would have been a lot of material waste. Here, the secondary use was divided into three parts: the outer bamboo wrap became a poster; the outer box became a serving tray; the interior platform was used as a display or storage unit for the products. The angle of the platform not only allows for easy removal of the products, but it mimics the shape of the paperboard chopstick package in the previous unit, thus branding the line with a distinctive shape.

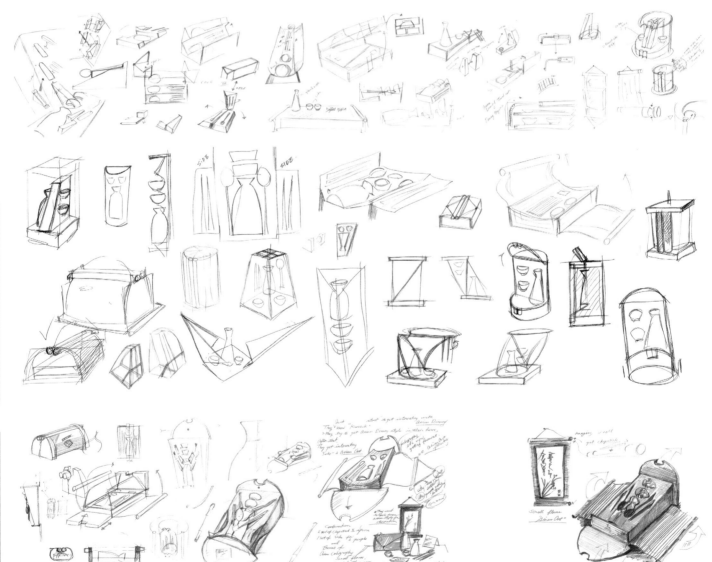

Using sketching as a method of making ideas concrete is an important skill for designers. Here, with a sense of investigation and play, the designer explores many forms, some of which grapple with the inherent problem of ensuring a secondary use for such a large outer package.

A very early exploration made use of scrap material to explore a cylindrical form that could be stood on its end. Visiting a print-shop to ask for discarded print-runs supplied the designer with ample material.

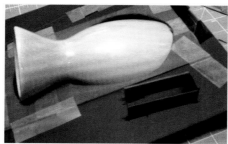

The next step involved laying the package on its back, and developing a top that peels off. As is often the case with such packages, a major hurdle was the amount of material required simply to cover the products. This led to the innovative use of a bamboo wrap that had as much value once unwrapped as it did while it protected the contents of the package.

By thinking ahead in the construction, you can avoid a lot of serious problems with wrapping a platform. Here, three slots were made to secure the U-shaped holders on either side of the sake dispenser. This allowed the designer to wrap the platform and the U-forms individually. In this image, taken before the pieces were wrapped, the designer is making sure the fit is snug.

When dealing with angled platforms and curved products, it can be time-consuming and material-intensive to ensure that the holes for the products accurately nestle them. By using a small grey board to test the shape of the holes, recutting the entire platform for every attempt was avoided. Instead, all minor changes in the shape were executed on the smaller boards.

Much of the illustration board seen throughout the book was reused from scraps that had been discarded from other projects.

Wrapping platforms

Wrapping the paper onto the illustration board requires forethought to avoid awkward wrap-arounds and paper bunching. These shots show how the interior tray was wrapped before it was fully constructed. Red paper was then glued over the inside surface. Gluing can be done with rubber cement, making sure that both surfaces are fully covered and dry, or with spray adhesive. Less-toxic sheet glue is also available. Whatever adhesive is used, there must be enough to account for the absorbency of the specific paper used. Some papers require much more glue than others – test to determine how much is needed for the paper you are using.

These images show how each individual interior piece was covered with the appropriate paper before final assembly. The fan-cutting of the light brown paper (left) is necessary to follow curved holes, but must be done with finesse in order to prevent the resulting hole from appearing faceted. Another option is to paint the interior edge of the board with a paint or dye mixed to match the colour of the paper. The paper is then wrapped onto the platform (below left), and trimmed so that it is flush with the hole. As with so many other things, the colour of the paint should be tested on separate pieces of board before being applied to the final piece; the colour often looks much darker once it is painted onto the board.

This is especially so if the board is black, as shown here. Notice in the below image how the paper has been wrapped before the corners are taped. This is an alternative method to the one shown in the earlier tutorial (page 122), but should be used only if the platform is an interior platform (so the edge is not visible when the package is closed).

Chapter 5: Case Studies in Building Prototypes

The wrap for the entire package is made from discarded bamboo blinds which, while working well for making several comps, could also become a part of a corporate process or reuse. Notice how the initial package form stood taller in an early exploration: by squaring the top off, it saves a lot of volume for both shipping and shelving, and makes the package less vulnerable to damage.

Photographic concerns

This angle provides the designer with an opportunity to show how the package would be experienced upon first opening it. Extra space was left around the image so it can be cropped as necessary.

Section 2 – Re:structure

Photographic concerns
This crop reveals the material handiwork as well as the individual components of the set, which function independently once the package is unwrapped. The interior platform acts as a display and storage unit for the products. The cardboard shell, which performed as a skeletal structure for the outer bamboo wrap, has a second life as a tray with handles. Meanwhile the exterior wrap, which contains a poem, can be hung from a wall.

The designer made sure to build a secondary bamboo wrap so it could be shown in both of these photographs.

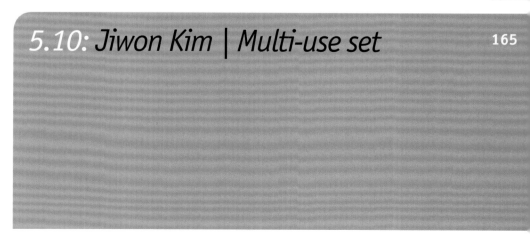

5.10: Jiwon Kim | Multi-use set

5.11: Yichun Yeh | CD burn kit

Objectives

Despite the growth in portable hard drives for digital data, and mobile music players for music data, the need for 'burnable' compact discs continues to remain strong. The motivating factor behind this project was to develop an attractive and portable CD burn kit that held 20 CDs, two markers and enough sleeves to hold the CDs once burned.

The designer was interested in attracting the curiosity of creative people by devising a playful and modular package-as-product that remained compact even as it could be transformed and personalized in its functional form to fit any work environment.

Sometimes you just have to build it, and see for yourself. While extensive two-dimensional exploration combined with a familiarity with material strengths and tendencies allow the seasoned package designer to limit the amount of three-dimensional building that needs to be done, for those still cutting their teeth in the field, it can be advantageous to long-term learning to build various prototypes in three dimensions with scrap materials, as seen here.

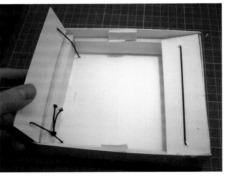

Left – Spring-loaded sides were explored in the context of a cube that would rotate on a Lazy Susan. While the spring-loaded mechanisms worked very well, it was decided that better access was needed for all of the products, not just the CDs.

Right – Various materials were explored, and mechanisms such as snaps and tension-release corners put to the test. The initial idea of using raw corrugated board as the final material was abandoned after playing with various weights and finding it structurally incapable of carrying the product weight.

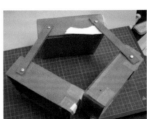

Above – An early study explored the potential for using three different thicknesses in order to reduce the amount of overall material used.

Above and right – The thinner corrugated board required too much height along the top and bottom of the package.

Near right – Simply as a means of exploring material qualities, silver paperboard was tried. Metallic papers are much less ecologically-friendly due to the heavy metals in them.

Far right and below – This late-stage prototype has resolved all issues of scale, functionality and material quantity. Acetate with the right amount of flexibility has been found, and reduced to a minimum thickness. The result is small quarter-round brackets that flex easily at the push of a finger, yet hold the content securely otherwise.

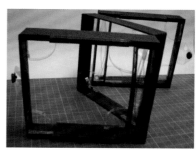

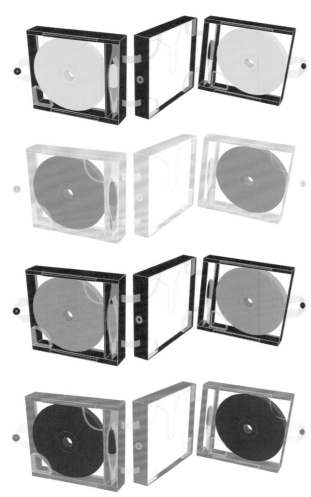

Digital colour studies helped speed up the process of finding the right contemporary colour scheme. The product line, if extended to various memory sizes, could take advantage of several colour schemes for product differentiation.

The wrapping of the final comp was a tedious and exacting process that required careful planning. The red paper was glued onto an illustration-board structure, and while the tension corners were glued directly on top of the paper, the acetate hinges were glued underneath the paper. The horizontal bars that protrude from the top and bottom of two sides portray how those structures would interlock with the middle one when the package was closed.

Chapter 5: Case Studies in Building Prototypes

Because most consumers have become accustomed to seeing the retail package as something that is discarded after purchase, any package that provides a secondary function should call attention to that function. As consumers hold packages in their hands they are in a constant state of decision-making, and it can be the added value (or the novelty aspect) of a secondary function that helps them with the split-second decision. In this example, the illustrations begin on the front surface, and contribute to the overall aesthetic. As the consumer picks up the package, the illustrations continue onto the bottom of the package, allowing for a degree of surprise – the bottom of a package!?

Photographic concerns
A different angle presents a more playful side of the product (above).

Clear and concise descriptions of the products, the package and the various ways in which the package can be used (left).

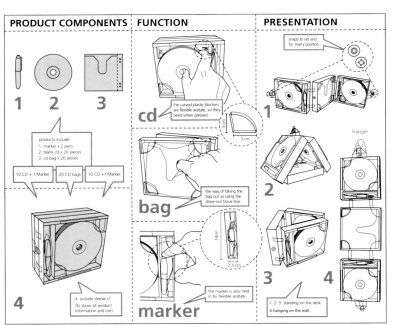

168

Careful attention to all of the details was essential in creating a convincing comp. The CDs were airbrushed, then a self-adhesive, clear output of the logo and line pattern was placed onto them. The tension-release corners proved to work very well for the final once an acetate with the proper amount of flexibility and strength was found. The red arrows in each corner, printed on acetate, make the dispensing method easily understood.

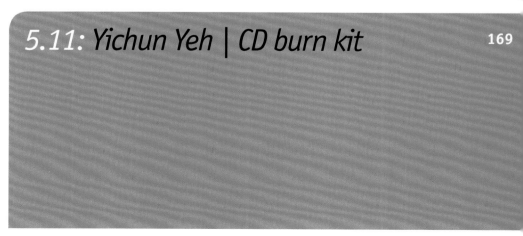

5.11: Yichun Yeh | CD burn kit

Objectives

In news accounts about recent natural disasters, stories abound of people forced to leave their homes so quickly that they did not have time to gather important documents relating to things such as home ownership, car ownership and medical insurance. With the ferocity and sudden nature of some of these disasters, individuals had no choice but to run or swim for their lives with whatever they could grab on the way out the door. Those news accounts were a motivating factor behind this project.

The goal with this package was to supply individuals in disaster-prone regions with a single holding place for these valuable documents. But not just a container; something, rather, that could also serve as a valuable survival tool in its own right, in that it provides buoyancy and high visibility. The compact nature and shoulder strap allow it to be hung next to a door, so that when an emergency did occur individuals could throw this pack over their shoulder so that both arms could remain free to grab children or more valuables. The combination of first-aid equipment, ultra-thin thermal blanket, emergency phone, survival knife, torch, compass and whistle provide a rudimentary survival pack, while other containers provide waterproof protection for important personal documents.

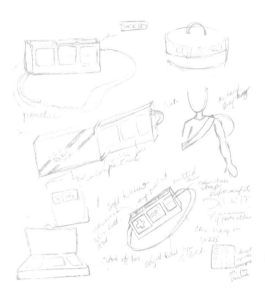
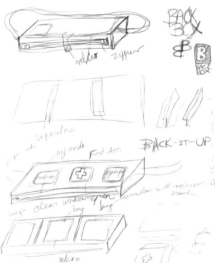
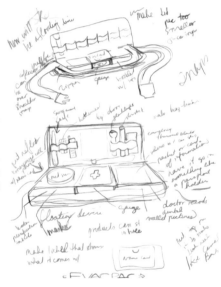

How much can a single person carry on his or her back? This was one of the first questions to answer since this package-as-product had to be lightweight and comfortable enough for a man, woman or child to carry in a time of emergency.

Issues of scale, and weight-bearing tendencies dictated the dimensions of the 'package', so early sketches were dedicated to configuring the departmentalization of individual products.

A strip of semi-rigid foam is cut and wrapped in orange, tear-proof fabric using PVA glue, then the internal section is wrapped in beige fabric. Before the two are glued together, the elastic loops are sewn to the beige panel.

170

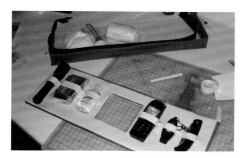

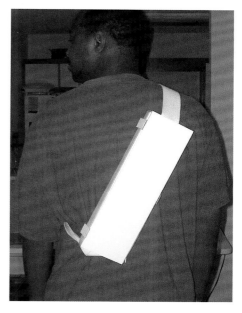

The other pieces of the package were created in similar fashion to those in the panel above. The case itself was more challenging than the flat panels due to the need to build corners. While sewing these kinds of materials is very effective, this particular package was built using hot glue.

The early prototype was tested for comfort and functionality. In this picture, the package is tested on a large man. While it could have been made larger for such a bodyframe, this size also worked very well for a woman.

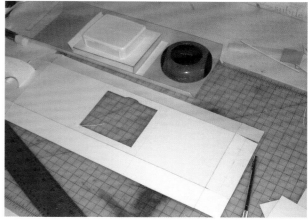

A hard case (above) was considered early on in the process to provide protection against crushing. The inclusion of a standard-sized sticking plaster kit which was accessible without having to open the rest of the package was also explored. While the opening was eventually customized, the initial idea of providing a separate opening was carried through to the final solution to make sure that the contents of the entire case would not fall out if the user was accessing a bandage (above right). It was quickly determined that the small, zipped opening, while providing the necessary containment, was simply too restrictive. It also prevented easy access to certain products that might be needed at a moment's notice.

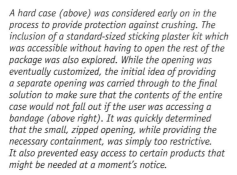

The zip is pinned into place before gluing (above). Then, the straps, which have also been wrapped in the orange fabric, are pinned into place.

Chapter 5: Case Studies in Building Prototypes

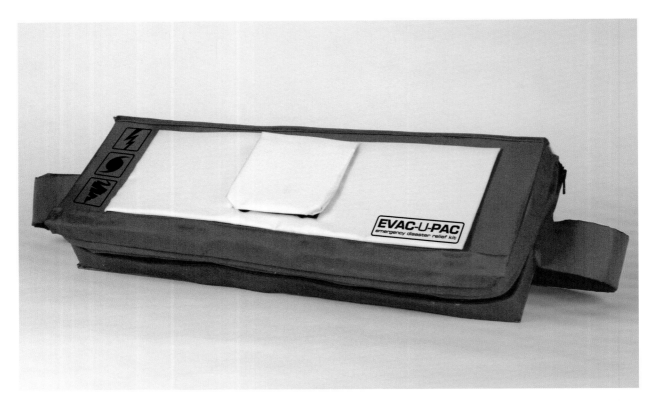

Some external, late-stage design modifications that occurred after the photoshoot (above) were applied to the original digital image (right).

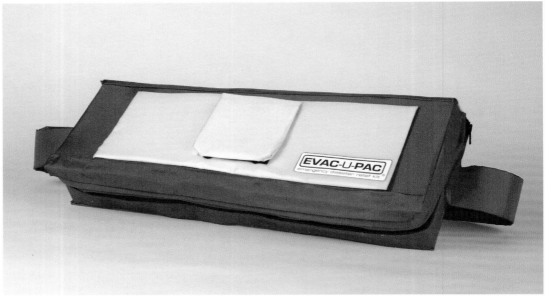

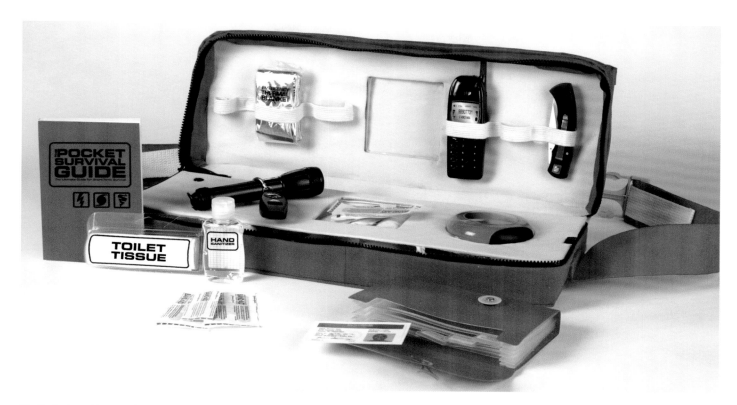

The final set provides enough rigidity for ease of handling and protection, combined with enough 'give' in the material and structure to make it comfortable to wear. The products that would be needed in an emergency are easily accessible, while personal documents and the survival guide are safely held in the bottom by a platform secured by Velcro™.

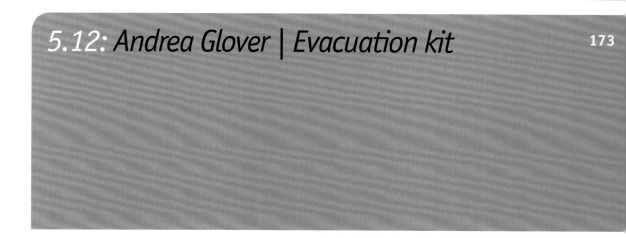

5.12: *Andrea Glover | Evacuation kit*

Objectives

Skateboarding is an activity born of creativity and improvisation, and The Molotov Cocktail Party Set is based on the general belief that skating is about all of the activities involved in making something rideable – not simply standing on a board with wheels. The package attempts to address the natural mistrust that exists between city officials and skateboarders by initiating a collaboration between the two parties, even as it celebrates skateboarding as a genuinely creative form of athletic street performance. For cities interested in bridging this often antagonistic divide, or for skate companies interested in

unifying these groups as a public-interest project, the first step is coordinating a joint effort to dismantle old road signs. Interested skaters aid city workers in this dismantling, and then in the putting-up of the new signage. The old signs are then cut and built into the outer casing for the skateboarding set.

The set includes a hacksaw, gulf wax, resin compound kit, a skate VHS, a roll of tape, two cans of spray-paint, stencils and stickers and a belt that serves a dual purpose as a strap for the box set. While some of these may be perceived by the establishment as tools to be used to deface public spaces, the goal of the set is to

encourage individuals to create micro-environments that are safe and open to skate culture. While the contents might seem provocative, the spray-cans contain water-based chalk, and the hacksaw is intended to help skaters rid designated skate spots of dangerous hazards so that city workers can be relieved of that time-consuming task.

The Molotov Cocktail Party Set seeks to attract consumers on their own terms and their own turf. There is no room for pretence in this market. That understood, this product has all the ingredients to differentiate itself and become both useful and collectible.

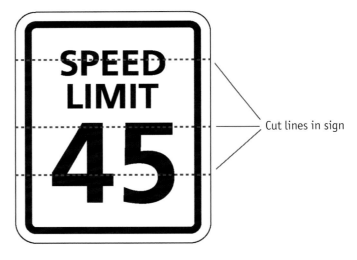

Cut lines in sign

Using hinges to hold the exterior together proved to be problematic in a number of ways. Not only did it add a substantial amount of weight to the package, but after testing them, they failed to withstand the repetitive use of skating over them once the sign was flattened over an edge.

Unlike most other package-design projects, this package had to be defined not by the shape and volume of the products alone, but also by the size of the road sign that would serve as the exterior package. Once the volume of the package and its ingredients was determined, a cardboard dummy is cut to the exact specifications of the road sign to ensure there will be no surprises.

Front view of hinge

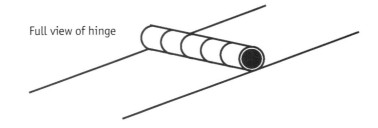

Full view of hinge

100.70.0.0
0.0.100.0
10.100.100.10

100.70.0.0
0.20.100.0
10.100.100.0

70.20.0.0
0.0.100.0
10.100.100.10

20.0.10.0
0.0.100.0
10.100.100.10

100.100.0.0
0.70.100.0
10.100.100.0

100.80.0.0
100.0.100.0
0.40.100.0

90.40.0.0
30.0.60.0
10.100.100.0

100.70.0.0
0.0.100.0
0.70.100.0

0.20.100.0
0.0.100.0
10.100.100.0

0.20.100.0
0.0.100.0
90.40.0.0

Early inspirations for a colour scheme included: guerilla tactics, urban vibe; tonality of street sign systems; discretion (to connote the idea of secret skate spots).

MOLOTOV

Left – A stencil of the logo is cut, then placed directly onto the sign. Because of the hand-crafted nature of each package, the set becomes an instant collectible.

Below – The Molotov cocktail was chosen as the emblem because of the improvisational qualities of the weapon. Three items (rag, bottle, petrol) that would normally serve separate purposes, when brought together, become a devastating object.

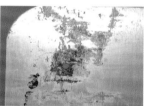

Left – This sequence (from top to bottom) shows the preparation and planning that went into adhering the rubber mat to the road sign. First of all the rust had to be sanded off, then the sign was carefully cut. It was then glued using contact cement, one section at a time, onto the rubber matting.

Right – Contact cement is a volatile substance and, because the rubber mat had to be glued in one large sheet, the materials were tested extensively before doing the final kit.

NB: Contact cement is decidedly not a sustainable material. Due to its properties as a multisurface adhesive with unmatched bonding strength, it was the only possible substance for this kind of job.

175

Chapter 5: Case Studies in Building Prototypes

The two internal trays nest into each other, and scrap foam was used to cushion the materials within the package. While virgin materials were used for this prototype, recycled-content fibreboard could be specified for the entire structure, and the black foam could be replaced with biodegradable foam.

The logo design is stencilled directly onto the old road sign, reminding people that each kit is a one-of-a-kind package. Package contents, meanwhile are silk-screened onto the bottom, opposite the logo.

In order to stay true to skate culture and not fall prey to over commercialization, this package is categorized as a limited edition, and hand-crafted speciality item.

The two interior trays can be emptied and reused for almost any purpose due to their solid construction and materials. Water-based chalk spray-paint ensures that any misuse of the sprays can be easily wiped away. The interior boxes are made from post-consumer content paper, and the graphics are minimal, requiring only small amounts of ink.

Cotter pins hold the box closed, while the strap, which is made from a waist belt and intended to be used either as a belt or a shoulder strap for the case, allows skaters to carry the entire package with their hands free.

176

SET INCLUDES:
1 STREET SIGN - 1 HACKSAW - 1 BAR OF SKATE WAX - 1 RESIN COMPOUND KIT
1 VHS - 1 ROLL OF TAPE - 2 CANS OF SPRAYPAINT - STENCILS - STICKERS

MOLOTOV
COCKTAIL PARTY SET

5.13: *Eddie Jacobson | Skateboard kit*

5.14: *Clark Delashmet | Flyfishing promotion*

Objectives

Individuals who are passionate about the sport of flyfishing are often especially enamoured with finely crafted wooden objects, such as hand-crafted wooden boxes. It stands to reason then, that a promotional gift to inform flyfishing clients of a new product-line can establish an intimate connection.

Beautiful boxes introducing a new reel, specialized flies and maps pertaining to the local water bodies were sent out to inform a select group of dedicated clients of the new items available in a line of flyfishing products. The box not only functions as a promotional vehicle for the flyfishing company, but doubles as a stand on which

clients can display their prized flies. The finished piece is large enough to have a presence on any desk, bookshelf or office setting, yet small enough to remain unobtrusive. Magnet closures and hinges recall features of tackle baskets.

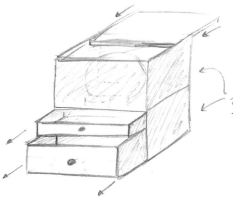

Numerous joints were studied in order to find out which would provide the strongest and most aesthetically pleasing result.

Early studies included making three compartments to house the individual components. The form was a solid box with a sliding top and two lower drawers. This made for a bulky design and a boring package.

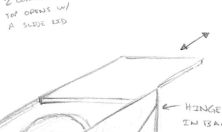

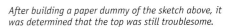

After building a paper dummy of the sketch above, it was determined that the top was still troublesome.

The second form was made of two compartments that hinged in the middle with a top sliding down to close the box. This form provided a more dynamic box but proved hard to open and still lacked an innovative form for secondary uses.

As the package was refined, it combined ideas from the first two forms: the hinged compartments and sliding top.

A paperboard form was constructed to see how the structure functioned, and to make sure it felt comfortable in the hand and managed the volume of the products efficiently.

The final paper dummy is seen here. It provided a reference point as the construction moved onto the wooden versions of the box.

Working with wood

When working with wood there are many factors to consider. Elements that can affect the outcome of a wooden package are: the type of wood; the colour and/or the stain of the wood; methods of construction; and cost. The type of wood chosen can greatly affect the look of the finished piece. Some factors that have to be looked at when selecting wood are hardness, colour, grain and price.

The type of construction can also affect the feel and functionality of the finished piece. How will it open? Are there drawers? Can it lock? What type of additional hardware will be required? What joints will be used? These are just a few of the many questions that must be asked before undertaking such a job.

Most wooden packages are custom made and require skilled craftsmen to make them. So it's often necessary to research and work with someone who is locally available. Price can also be a major factor in the production of wooden packages. Since the materials involved are usually more expensive than paper products the price per unit will be higher. Keep this in mind when designing with wood.

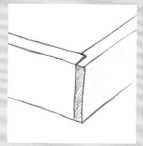

Four common joints used in wooden box construction are shown here. Finger joints offer a strong joint due to the large glue surface.

Butt joints are the simplest and quickest way to build a box, but provide a weak joint.

Lap joints are a little stronger than butt joints due to the slightly larger glue surface and the nesting of one of the sides.

Dovetails are the strongest.

A finger joint was decided upon. It was constructed using a dado blade set on a table saw with a jig allowing for the accurate spacing and cutting of the finger joints.

Different thicknesses were studied to determine a comfortable scale between 'finger' size and the height of the final box.

Wood stain

Choosing the right colour of finish can often make or break the final package design. But don't just consider the colour of the finish, think about the protection the particular finish provides as well. Understanding where the product will reside and how much it will be handled can give a good indication of what type of protective finish should be used, and how many coats should be applied.

Above – Multiple finishes were layered on top of each other to test for the finished stain colour. Once the colour was determined, darkness was studied to see how dense the colour should be. These three shades of stain (left to right) are:
1) Two layers of stain with one layer of finishing wax.
2) Two layers of stain.
3) One layer of stain.

Above – Different finishes were studied to ensure a high quality look and feel to the finished product.

179

Box diagram

The box was constructed of three sections. The bottom two sections were hinged at the back of the box, while the top of the box attached to these sections with magnets in the walls of the top and middle section.

Magnets were mounted to the box by drilling 2mm (¹/₈ in) holes, the diameter of the small magnets. The holes were filled with glue and the magnets were dropped in. The result is a seamless connection between the top and middle sections of the box.

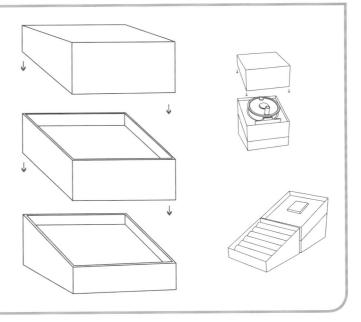

An early illustration was used to study form, surface graphics and colour.

Photographic concerns
Different environments can affect a product's look and feel. Placing the product on a white background could prove necessary to show details of the package. In the image to the right the package is in an environment that accentuates the form and gives it more personality and appeal.

Photographic concerns

In the final product shot, the package was shot on a wooden floor to give it a fishing-camp feel. The image was arranged so that the flyfishing reel, maps, flies and promotional letter on the inside of the top could all be seen at one time.

These two shots were taken at different angles to see which featured the product better. Different angles of shot can make a huge difference to the look of the final package.

5.14: Clark Delashmet | Flyfishing promotion

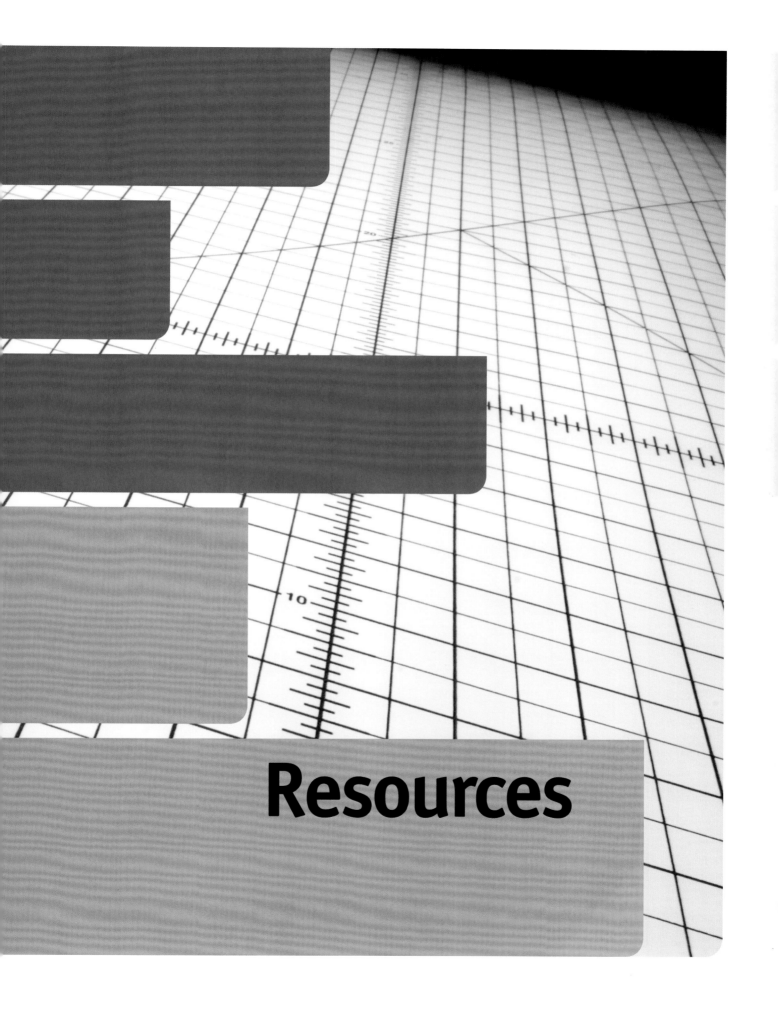

Resources

Afterword

What we hope to find at the end of any question is an answer of some kind. That answer almost always reveals more questions, and these new questions could never have been articulated without first answering the original question.

This book has aimed to provide some answers to questions that today's graphic designers have been asking about sustainable practices. By embracing a workable framework, we can better determine how each new piece of information can fit into the larger picture. The parameters of a sustainable framework can be defined with a few key points of advice:

1) Close material loops so that material usage can be optimized, and strive for longevity of material use and reuse.

2) Even as biologically harmful (technological) loops of material usage are improved, find ways to replace these technological materials with materials that are less toxic to ecological systems.

3) Wherever possible, enhance the longevity of product reuse in order to lessen the burden of these perpetual material recycling loops. Among other things, this 'life-extension' of products reduces the need for energy consumption that exists throughout any manufacturing and distributing scheme.

Even as we understand that biologically harmful substances are necessary for certain products and packages, we must strive to find biologically benign substitutes that may one day replace those substances. We can't make computer circuits out of potato starch, for example, so until that day (which might be sooner than we imagine), we must wisely manage the substances that do provide us with that sort of ability.

While our ultimate objective is to permanently replace harmful materials, we should not in the meantime stop finding ways to improve them. The promising advancement of biopolymers such as PLA and Plantic, for instance, shouldn't prevent us from also finding better ways to reuse petroleum-based polymers. In fact, it is important to push beyond biopolymers derived from potential food sources, and focus instead on 'second-generation' biopolymers which are derived from agricultural waste. We have also seen, innovative companies such as Innocent have finally reached the goal of creating new bottle plastic from 100 per cent post-consumer recycled content, something that had long been considered impossible. Likewise, scientists in Japan have recently realized the goal of 'depolymerizing' certain plastics rather than simply melting them down. By breaking them down into their original chemical components, these scientists have found a method of closing the loop on petro-based polymers. Soon, we might very well see a world where all plastics can be recycled continuously rather than downcycled, and such an advancement would suddenly make old plastic a highly sought-after commodity.

This promising new ability to depolymerize plastics will allow us to use plastic much as we use glass and steel today – to reconstitute them at their original integrity in an endless loop. So, at the same moment in time when the discovery of agribased polymers has provided us with

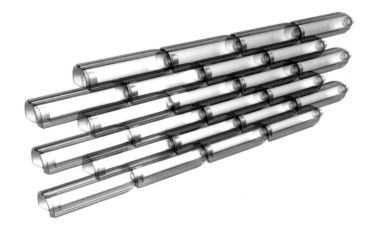

the opportunity to make plastics from renewable and biodegradable sources, we have discovered methods of reusing the old, petroleum-based plastics in more efficient and more sustainable ways.

In order to ensure continued sustainable development, package designers must learn to appreciate what each of these two parallel developments has to offer to the world of design. A large percentage of petro-based plastics will be replaced over the next few decades by biopolymers, and the net gains in sustainability will be nothing short of revolutionary. A lower demand for petroleum will result, as will an equivalent reduction in harmful extraction techniques.

Because petro-based plastics remain in the environment for hundreds of years, however, and because many of the plastics that were at the very beginning of the 'plastic era' still reside among us, aiming to make use of their persistent properties in order to devise long-term secondary uses for them is of great importance.

Innovations in secondary use of packages must adjust to the functional capabilities of biopolymers as well. Many of the case studies presented in the last section of this book provide secondary uses that are temporary. They reflect the nonpersistent qualities of the substrates used to make them – paper and paperboard are not materials known for their longevity. In the same fashion, biopolymer packages can be designed to fulfill temporary secondary needs.

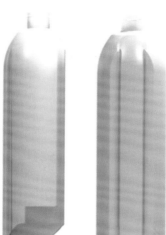

Designers are finding innovative ways to sequester petro-based polymers in long-term secondary uses. At the same time, advances in depolymerizing plastics so that they can maintain their original integrity in ensuing product or package 'lives', combined with advances in biopolymer development, offer designers a more versatile choice of sustainable packaging materials.

The bottle system above, devised by Rinus Berg-van-den, DMG of the Netherlands, takes advantage of the persistent qualities in plastics in order to create an architectural building system. The groove-and-snap system also provides an opportunity to 'bundle' the bottles in consumer six-packs that do not require a lot of secondary packaging.

The answers in this book define a working knowledge about the interplay between creative ingenuity and the technological practicalities that determine their scope but, perhaps more importantly, they define the opposite side of that interplay as well; that between technological practicalities and the creative ingenuity that determines their scope.

The disparity between persistent plastics and biodegradable biopolymers requires a new structural framework that addresses the ideal loop, or recovery system for each material. Sequestering petroleum based plastics in ecologically-benign functions, like building materials, best utilizes their properties.

Like human metabolism, where our bodies use different forms of nutrition for different purposes, package designers must understand the most beneficial attributes of a wide variety of materials, and use them, according not to our demands, but to their unique properties. These properties become the signals designers must pay attention to. Much like glass and steel before them, plastics and biopolymers can be applied to immediate secondary use, or can be designated to 'feed' the material loop to which they belong. They can be reused in their constituted forms, or broken down to be reborn as new packages. Package designers must accept that the role of a practitioner is not merely to practise, but to practise in a way that reflects the depth and breadth of the knowledge-base available to them. In so doing, they can provide ways to help societies understand the complexities of these nutrition systems, and provide guidance through those complexities.

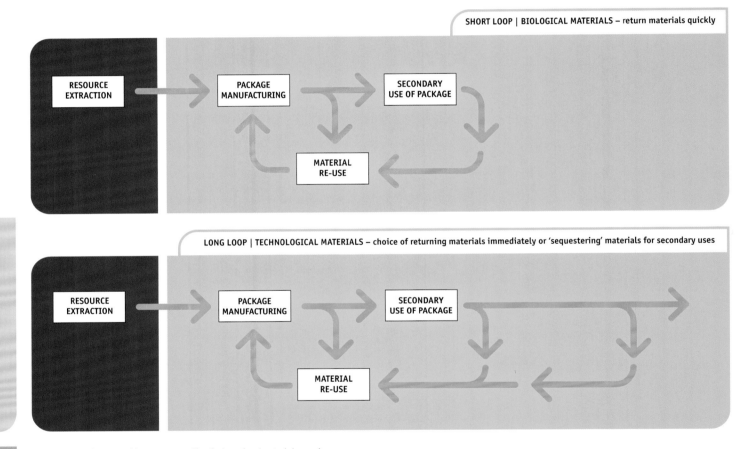

The diagram above provides a useful guide to how designers might consider the role that their material choices play in the various closed-loop systems that the materials naturally provide.

The designation 'material reuse' in the short-loop diagram can be defined as a manufacturing term or as one that denotes composting. The goal is to exclude the 'resource extraction' arena as often as possible.

Glossary

After Market Product
The utility of a product in an area that is not defined by its initial intent. Specifically, in the packaging realm, it defines a secondary use of the package in one of three ways as defined in this book; reuse by default, reuse by innovation, and reuse by prescription.

Biomass
When describing alternative energy sources, this term references a broad array of fuels derived from dead biological materials. These sources can be harvested for the specific purpose of fuel production or harvested as an agricultural by-product. Biomass can be converted into biofuels or burned. Burning biomass in a carefully controlled and energy efficient manner, while contributing to global warming, is less damaging than burning fossil fuels, because it does not release carbon that has been sequestered for thousands of years as does fossil fuel. Instead, the carbon release from biomass has been available to the earth's atmosphere. Biofuel production, on the other hand, can be derived from many plants, including switchgrass, corn, sugar cane, and most promisingly, algae. While some first-generation biofuels are problematic in that they require energy to grow and they create competition from food sources, second-generation biofuels hold great promise.

Bioplastics/Biopolymers
An umbrella term that defines biodegradable plastics from renewable sources, which are quickly becoming viable and environmentally friendly alternatives to petroleum-based plastics. It must be stressed that 'second-generation' biopolymers, which are derived from agricultural waste, are developed so as to prevent competition with needed food sources. Considering the amount of agricultural by-product (husks, stalks, leaves, shells, starch residues, etc.) created in farming enough food for six billion people, there's good cause to explore these potentials. Biopolymers are presently grouped into the 'number 7' resin designation, and very little can be done with the resulting recycled content. As biopolymers grow in popularity there will be a need to create a new resin category so that bioplastics can be treated together.

Blow Moulding (Injection, extrusion, stretching)
A manufacturing technique for creating hollow plastic forms, also called blow forming. Compressed air is blown into mouldings, forcing the plastic to the edges of that moulding in three different ways; through extrusion, injection or stretching. Extrusion moulding, while less accurate than injection moulding, is more suitable for shorter production runs. End products include bottles, tubes, containers, moulded parts, etc.

Carbon Footprint
Through the course of each day and night, individuals and companies perform numerous tasks. Many of these tasks require some input of energy, and thus some burning of carbon and pursuant release of CO_2 and other greenhouse gasses. Over the last decade, measurement tools have been developed to help companies determine the amount of energy they expend on activities both large and small, and so a big-picture assessment, such as the total impact of one's operation, can be an effective tool in helping companies determine ways to find reductions within their daily operation. Some tools break down the CO_2 emissions into a primary footprint, or a measure of direct energy use, and secondary footprint, or a measure of indirect energy use, or energy that is embodied in products and services already rendered.

Carbon Neutrality
Carbon neutral is a term to define a state of balance in energy usage where, for every pound of CO_2 emitted on behalf of a company's operation, an equal amount of CO_2 reduction is realized. Carbon neutrality can be achieved through a combination of purchasing carbon offsets, reducing energy consumption and purchasing renewable energy. The first step in becoming carbon neutral is determining your carbon footprint. While achieving carbon neutrally can be difficult, dedication to the goal inevitably results in a reduction of CO_2 emissions. Also called Zero Carbon.

Carbon Offsets
If energy consumption has been reduced, and renewable energy has replaced the use of non-renewable energy, but there are still sources of CO_2 emission within a business operation, that business may elect to purchase carbon offsets, which are measures to fund conservation efforts through carbon offset programmes. Carbon offsets—or carbon credits—vary in their application, but most frequently take the form of tree-planting programmes, funding renewable energy development and production, efficiency standards or similar CO_2-reduction programmes. While this effort is seen as beneficial to the climate change dilemma, many worry that such purchasing trends do not address the problem, but instead allow companies to feel less guilty about their CO_2 emissions. Some have likened carbon offsets to religious indulgences paid to the church that eventually led to the Reformation.

Closed Loop
Many environmental problems occur when manufacturing processes create materials that combine biological materials with non-biological, materials (referred to by most industrial ecology advocates as technical materials). True cradle-to-cradle methods cannot be applied unless materials return to the manufacturer in non-contaminated states (for example, the many layers of foils and polymers used to make a potato chip bag makes it impossible to recover any one of those material layers. So, a closed-loop system of biological materials—any material that can biodegrade safely—and a closed loop system of technical materials allows for more efficient recovery systems. DfE (Design for Environment) techniques ensure that the various materials used in any package or product can be easily isolated and put into its own closed loop of material usage.

Comp/Prototype
While these terms are often used in a generic and somewhat interchangeable fashion, there is a difference. Comp is short for comprehensive, which is a term that describes a singular (or short-run) model that replicates how a package will look once it is mass-produced. A comp is the finally realized solution recreated in three-dimensions. While also a singular (or short-run) three-dimensional object, a prototype, in the strictest sense, is built to explore the viability of the form and function of the object. So, whereas a comp represents the final solution, a prototype is intended to reveal any shortcomings in the initial solution with the idea that another, more refined, prototype will be built to remedy any problems discovered through handling of the initial prototype. You can comp a prototype.

Cradle-to-Cradle
As opposed to the all-too-common cradle-to-grave manufacturing model that generates a one-way waste stream toward the eventual disposal of a product or package, the cradle-to-cradle philosophy considers the end of one lifecycle as the beginning of another. As a core tenet of industrial ecology, and so well expressed by William McDonough and Michael Braungart as 'Waste=Food,' cradle-to-cradle thinking is inspired by nature's capacity to absorb any refuse produced as nutrients for other biological purposes. Once could argue that modern manufacturing requires more bottom feeders; more mechanisms to create new uses for discarded materials.

Die-strike
A term that defines the physical template, usually metal blades set into pre-cut wood, used in the production of folding cartons to create the trimmed and scored edges. The term is also used to define the line art, some would say mechanical, that is drawn to define that physical object. The term die-cut is also used to describe the physical template, while the term die-vinyl is used to describe the drawn (or printed) guide. Due to the prevalence of the computer in today's production process these terms, which once described clear differences in the artifacts as they existed in the sequence of production, are now often used synonymously.

Downstream Impacts
A term that refers to any environmental impacts that transpire after the package leaves the consumer's hands (also referred to as 'back-end' or 'post-consumer'). These impacts include landfilling, and open burning, and they can be reduced or mitigated through processes such as recycling, composting and waste-to-energy incineration.

Ecological Persistence
While many chemicals associated with the manufacturing of plastics and other harmful materials exist in small amounts, their tendency to remain molecularly intact even after long periods of time (ecological persistence) contributes to a phenomenon called bioaccumulation. Bioaccumulation occurs when animals and natural systems cannot metabolize toxins and they slowly build up to greater and more harmful levels. This occurs not only within individuals species, but it builds steadily along the food chain, where smaller animals are consumed by larger animals. Because humans are at the top of the food chain, the ecological persistence of hazardous chemicals directly impacts human health.

Extended Producer Responsibility (EPR)
A method of assuring that manufacturers factor in the environmental costs of their product's production at the earliest stages of a business plan, many EPRs are written into law to encourage life cycle accountability.

Film Extrusion
A manufacturing technique of creating thin plastic films frequently used in food packaging and for various other packaging sectors. End products include plastic bags of all kinds, shrink wrap, insulation films and product liners.

Geothermal
When describing alternative energy sources, this term refers to the technique of collecting heat from underground sources or using more consistent temperatures within the earth's core to generate cooling or heating. Small-scale systems can make use of more consistent temperatures within the ground as shallow as 3-4 metres to create a moderate temperature range for building interiors. Industrial geothermal power plants, on the other hand, derive their power solely from the heat found deeper below the earth's surface, either through extracting heated water or through running water through heated rock formations. Geothermal heat, which has low

environmental impacts, accounts for approximately 1 per cent of the world's power, but is growing steadily.

Hemp
One of man's earliest sources of cloth fibre and paper, hemp is well suited for a vast array of sustainable industrial applications. It is fast growing, naturally grows in many climate zones, and requires minimal cultivation to flourish. Along with its significant nutritional qualities, hemp can be converted for use in products such as paper, biofuels, biodegradable plastics and sustainable clothing, all of which can be manufactured in less environmentally damaging methods than are presently being applied. Industrial hemp (sativa) contains little of the psychoactive drug that some other plants within the cannabis genus contain.

Industrial Ecology
Many, if not all, of the sustainable frameworks discussed in this book can be described as espousing the industrial ecology philosophy. The term was first coined in 1989 by Robert Frosh & Nicholas Gallapoulos. By using the natural ecology as the key metaphor, proponents of industrial ecology attempt to create industrial systems that mimic natural systems in their energy flows, diversity and feedback mechanisms. At the heart of this philosophy is the understanding that all economic systems are subsystems of the natural ecology.

Industrial Grade Composting
While backyard composting can efficiently decompose biological matter into nutrient-rich compost, there has been an increase of industrial composting facilities that can break down some of the new bioplastics and 'compost safe' commercial materials. Industrial composting is carried out in carefully controlled settings, often in enclosed spaces, so that all facets of the process can be controlled (humidity level, oxygen content, etc.). Bioplastics cannot effectively biodegrade on their own; they require the ideal levels of heat and humidity to trigger their decomposition.

ISO 14000 Standards
The International Standards Organizations (ISO) has devised the ISO 14000 family of standards as a comprehensive set of standards for creating, managing and improving environmental management systems. Resulting from the United Nations Conference on Environment and Development in Rio de Janeiro in 1992, these standards provide tools for organizations to manage their environmental profiles and improve their performance in this arena.

Kenaf
A fast-growing, low-demand and fibrous plant that has been used for centuries as materials for rope, coarse fabrics and paper. After surveying over 500 potential replacements for tree pulp in the newsprint paper-making process, the USDA determined in 1960 that kenaf would be the most viable and sustainable alternative. The amount of usable fibre per acre of kenaf is roughly 3-4 times the volume of a standard pine tree farm, the energy required to break kenaf fibre into pulp is significantly lower than pine tree fibre, and kenaf can be harvested more frequently.

Life Cycle Analysis (LCA)
A systematic investigation of the entire life cycle of any method of production, and the peripheral efforts required for this production, as a means of assessing the total environmental impacts associated with it. Complex software programs have been developed (like the MERGE system used by the Sustainable Packaging Coalition) to aid package engineers and designers in their assessment, not only of the environmental repercussions of the material nature of a package, but of the entire package distribution system.

Methane Extraction/Capture
As a greenhouse gas, methane is almost 25 times more potent the carbon dioxide, and an estimated 60 per cent of methane results from human activities such as animal husbandry, fossil fuel production and waste management. Because methane gas is also an energy-rich form of fuel, many efforts are being made to capture methane escaping from landfills and farm animal waste pools and convert it into a source of energy production. This would simultaneously reduce the demand for energy and reduce the emissions of greenhouse gases into the atmosphere.

PCW
An acronym for post-consumer waste and a designation for materials that have travelled through the consumers' hands and into the waste stream, at which point they are harvested and reconstituted for another use. Other acronyms for this kind of material are PCR (post-consumer recycled), and PCC (post-consumer content). As a sustainable material, post-consumer waste is more efficient than post-industrial waste because it closes a material loop, turning what was considered waste into a viable product.

PIW
An acronym for post-industrial waste, which describes the industrial practice of collecting the excess materials resulting from a production process as material for the next production cycle. This practice has long been common due to its obvious financial benefits of using as much of the material in question as possible.

Resource Curse
Coined by geologist and author Richard Auty in 1993, this phrase refers to the perplexing tendency for many regions and countries in the developing world that possess a wealth of natural resources to stumble down a path of low economic growth, poverty and corruption. While the reasons for this are debated, a common phenomenon that leads to this social stratification and inequality is a willingness of multinational corporations to pour tremendous amounts of money into the local governing bodies in order to exploit these natural resources, all the while looking the other way as abuses of power and corruption run rampant as tools to funnel the money into the arms of those leaders. Also referred to as the 'paradox of plenty.'

Rightsizing
A term to describe the process of reducing the size of a package within reason. Reduction to the point of elimination is the best practice, but it is not always reasonable, nor is reducing the amount of packaging to the point where the product is vulnerable to spoilage or breakage. This is why this particular term is used; 'size minimization' ignores the fact that there are factors that must be taken into account when reducing package sizes.

Service and Flow
A key part of any industrial ecology system, service and flow refers to a fundamental shift in material consumption, from one of product offerings to one of service offerings. From rugs to computers, people do not necessarily need or want the object as much as the service it provides. Service and flow defines an approach to commerce that provides consumers with the service a product provides without burdening them with a product that will eventually become obsolete and need to be discarded. If products are designed to be collected for their valuable materials once they have performed effectively for a period of time, consumers can then 'trade' their old product for the services of a newer model. Thus, garbage is eliminated from the cycle.

Switchgrass
A robust, fast-growing prairie grass that can be converted into high-yield ethanol capable of generating 4-5 times as much energy as is required to produce it. In addition to its fibrous stem and leaf formations, switchgrass has a dense, finely textured and massive root system that contributes to soil biodiversity, resists erosion and works as a filtration system for toxins.

Take Back Regulations
A tool used to ensure compliance with extended producer responsibility, these regulations require manufacturers to take back hazardous materials within their products. Certain take back programmes can be voluntary, and are seen to be one of several ways that extended producer responsibility can be achieved.

Thermoforming
A manufacturing technique that converts thermoplastic sheets into products such as disposable lids, containers, trays, blister packs and clamshells. The technique most often makes use of vacuum forming.

Triple Bottom Line
Also called 'people, planet, profit,' this terms is used to describe a business model that defines successful performance through the three lenses of social, economic and environmental health. This focus on a holistic assessment of business operation is a key tenet of sustainability, and is often reflected in statements of corporate social responsibility (CSR).

Upstream Impacts
A term that refers to any environmental impacts that transpire before the package reaches a consumer's hands. This would include the energy loads, labour stresses and ecological wastes connected to material extraction, processing, production and distribution. Upstream impacts (also referred to as 'front-end' or 'pre-consumer' impacts), far outweigh 'downstream' impacts.

VOC
An acronym for Volatile Organic Compounds, which are chemicals that vaporize and enter the air under normal atmospheric conditions. Their vapours contribute to a range of air pollution, including smog, ozone and greenhouse gases.

Wicked Problems
The mathematician and designer Horst Rittel defined a wicked problem as, 'a class of social system problems which are ill-formulated, where the information is confusing, where there are many clients and decision makers with conflicting values, and where the ramifications in the whole system are thoroughly confusing.' In his seminal essay, 'Wicked Problems in Design Thinking,' Richard Buchanan uses Rittel's definition as a stepping stone to challenge designers to think more broadly about their efforts to ensure solutions that contribute to the solving of wicked problems rather than to their exacerbation.

Glossary

Index

Further reading

That's right, these are books – paper-based books. If they are looked after and shared, they will provide renewable supplies of knowledge and insight, all without ever turning on an energy-hungry computer...

Benyus, Janine M., *Biomimicry: Innovation Inspired by Nature*, Harper Perennial, 2002

Calvino, Italo, *Six Memos for the Next Millennium*, Vintage Classics, 1996

Capra, Fritjof, *The Hidden Connections: A Science for Sustainable Living*, Anchor Books, 2004 (reprint)

Csíkszentmihályi, Mihály, *Creativity: Flow and the Psychology of Discovery and Invention*, Harper Collins, 1996

Denison, Edward, Guang Yu Ren and John Suett, *Packaging Prototypes 3: Thinking Green*, RotoVision, 2001

Ewen, Stuart, *Captains of Consciousness: Advertising and the Social Roots of the Consumer Culture*, Basic Books, 2001, 2nd ed.)

Foucault, Michel, *Power/Knowledge: Selected Interviews & Other Writings, 1972–1977*, Pantheon, 1980

Frank, Thomas, *One Market Under God: Extreme Capitalism, Market Populism and the End of Economic Democracy*, Doubleday, 2000

Frank, Thomas, *The Conquest of Cool: Business Culture, Counterculture, and the Rise of Hip Consumerism*, University of Chicago Press, 1997

Fuller, R. Buckminster, *Critical Path*, St Martins Press, 1981

Hawken, Paul, Amory Lovins and L. Hunter Lovins, *Natural Capitalism: Creating the Next Industrial Revolution*, Little, Brown and Company, 1999

Hawken, Paul, *The Ecology of Commerce*, Collins Business, 1994

Imhoff, Daniel, and Roberto Carra, *Paper or Plastic: Searching for Solutions to an Overpackaged World*, University of California Press, 2005

Johnson, Mark, *Moral Imagination: Implications of Cognitive Science for Ethics*, University of Chicago Press, 1993

Küng, Hans, *Global Responsibility: In Search of a New World Ethic*, Wipf & Stock Publishers, 2004 (first published 1990)

Margolin, Victor, *The Politics of the Artificial: Essays on Design and Design Studies*, University of Chicago Press, 2002

Mau, Bruce, Jennifer Leonard, and the Institute Without Boundaries, *Massive Change: A Manifesto for the Future Global Design Culture*, Phaidon Press, 2004

McDonough, William, and Michael Braungart, *Cradle to Cradle: Remaking the Way We Make Things*, Rodale Press, 2002

Papanek, Victor, *The Green Imperative: Natural Design for the Real World*, Thames & Hudson, 1995

Simon, Herbert, *The Sciences of the Artificial*, The MIT Press, 1996, 3rd ed.

Singer, Peter, *One World: The Ethics of Globalization*, Yale University Press, 2004, 2nd edition

Steffen, Alex (ed), *World Changing: A User's Guide for the 21st Century*, Abrams, 2006

Thackara, John, *In the Bubble; Designing in a Complex World*, The MIT Press, 2005

Picture credits

The author and publisher would like to thank the following institutions and individuals for providing material for use in this book. In all cases, every effort has been made to credit the copyright holders, but should there be any omissions or errors the publisher would be pleased to insert the appropriate acknowledgment in subsequent editions of this book.

p14 design and photography Mark Schnoebelen
p13 design Zoe Hsiao Han Pu and Tsai-Ting Li; photography Veronica Krakowiak
p19 design and photography Alison Johnson
p20 photography Bailey Davidson
p26-27 design Christine Kingerski; photography Jessica Johnson and Nicole Sellers
p32 photography Nicole Pike
p34 design and photography Seth Akkerman
p35 photography Adam Williams
p53 design and photography R.P Collier
p54-55 photographs courtesy John Habraken and Rinus Berg-van-den
p56 photographs courtesy Method
p58 photographs courtesy Scott Stowell, M&Co.
p65 design Sara Jo Johnson; photography Andrea Clatworthy
p69 photographs courtesy Starbucks
p70-71 photographs courtesy Hewlett Packard
p74-75 photographs courtesy Method
p76-79 photographs courtesy Pangea Organics
p77 origami Pangea carton photographed by Bailey Davidson
P80-81 photographs courtesy Innocent
p82-83 photographs courtesy Icon Development Group
p84-85 photographs courtesy Twist
p86-87 photographs courtesy Sandstrom Partners
p88-91 photographs courtesy Celery Design Collaborative
p92-93 photographs courtesy Chameleon Packaging
p95 photography Larissa Thut
p99 design Ji-Hye Kim; photography Jenna DiGiore
p100 photography Bailey Davidson
p110-115 photography Bailey Davidson
p116-123 photography Larissa Thut
p124 photography Larissa Thut
p126-129 photography Brittany Brett
p131 design and photography Devin O'Bryan
p135 photography of pop-up mechanism Bailey Davidson; pack photography Megan Cummins
p138-141 design and photography Larissa Thut
p143 design and photography Julien Foo
p147 photography Amber Parker
p151 design and photography Jon Orchin
p155 photography Larissa Thut
p159 design and photography Kate McElwain
p164-165 photography Larissa Thut
p168-169 photography Brittany Brett
p172-173 photography Larissa Thut
p176-177 photography José Márquez
p181 photography Amber Parker